The *Liberal* Presidents

The *Liberal*

Presidents

A STUDY OF THE LIBERAL TRADITION

IN THE AMERICAN PRESIDENCY

J. C. LONG

KENNIKAT PRESS, INC./PORT WASHINGTON, N.Y.

THE LIBERAL PRESIDENTS

Copyright 1948 by J.C. Long
1965 edition published by Kennikat Press
by arrangement with the author.

Library of Congress Catalog Card No:64-24460

Manufactured in the United States of America

Indexed in the ESSAY & GENERAL LITERATURE INDEX

To My Father
JOHN DIETRICH LONG
an indomitable liberal
in whom there was no guile

O beautiful for pilgrim feet,
Whose stern, impassioned stress
A thoroughfare for freedom beat
Across the wilderness.
America! America! God mend
  thine every flaw,
Confirm thy soul in self-control,
Thy liberty in law!

Katherine Lee Bates,
America, the Beautiful

Preface

To offer any work to the public employing the term "liberal" is a risky business.

The few who wish no part of the liberal tradition under any interpretation will merely turn away; but each one of the host of liberal thinkers will have his own special concept of what the liberal tradition means. That is his individual right, and the author merely claims his own right of understanding and affirmation.

The author acknowledges indebtedness to Jacques Barzun, Henry Steele Commager, Bernard De Voto, L. H. Gipson, Louis M. Hacker, Carlton J. H. Hayes, Hamilton Holt, Allan Nevins, J. H. Randall, T. H. Weldon, and numerous others, for stimulating comment on the issues presented here, but implies no responsibility or endorsement on their part for the writer's conclusions.

Acknowledgment also is made particularly to Professor R. G. Cowherd, of Lehigh University, for detailed reading and criticism of the manuscript. Here, too, the responsibility is wholly the author's.

The men who occupied the White House, by their deeds and words, obviously have been the chief molders of the tradition of the presidency. Sometimes they have been subject to misinterpretation because their words were too sparsely quoted. The general reader, however, is said to reject long quotations. Hence I usually have summarized the issues, but on neglected or on controversial matters have given full direct quotations in the appendix so that the skeptical reader may judge for himself. As examples, Jackson's pronouncements on the Indians and Andrew Johnson's words in his Reconstruction veto messages reveal the immediate presidential influence on those questions better than any commentary could do.

Finally, this discussion of the presidency cannot be assumed to further either Democratic or Republican purposes. Neither party has had a monopoly of the errors or virtues. In the words of de Tocqueville who surveyed the American scene more than a hundred years ago: "This book is written to favor no particular views, and in composing it I have entertained no designs of serving or attacking any party; I have undertaken not to see differently, but to look further than parties, and whilst they are busied for the morrow I have turned my thoughts to the Future."

J. C. LONG

Contents

1

Preview of the Liberal Tradition

The dogmas of the quiet past are inadequate to the stormy present . . . As our case is new, so we must think and act anew. We must disenthrall ourselves, and then we shall save our country.

ABRAHAM LINCOLN

I

The United States of America from its beginning has been a liberal enterprise.

The purpose of this book is to show how that liberal tradition has persisted and grown, and to what extent the presidency has expressed or promoted the evolving phases of liberalism.

The story is not one of a prettily patterned progress, not orderly, not logical. The presidents have rarely been the forerunners of new ideas, or even the purest exponents of the causes with which they have been identified.

John Randolph was a more uncompromising Democrat than Jefferson. William Lloyd Garrison and a score of eminent Abolitionists prepared the way for Lincoln as the Great Emancipator. Bryan was a forerunner of Theodore Roosevelt's doctrines. A whole generation of liberal writers, historians and politicians laid the groundwork for the administrations of Wilson and F. D. Roosevelt.

History, as Parsons has said, is "a stream of mingled fact and theory, now clear, now muddied by passion and prejudice, eddying about this hero and that, and reaching each generation through the shifting channels of individual minds." [1]

The liberal tradition in the presidency has been carried on through the shifting channels of individual minds. Nearly every president may be regarded as a hero in the Greek sense of a man of eminence tortured by human fallibility. The presidents, however, have not been heroes in the perfectionist sense.

There is always a temptation for the exponent of any cause to set up Galahads and villains, each following well-defined courses, to the distortion of what has taken place in human events. Thus we find A. J. Beveridge in his *Life of Marshall,* by selected facts, making a poltroon out of Jefferson, while under the pen of Claude Bowers, Jefferson could do no wrong. Again, the liberal of any era tends to be a zealot and thereby to measure the men of the past according to their conformity to the liberal ideas of the moment.

These warnings are sounded because the liberal tradition in the presidency

[1] Geoffrey Parsons, *The Stream of History,* p. v.

can best be presented by regarding particularly the administrations of certain pivotal men in the White House, though not to the exclusion of others. In this fashion the shape of liberalism can be seen in actual exercise of the office. Washington was the exponent of eighteenth century liberalism, which emphasized constitutional government, both in Great Britain and here. Martin Van Buren, who in many respects was the political and philosophical brains of Andrew Jackson, became in his own administration a notable example of nineteenth century liberalism, holding that he governs best who governs least, and thereby demonstrated his inadequacy for the new times. Jefferson and Jackson who came in mid-era, were men of transition, wavering between their anti-federalist leanings and conversely their impellment to assert the national authority in times of crisis.

Lincoln was the president under whom the nation survived during the chief threat to its unity. In his time competitive ideas of liberalism involving union, home-rule, and slavery, clamored to be resolved in terms of action. Theodore Roosevelt was the first modern president of the early twentieth century pattern. Not until that period did the conditions of urban life, employment in large groups and the power of trusts directly affect a majority of the population.

The administrations of Wilson and F. D. Roosevelt, though differing in the personalities of the men and in detail, were much alike in both domestic and foreign principles. Each believed in a planned society, with limitations, on the home front. Each looked to the extension of free government over a world area. In them the liberal tradition entered new phases as the nation experienced ever-increasing concentrations of population, industrial management, mass publishing, mass distribution and swift communication.

In foreign affairs, Wilson and F. D. Roosevelt came nearer to the philosophy of George Washington than any other president, as shall be seen in due course. Meanwhile, it may be noted that Washington's caution against foreign alliances was specifically defined as to the particular circumstances. He sought isolation as a containing wall so that free government for the Continental United States might develop unimpeded. For this vast area, he envisaged a government more unified than a league or group of nations.

The liberal tenor in the United States has not been limited to changes in the structure of government or to economic control. The note of moral reform has been constantly present. Corruption in municipal and state governments has been steadily counteracted by the rise of honest citizens and their leaders, who recurrently have thrown the rascals out. The federal government has been notably free from financial scandal, the instances being rare exceptions. The post Civil War period was the blackest in respect to corrupt practices and the redemption of the country from political stockjobbing may be credited to Rutherford B. Hayes. Hayes was called upon to affirm principles of honesty which might have been assumed to be matters of course, but in his time needed emphasis. He rescued the government from the cancerous sins of cynicism and corruption.

If the liberal tradition in the presidency be measured by the rise of the plain man, the life of Andrew Johnson deserves especial attention. The son of a tavern porter, a merchant tailor from a small town, without formal education, he had the humblest origin of anyone to occupy the White House. Johnson also was an exponent of freedom because of his stalwartness of character. He was unsurpassed by any who have held the office in his devotion to principle, in adhering to the course which he believed right, though it led to political self-destruction. Further, in his administration the authority of the presidency met and survived its only serious challenge.

Washington, Jefferson, Jackson, Van Buren, Lincoln, Johnson, Hayes, T. Roosevelt and F. D. Roosevelt—these men were outstanding liberal beacons, but not the only ones. The liberal commitment was made at the beginning. No president has repudiated it. Though some were quite passive custodians, many had some part in shaping it. Their part in carrying on the American idea in turn was shaped by their lives, by their opponents, and the condition of their times. To measure the degree by which they advanced the liberal concept in the presidency, it is desirable to have a chart of what liberal means.

2

T. D. Weldon, in his closely reasoned analysis of liberty in government entitled *States and Morals,* has the engaging habit of telling the reader that he may skip the remainder of the chapter if it seems like too hard going. To linger here a few moments on the definition of what is meant by liberal, or the liberal tradition in the presidency, may seem a bit arduous, but it is almost inescapable, as it may be useful in clarifying the sense of direction in the chapters which follow.

Any liberal, of course, is free to take issue with the definitions and conclusions, and many doubtless will. In any event, before pointing to definitions which mark the liberal path, I should like to clear the way by challenging some misleading markers.

A popular confusion of the moment is the notion that a strong president and liberal tendencies are synonymous. The idea is reminiscent of Alexander Hamilton, who said that "energy in the Executive is a leading characteristic in the definition of good government. It is essential . . . to the security of liberty against the enterprises and assaults of ambition, of faction, and of anarchy." [2]

Entranced by the idea of power in the presidency, some liberals, such as Harold Laski, have hailed John Tyler, an inconspicuous president, as a forgotten strong man who deserves high consideration. Tyler was personally

[2] "Publius," *The Federalist,* No. 70, March 18, 1778.

amiable, but stubborn and strong-willed. Coming to office because of the death of President Harrison, he had little excuse to act as though he had a mandate from the people against the legislature, yet he soon broke with the party who elected him. He also had been a lone wolf, sometimes Whig and sometimes Democratic in policy. He had been an ardent states-rights man, and had cast the only vote in the Senate against Jackson's "force bill," which suppressed nullification of federal authority. Tyler's vigorous use of the veto and his considerable success as an administrator do little more than mark him as an original and industrious mind, lacking either the flexibility or the catholicity necessary for popular leadership.

James K. Polk would be a more logical candidate for resurrection on the basis of strength and general effectiveness. He achieved tariff reduction, reform in the treasury, settlement of the Oregon boundary dispute, and the acquisition of California. He had, moreover, the unusual fortitude to decline to seek a second term.

George Fort Milton in *The Use of Presidential Power* tells us that the great presidents were the strong ones, great presumably including the idea of good for the people. The implications of such a doctrine are hazardous to liberty.

A president who assumes that he exclusively knows what the public desires, and that the elected representatives in Congress do not, is treading on dangerous ground. The structure of the Constitution was designed to prevent such assumptions.

The beginnings of dictatorship and of unlimited monarchy have relied on the theory that the head man actually expresses the will of the people as contrasted with their legislature. Such was the thought of Bolingbroke in *The Idea of a Patriot King,* when he advocated the Tory theory of monarchy. The American habit of free thought is so deep-rooted that no president to date has seriously contemplated a dictatorship, even when exercising extraordinary war or emergency powers, but that does not give sanction to the concept of a strong president as the measure of liberty.

Jefferson exercised unusual powers only in the case of the Louisiana Purchase, the Act for Governing Louisiana, and the Embargo Acts. Lincoln repeatedly resisted taking extreme measures, even though urged to do so by the other leaders of his party. A liberal president can quite as readily be marked by a sharing of his powers as by their exercise.

One of the high features of F. D. Roosevelt in the White House was his conduct of the war, in which he enlisted in his Cabinet men from the opposite party, steadily consulted and collaborated with the leaders of Congress, and refrained from the persecution of conscientious objectors and political critics.

Indeed, the cautious use of power is an earmark of the liberal mind.

3

Popularity is no surer measure of liberalism than power, at any given moment. In fact, in many instances the president has had no right to assume that he spoke for the majority of the people as measured by the election returns.

There is an impression, fostered by the mechanics of the electoral system, that presidential elections have been characterized by frequent landslides. In terms of the popular vote, this is a fallacy. A candidate obviously could run a close second in every state, yet win no electoral votes. Virtually every presidential election has been closely contested since 1824 when the electors began to be chosen àt the polls rather than by state legislatures.[3]

In eleven elections the successful candidate has had less than 50 per cent of the popular vote for all the candidates, and in only ten elections has the president won 55 per cent or more of the total; but, except in the cases of John Quincy Adams and Hayes, the winner has had a larger vote than any single one of his opponents.

The largest percentage of the popular vote enjoyed by any president was that of Harding who polled 60.48 per cent of the total in 1920. Franklin Roosevelt had the next largest in 1936 with 60.19 per cent. The opposition vote since 1824 has always exceeded 40 per cent.

Though not chosen in an era of wide popular elections, James Monroe, after Washington, was the only president to be overwhelmingly the public choice. In his second election Monroe was opposed by but one electoral vote, cast by a New Hampshire man who believed that no other president should duplicate Washington's record of being unanimously chosen, and none has. In only a few states was there popular polling for electors in Monroe's time, and the vote in those instances is no longer known, but the absence of any ticket opposing Monroe suggests a well-nigh unanimous acceptance of his candidacy.

The American public, moreover, has not voted habitually for candidates who advocate improvements or change. Bryan, Theodore Roosevelt's Progressive campaign, and the elder LaFollette certainly offered more liberal programs than their successful opponents—more liberal in the modern sense at least. Yet they were defeated by public test.

The majority are often conservative. In prosperous times the people are disposed to "leave well enough alone." Monroe's phenomenal popularity was due to a public who did not wish a change. Monroe was a slaveholder, a member of the Virginia coterie. Though reform was on the march, led by

---

[3] In the election of 1824 as referred to later in the chapter on Jackson, the popular vote figures were scantily reported. For detailed reports of this and other elections see Edward Stanwood, *A History of Presidential Elections.*

various bands of freethinkers, the mass of the public was contented. Monroe's administration was in the "era of good feeling."

Harding's case was somewhat similar, in that he benefited from a time of prosperity. Also, his victory was a revolt against Wilson's brand of liberalism, wartime regimentation, and advocacy of a world government. Harding's "back to normalcy" doctrine has been jeered at repeatedly by social reformers, but he received the largest popular majority of any president since the Civil War.

Each wave of liberalism which has swept America has raised different fundamental issues, so that the liberal of today has frequently found himself to be the conservative of tomorrow. Occasionally, the conservative of a given period ultimately becomes regarded as more liberal than his supposedly freethinking contemporaries. It cannot be assumed that the liberal presidents were the sole presidential advocates of major economic changes. The eight-hour day was introduced in the coal mines during the administration of McKinley, and in the steel industry under Harding.

The liberal presidents, further, cannot be said (war periods excepted) to have been especially notable for creating prosperity for the masses. In the last half-century administrations of the conservative William McKinley, Harding and Calvin Coolidge were noted for "full employment" and the "full dinner-pail," even though opponents denied them the credit therefor. True, the liberal Jackson was president in lush days. It is to be expected, however, that the liberal presidents, the apostles of change, will arise not in comfortable eras but in the winters of our discontent when the public is sharply aware of the failures of the *status quo* and welcomes new ways.

While not even two-thirds of the popular vote has ever been cast for a single candidate, and while liberalism has not been kept in the custody of any single party, it is not to be inferred that there has been no change. Frequently it has happened that the whole nation has moved in a given direction, so that presidential contests in a given cycle may revolve around personalities rather than principles, and not around good men as opposed to bad, but around men differing only in degree, detail, and temperament, as Willkie and Dewey differed from F. D. Roosevelt. The liberal tradition, in short, has been a series of departures from the past, led by men who represented the trends of their eras.

4

It is apparent then, that such ideas as good, strong, or popular do not suffice to give definition to the liberal tradition; yet the elements of the liberal as opposed to the authoritarian concept in government and public policy have been marked by several broad principles.

First is the belief in government by consent. The doctrine of the consent of the governed, nurtured in Greece, was revived by the Anglo-Saxon race for the modern world. The Magna Carta, even though granted only to the nobles, set forth the underlying principles. By the Revolution of 1688 the English government established supremacy of the Commons and limited the monarchy to being a symbol of the state. George II was no more an actual ruler than George VI.

The failure of Great Britain to extend this constitutional liberty to her colonies and the untimely attempt of George III to re-establish a personal monarchy forced the Colonies to rebel and form the United States, in order that the inhabitants might have the constitutional liberties enjoyed by Englishmen in the home country. The written constitution of the United States aimed to preserve the consent doctrine inviolate. All acts of the government are predicated upon the consent by the people, and in theory therefore, the government always has been liberal.

The principle of consent, however, had two dynamic implications which excited popular struggle for many generations. The first of these was the right to vote. The consent of the governed obviously implies the right of suffrage to every adult person, regardless of creed, color, or sex. The Constitution initially left the franchise question to self-determination in each state.

In the early days of the nation, the vote was limited by property qualifications in many states, by religion in some quarters, and almost universally denied to women and Negroes.

While the suffrage was rapidly extended to all white males, embracing virtually all in that category by 1828, the issue was rarely a concern of the inhabitants of the White House. The American presidency consistently ignored this phase of American freedom until the question of enfranchising the blacks was forced upon its attention during and after the Civil War. Again, the enfranchisement of women never had ardent or major support from any occupant of the White House. The consent of the governed was accepted as a passive rather than an active principle.

The other dynamic issue emerging from the consent principle was the extent of sovereignty. Does the federal government, on national and interstate matters, have the ultimate sovereignty? The presidency has been obliged to be concerned with that issue throughout the existence of the office. Until the question was settled in many essential respects by the Civil War, it involved the very continuation of the nation and, hence, of the presidency.

The consent of the governed theory, however, posed certain conflicts with the doctrine of sovereignty. On the one hand, national sovereignty was regarded by Washington and his successors as essential to the continued existence of the American experiment. On the other, the separate states, notably those of the South (though there were earlier abortive revolts in the North), claimed that their consent to be governed included their right to secede. Here was an issue similar to the eternal compromise between organized society and the individual. Theoretical anarchy, with each individual acting according to his conscience or desire, was obviously impractical, but in the interest of man-kind what was the ultimate unit of government—the family, tribe, town, state or nation? For the United States, by the terms of the Constitution, the essential governing unit was the nation, and Washington stretched this to include continental sovereignty as he envisaged the expansion toward the West. The government ruled not only over the States, who could dictate policies through their representatives; but also over the territories governed by appointive officers.

To a citizen of the United States in the twentieth century these considerations may seem ancient and irrelevant, but from a world point of view they continue to be pertinent. Since every nation today is close in point of time to every other, and since the presidency cannot be isolated from world affairs, principles of government hitherto valid cannot be comfortably assumed as an enduring matter of course.

As Weldon has pointed out, historically and currently there are three main theories of governmental organization—organic, force and consent. The organic theory assumes that a ruler or an elite group is in power by Divine Right, or destiny. Such for centuries was the theory in Japan, the theory in Germany under the Hohenzollerns, and in all monarchies where the legislature is not supreme.

The force theory, in turn, is a near cousin to the idea of the God-emperor. Mussolini and Hitler dispensed with free legislatures, preserving only the right to vote "yes." The countries who affirm belief in government by consent of the people currently have survived as victors in a World War. That is one important test of validity, but not conclusive. On a challenge of sheer material power, the American republic could not have persisted in its early days. Yet it continued.

H. S. Maine in *Popular Government* a half century ago affirmed that America's democratic institutions had endured under "peculiar" conditions "not likely to recur." Granting that they have been peculiar and are being modified, the presidential office is faced with the question not only of whether democratic institutions can be established elsewhere, but also of whether the United States should surrender a part of its sovereignty to the United Nations of the future in order that the unit of popular government, which Washington envisaged on a continental scale, may be enlarged.

As this issue will continue to face the country in the coming years, the early struggles of the presidential office in respect to union and sovereignty as providing a broad base for freedom, have a renewed pertinence.

Next to consent and sovereignty, the burning issue for the first seventy-five years of the United States was slavery. Not all the scents of Araby can conceal the fact that on this crucial question, the presidents of the republic took little or no action against slavery until it came to a crisis under Lincoln.

Fortunately for the young country, and for the peace of mind of those in the White House, the early economic struggles were not crucial. Nearly all citizens had a moderate prosperity, and the financial contests, such as the tariff, were largely among the elite in which such notables as John C. Calhoun and Daniel Webster reversed themselves as occasion might seem to require. The tariff, for example, was not an issue between the people and "the interests," but between different groups and sections. The Southern planters and the New England shippers desired a low tariff whereas the young manufacturers and Hamiltonian federalists sought protection for American industry.

The general idea of economic controls by government was considered illiberal in those first seventy-five years. Nineteenth century liberal doctrine demanded freedom from governmental interference in private affairs. Hence, many of the doctrines of Jefferson and Jackson would seem shockingly reactionary today. As shall be seen, the liberal tradition in economic matters has undergone revolutionary changes.

Since the Civil War, presidential office has asserted continuing and enlarging controls over finance and business, preservation of national resources, regulation of hours, wages, taxation, and various forms of social security. The control trend began with the rise of industrial America in the late nineteenth century, and has continued under every president, including those usually considered to be conservative.

Anti-imperialism is another yardstick by which the liberal tradition may be measured. Where the nation has acquired new lands by purchase, both the American public and history have approved. Where empire has been achieved by conquest, the public at the moment has usually applauded, but it is difficult to include the action in the liberal tradition. In fact, the entire history of the seizure of land from the Indians is an inconsistency which highlights the difficulties of achieving a just and free state. President Jackson, as shall be seen, tried elaborately and ingeniously to defend America's Indian policy on the highest moral grounds, ending in a morass which encouraged silence on the part of his successors in office.

Peace, the active use of the presidential office to avert war and to achieve world peace, is a phase of liberalism in which the presidency has been conspicuous. Jefferson risked his popularity to avert war. Lincoln and Johnson set a new example in attitude toward the vanquished and the restoration of peace. Cleveland and Taft, for a time Theodore Roosevelt, and notably Wilson and F. D. Roosevelt, gave the fullest influence of the presidency toward creating new means for the effectuating of peace among all nations.

The liberal tradition in the American presidency is then to be measured by its relationship to the consent of the governed, to union and sovereignty, to slavery and race issues, to justice between sections, to anti-imperialism, to economic protection of the citizen, and to world peace.

Not all of these issues have involved the presidential office, at any one time. The office is presented in terms of issues and men, however, because that has been the realism of its development. Its theoretical place was fixed by the Constitution. Few legal changes have been made in its powers except in cases of emergency and in the expansion of appointive powers.

While trying to appraise the liberal tradition in the presidency in terms of the major issues in our national development, it may be worthwhile to comment briefly on some of the usages of "liberal" as a descriptive adjective.

The word "liberal," to be sure, is a loose term, having many connotations depending upon the individual. Consider first its historic and strictly political sense. It was first applied to the more radical section of the Whig Party in England, early in the nineteenth century, the party which had earlier supported the cause of the American Colonies. The various anti-Tory groups in England united under the Whig banner in 1832, and in 1839 became officially known as the Liberal Party which embarked on a long career of political reform.

The *Oxford English Dictionary* defines "liberal" as "favourable to constitutional changes and legal or administrative reforms tending in the direction of freedom or democracy." Webster amplifies the thought by saying "not bound by authority, orthodox tenets, or established forms."

Joseph and Stewart Alsop contribute a further refinement to the term by introducing the element of speed. The conservative, they hold, wants change "to be as slow as possible," whereas the liberal political leader is discontented with the existing order, positively likes social change, and wants it to be rapid.[4]

Bernard DeVoto adds the thought that "the intellectual climate of their time" affects historians, and that "fashions, in thesis and dogma, sift under their study doors." [5]

Hence, intellectual fashion and climate have had their part. In each period, there have been influences which marked certain men as liberal or illiberal, because of their relation to measures or beliefs of transient interest. A few fundamental goals and the basic intent, seem to be the most reliable means for appraising the liberal tradition and the presidents who have been its chief beacon lights.

In the present "climate" America continues, like the early Greek republics, to be torn between a desired maximum of freedom for all individuals, and a reasonable amount of policing in order that society may provide the citizen with an opportunity for life, liberty and the pursuit of happiness. Every president has been obliged to face this dilemma in varying degrees; and a reexamination of the subject over the span of our history may not only be provocative, but may give us renewed courage to tackle its complexities.

To use Lincoln's words, the liberal tradition has implied a willingness "to think and act anew. We must disenthrall ourselves, and then we shall save our country."

[4] Joseph and Stewart Alsop in *Life,* May 20, 1946.
[5] Bernard DeVoto, *Harper's Magazine,* February, 1946.

Thirteen cozy little states nestling on the Atlantic seaboard, their population composed of planters, farmers, woodsmen, trappers, fishermen, with a few rich shippers, merchants and importers clustered in the major seaports. The total populace was under four million.

There were no factories. The capital city was New York, with 33,000 population living on Manhattan Island.

The states had proclaimed themselves as United States in brave language conceived by a few statesmen, yet their differences were extraordinary.

In New England, the merchant and shipping adventurer contrasted with the religious Pilgrims, the Wesleyan Methodists, and the Rhode Island Baptists.

In New York, the Dutch, the English, the Spanish and Portuguese Jews, the traders from all nations were founders.

In Delaware were Swedes; in Pennsylvania were Quakers and sects from everywhere to whom William Penn gave sanctuary, notably refugees from Germany and Czech areas.

Maryland was a Catholic refuge. Georgia harbored debtors. Virginia had received both "cavaliers" and "roundheads" as fortunes changed in England.

North Carolina was a thriving and peace-loving cross-section of Scotch, Scotch Irish, Moravian, Swiss, and English settlers.

South Carolina was mainly British, Huguenot and Czech. It was also cosmopolitan; churches of many faiths and racial origins were to be found there.

All of these differences had a unity of voluntary agreement. They chose to live together under mutually agreed terms, rather than to live separately under previous terms with the mother country.

The revolutionary war had banded the colonies together in revolt against what they would not do. Successful in that, they were faced with what they would agree to do collectively in the future.

2

First Patterns for the Presidency

Washington was an Englishman, you know, after all.
ANDREW JOHNSON

Every valuable end of government is best answered by the enlightened confidence of the people, and by teaching the people themselves to know and value their own rights.
GEORGE WASHINGTON, *First Message to Congress*

I

The intrinsic character of George Washington established the liberal tradition in the American presidency. The unanimous choice of him for the office by contemporaries, who were divided into many different camps of opinion, was significant of his uniqueness. The trust which the quarreling factions placed in him enabled him to mold the first patterns of the presidency in accord with his convictions.

To the modern mind the traditional George Washington is a figure unreal, vague, with a surface of plaster of Paris. The wig, the colonial costume, the ubiquitous Gilbert Stuart portraits give him the remote aspect of a character of a period drama. His predominant repute as a military man also tends to alienate him from the civilian mind.

It is important to bring the man alive before we can comprehend the influence which he had on his times, an influence which has flowed down to succeeding generations. Andrew Johnson gave a key to Washington's nature when he said, "Washington was an Englishman, you know, after all." A sage remark. Washington was as English as roast beef. He had the heartiness, the tenacity and the dogged sense of individual rights which have characterized the Britisher.

Born in 1732, forty-four years before the American Revolution, he had come to middle age as a British subject. He had engaged in soldiering from the age of twenty-one to thirty-two and had fought alongside of professional British troops against the French. In 1775 he had been appointed in command of all the Virginia forces to defend the western frontier of that colony against the Indians. Here he gained a broad military training, but he found that as a colonial he received scant consideration from the British military authorities, and in 1758 he retired from active Army service.

By the time of the American Revolution, Washington, through inheritance, marriage and skill as a planter had become one of the richest men in the colonies, possibly the first in wealth. He was a country gentleman on an ample scale, a devotee of horse racing, hunting, dancing, fine food and drink, and an astute manager of his financial affairs. He had occupied the office of local magistrate, had sat in the Virginia House of Burgesses, and in Williamsburg had come in contact with that extraordinary and brilliant coterie which had included Jefferson, Mason, Patrick Henry, Madison and the like.

As commander-in-chief of the Continental Army, Washington was forged by a new set of experiences. He was obliged to be not only a fighter and strategist, but also a master politician. It fell upon his shoulders to obtain money and supplies from the Congress and various colonial governments. He had to cope with disloyalties among his officers, to negotiate with foreign allies, in fact, to deal with virtually every aspect of government and under the disadvantage of improvised and changing conditions.

Throughout the war, the ease of Mount Vernon was left behind, and his daily contact was with all conditions of men, including the common soldier. The Continental army was a volunteer informal affair and as its chief, Washington came to know the common people through intimate association on the camp ground, as few other presidents have done. When the war was over he fought for the veteran's cause before a new Congress, though seeking nothing for himself. He sternly rejected the suggestion of some of his officers to make him a king, and he retired to Mount Vernon never expecting again to be associated with politics. He had loaned most of his fortune to the Revolutionary cause, was deeply in debt and never recovered financially. His later years were a struggling sharp contrast to his rich colonial days.

Accordingly, when we think of the man who became America's first president, the wealth, the portraits and the statues fade into the background. We observe a Virginia planter who was worried over his bills. We see a tall rugged man, large-faced, pallid, worn by his experiences in war. He has lived through every vicissitude of politics. He has been chairman of the Constitutional Convention and as such has heard the arguments advanced for the various plans for setting up a new government. He has reached the conclusion that the compromise arrived at is the best that could be obtained under the circumstances. He would be content to rest at home. But all parties persuade him that he is the one outstanding citizen who can give prestige and authority to the new enterprise.

This choice of Washington by his peers casts an odd light on such historians as J. S. Bassett who affirm that he "was not versed in the principles of Government." C. A. Beard is perhaps on less shaky ground in saying "It does not appear . . . that he ever set forth any coherent system of Government," though Washington's official papers deal with many phases of statecraft.

Washington, it is true was not a formal political philosopher, not given to theoretical speculations, but in his person as an eighteenth century British citizen who had risked all to insist on his rights, he embodied the traditional British freedoms transplanted to American soil. The free English heritage of Washington included freedom of speech, freedom of the press, freedom of assembly, the right to be tried by one's peers.

The Bill of Rights was British in origin, having been formally adopted in 1688, and incorporated in the first ten amendments of the American Constitution. The basic doctrine of consent, or representation, and the principle that the taxing and appropriating powers belong to the popular legislature were British concepts. In 1765 when resisting the Stamp Act in his capacity as a British citizen, Washington had said that parliament "hath no more right to put their hands into my pocket, without my consent, than I have to put my hands into yours for money."

Washington's approach started, then, with a solid body of old-school liberalism, rather than with a sense of mental adventure. He tried new paths without hesitation, but in the main he sought methods which would enable the old freedoms to prevail. His mind was colored by the fact that the English commonwealth was primarily a commercial one. Even the hereditary nobility were habitually replenished by commoners who had amassed fortunes in trade, finance, the law, or warfare. Washington sought to build a country in which the common man would prosper. The class struggle was not in his ken. He saw the New World as a land of opportunity for all.

2

While Washington had presided over the Constitutional Convention he had only once taken part in the discussions, holding that it was not his place to do so while occupying the chair. On the one occasion which was the exception, however, he had chosen to speak in favor of having a larger number of representatives in the Congress in order that the people's will might be more fully recorded.

Privately, Washington was deeply concerned over the fundamental method whereby the popular will was to be expressed. Should it be through a loosely knit government of independent units? The Articles of Confederation under which the new country operated for its first few years had proved to be impractical. "Persuaded I am that the primary cause of all our disorders lies in the different state governments and in the tenacity of that power," Washington wrote to David Stuart. "Whilst independent sovereignty is so ardently contended for it must render the situation of this great country weak, inefficient and disgraceful." He desired "a firm and permanent government for this union, that all who live under it may be secure in their lives, liberty and property."

The new Constitution as finally adopted did provide numerous specified functions for the federal government such as national defense, the raising of money, the issuing of currency and so on, but there was an undefined area in the Tenth Amendment. "All powers not delegated to the United

States, by the Constitution, nor prohibited by it to the states, are reserved to the states, or to the people."

Jefferson and his followers took the position that the rights reserved to the states barred the federal government from exercising any rights not specifically stated. It may be noted, however, that the Tenth Amendment reserved the undefined rights alternatively "to the people." This obviously could be interpreted to mean that the people through Congress likewise could exercise the reserved rights.

Jefferson said, "To take a single step beyond the boundaries thus specially drawn around the powers of Congress, is to take possession of a boundless field of power, no longer susceptible of any definition."

James Madison, however, recognized that an individual independence of the states was "utterly irreconcilable with the idea of an aggregate sovereignty." He looked for a middle ground "which will at once support a due supremacy of the national authority, and leave in force the local authorities so far as they can be subordinately useful." If such a broad attitude could have been accepted throughout the early years of the nation, much travail would have been avoided.

Washington on assuming the presidency hoped to compose the differences between those who would interpret the Constitution broadly and those who would limit it strictly, by appointing his Cabinet evenly from the differing groups. Alexander Hamilton at the Treasury was a broad construction man, while his *vis-a-vis* was Thomas Jefferson as secretary of state.

The activities of Alexander Hamilton in attempting to set up a sound financial structure put a severe strain on Washington's desire for harmony. Hamilton had several far-reaching proposals. He proposed to honor at par the Continental currency and to assume the debts of the separate states. He aimed to establish a central bank, somewhat on the pattern of the Bank of England. He advocated a federal sales tax on whiskey and a tariff to protect domestic manufacturers.

Hamilton's proposal to redeem the Continental currency at par and to assume the state debts was calculated by him to enlist the interest of the financial fraternity in the new government.

To the eighteenth century English mind a governmental alliance with commerce was plain common sense, a matter of course, commendable. What was good for British trade, was good for the country, was good. In time of war when a British ship seized an enemy vessel, all of the victors, from the captain to the least of the crew, were entitled to a percentage, according to a recognized schedule. It was assumed that national activities would be so conducted as to benefit the finances of the citizens. For example, certain colonists desiring to establish a college in western Massachusetts, presenting their petition to General Amherst, quite sincerely argued that it would promote "the Redeemer's name and the British interest." Neither government nor liberty were abstractions in the Anglo-Saxon mind, but rather methods for providing for a satisfactory economic life.

In the new country there was much to be said for that practical point of view, as expressed by Hamilton's program for meeting Continental obligations. There was scandal in the fact that a few speculators had prior knowledge that the government would honor colonial paper, and therefore had bought up quantities of currency at depreciated values; yet there was the advantage that the United States now would have a clean slate financially. The new management which had come in with the Constitution, thereby paid all creditors, even those brokers who had bought the notes at a discount.

The assumption of state debts by the federal union also strengthened the credit record. While the assumption in one sense was unfair to the solvent states and favored those less prudent, it bound all under a blanket commitment. The union, and all the states in it, were benefited by the financial restoration of the weaker elements. Washington was able to report to Congress at various times in his administration that loans had been floated with the Dutch government, which was notable evidence of the secure financial standing of the new country. As a further point in the policy, separatism for any state became less desirable as financial unity was achieved.

Even Jefferson at first was convinced by Hamilton that the federal financial measures were wise, and wrote to James Monroe, "In the present instance I can see the necessity of yielding to the cries of the creditors in certain parts of the union, for the sake of union."

Hamilton as a practical man had sweetened the proposition for the Southern delegates by offering to support the location of the capital city on the Potomac River, if the South would agree to his financial proposals. Virginia, in particular, and other Southern states, had been disturbed over the fact that the seat of the federal government was currently in New York and possibly would be located permanently in Philadelphia. Hence the South accepted the bargain, and Jefferson endorsed it.

Not long afterward, Jefferson wrote to Washington that he had been duped by Hamilton and "made a tool for forwarding his schemes, not being sufficiently understood by me." It seems difficult to believe that Jefferson actually was deluded by Hamilton, as to any particular proposition at any particular moment, but it is likely that when Jefferson first united with Hamilton's plans he did not realize the prestige that they would bring to the Hamiltonian views or to other measures that might flow from them.

Jefferson had had little contact with American urban life, having spent most of his years either in Virginia or as a diplomat in France. Accordingly, all of his preferences and prejudices were against the systems which Hamilton understood. Jefferson not only distrusted the financial and commercial groups, including the commercial working classes; but he was strongly opposed to anything which smacked of British tradition.

Hence the very devotion of Hamilton to various aspects of the British system was peculiarly annoying to Jefferson and helped to widen the chasm between the two men. Jefferson himself tells the story of a Cabinet meeting held in the absence of President Washington, in which the British system of government was discussed. Hamilton, Jefferson asserts, maintained that the corruption which existed in the British government was one of the things which kept it going. Hamilton is quoted as saying that the British government "as it stands at present, with all its supposed defects, is the most perfect government that ever existed."

The story rings true. Hamilton as a British subject, who had observed the strength of that mercantile nation, believed that the very things to which Jefferson objected, namely that government policy should favor the mercantile interests, was part of the strength of the system, and to Jefferson that was "corruption."

Hamilton also obviously believed that in the British Empire at that time was the greatest guarantee of freedom, the greatest protection to individual rights that had existed anywhere on the face of the globe up to that time. Jefferson leaped to the conclusion, however, that Hamilton would like to reproduce every detail of the British pattern in the New World and from time to time he accused Hamilton of favoring a monarchy and a House of Lords.

On another occasion Jefferson had the opportunity to discuss with Washington his objections to Hamilton's financial policies and found that the president was defending them at every point. Finally, Jefferson, discovering that the president was a believer in "the treasury system," pursued the subject no further.

Washington did believe in the treasury system as developed by Hamilton and at the same time in the words of Jefferson, he was "true to the republican charge confided to him." In fact Jefferson reports that Washington made this pledge the more earnestly because he knew of Jefferson's suspicions and doubts.

Obviously there was a gap somewhere between men who wished to serve the public causes by differing routes. Hamilton was described by Jefferson as "A singular character . . . disinterested, honest in all private transactions . . . yet bewitched and perverted by the British example." Washington, too, was regarded by Jefferson as a man of unequaled character. The records also show that Washington did not profit by the financial policies of the new government. He was not among the numerous holders of government paper who had benefited by the assumption of colonial debts, yet Washington supported the Hamiltonian policy, as helpful to the nation.

The moment comes for a flash back. We have seen Washington, the stalwart freedom-loving colonial fighting for his British rights. We have seen them won, a new country established, failure threatened because of weakness of the Confederation, a Constitution adopted which included the essence of the British Bill of Rights, steps taken to strengthen the unity of the new country, and thereupon the outcry of "British influence"! What events of history had produced the seeming paradox of American leaders affirming the principles of their heritage, yet denouncing their origin?

3

The words "monarchy" or "monarchical" were favorite epithets, used by those who opposed a strong central government, carrying the inference that support of federal administration was no more than a cloak for the desire to establish a royal system in the United States. During the Revolution, the anti-British propaganda of the colonies naturally had stated the issue in extreme terms. The Declaration of Independence had referred to the Throne as "An absolute despotism." That was a considerable exaggeration as Jefferson, drafter of the Declaration, knew. Other pamphleteers, including Hamilton, Paine and Madison, affirmed the tyranny of British kingship, when trying to arouse ardor for the American system.

The politically educated men of the time were aware that George III was a recent, and only moderately successful, exponent of Tory practice, and did not represent the traditional English concept of kingship or constitutional practice.

A student of the early years of the United States government may, then, be misled if he accepts at face value the language of the political literature of the time, which tended to characterize anything undesirable as British. To understand the heritage of the colonies, Washington's attitude toward the presidency, and the broad general issues which had led to the separation of the colonies and the defeat of the Tories at home, it seems worth while to digress briefly and review what had been taking place in the home country.

Long before the struggle for freedom in America, the fight for civil liberty had been waged recurrently in Great Britain. There had been cycles of freedom in England before the time of the Tory Stuarts. Cromwell staged a protest, then the Stuarts returned, only to fail ultimately and completely.

When in 1688 the English had been able to dispense with James II, bloodlessly, and summon a new dynasty, government by "divine right" was at an end. The Bill of Rights was written into law. The Parliamentary authority was solidified further in 1714, when the government chose George, the Elector of Hanover, as king under the Act of Settlement. George I, wholly ignorant of the English tongue, had little interest in the government conducted in his name. George II grumbled at the domination of his ministers, but accepted the realities.

There was no doubt as to where the source of power resided. The prime minister issued orders of state in the name of "his Majesty," but it was the prime minister and cabinet, dependent upon the support of the Commons, who determined what the orders should be. When any ministry failed to enjoy majority support of the Commons, it was obliged to resign. The monarch appointed his ministers, conferred titles and distributed most of the best sinecures in the government, but in all this he followed instructions from the prime minister. Even the king's "Address from the Throne" at the opening of Parliament, which was comparable to the American presidents' messages to Congress, was composed by a spokesman of the ministry and expressed its policy. The king was simply the embodiment of the state, without personal authority.

Throughout the long period from 1688 to the accession of George III in 1760 the Whigs had been the dominant party. In general, the same leading families held the chief offices, though brilliant critics such as William Pitt and Edmund Burke could occasionally force their way in. The threat of a return of Tory rule, abetted by French influence, served to keep the Whigs in power. Further, in the eighteenth century England enjoyed an era of prosperity for all classes (except the poorest city dwellers) such as had never before been experienced, and accordingly there was little discontent with the existing regime.

During the Whig supremacy the American colonies were frequently neglected and ignored, but not systematically opposed, or called upon for gestures of obedience. The Whig policy was zealous for civil rights, for constitutional liberties, and watchful against attempts at aggrandizement by the Throne. The inherent weakness of the Whig machine, a common fault in politics, was its disposition to hog all the favors of government, and to underestimate the potentialities of shrewd men in opposition.

Naturally the underprivileged Tories were eager for a change, and found their opportunity in the early reign of George III. The young George had been tutored by the Earl of Bute, a Tory, who had great influence over him. The primer of instruction had been Bolingbroke's *The Idea of a Patriot King*. George was taught that the nominal powers of the throne were or should be actual. Long before his disputes with the colonies, he had alarmed his ministers and started on a career of attempted seizure of powers. At the very outset he attempted to dictate his "Address from the Throne" without the approval of his Cabinet. The leaders of the government protested, and the king was obliged to modify his words for the official record.

Under Bute's guidance, George III resolved "to purge to his Court" of former officeholders, and new faces appeared everywhere. The king was able to defy constitutional precedent not only because of Tory revival, but likewise because of rivalry and dissension among the Whig leaders. The elder Pitt's ministry fell in 1763, and was followed by a series of weak administrations which were personal and factional rather than typical of any party. It was during these vacillating 1760's that the taxation issue rose in the colonies, and failed to be resolved.

Compared with the dictatorships witnessed by the modern world,

George III's attempts at personal rule were amateurish. The king and his ministers defied the unwritten constitution of the nation, but could not suppress public criticism. In 1780 Dunning rose in the Commons and offered the resolution, "Resolved that the power of the Throne has increased, is increasing and ought to be diminished."

When the colonies had declared their Independence, Pitt, Lord Chatham, was free to say in the House of Lords, "I rejoice that the colonies have resisted." General Amherst declined to take the sword against the colonies on the ground that success would be impossible, yet he lived to be a member of the Cabinet. Burke was not liquidated for urging the conciliation of the American colonies. General Howe, a sympathizer with American principles, was the most courteous and harmless invader that a rebel army ever experienced. Whig sympathizers in Parliament wore the buff and blue colors of the Continental Army.

Throughout the differences between England and America, Benjamin Franklin and other colonial representatives openly conferred with leaders of the government's opposition. Lord North, the Tory prime minister, 1770–1782, had no arbitrary police powers, even though he was the symbol of tyranny in the colonies. He was merely an unfortunate actor in an untimely cause. A nobleman of small means, and father of eleven children, he desired to continue in his lucrative government office up to a point. At his supreme moment of common sense he demonstrated the profound respect for law which prevailed even in Tory quarters. That moment was when the news of Cornwallis' defeat at Yorktown reached England. Lord North as an experienced politician knew that the Tory government could not survive that blow. Parliament would fail to give it a vote of confidence, and it would retire. Hence North tendered his resignation to the king ahead of the inevitable event. The young George III, educated in a fictional dream, having succeeded briefly in defying constitutional practices, commanded Lord North to continue in office, but the minister politely declined.

Popular report has largely forgotten that significant scene, so illuminating as to England's practice, so pertinent to America's beginnings. Consider the facts: The British king, allegedly an absolute tyrant, commanded his chief minister to remain in charge, was refused, and there was nothing he could do about it. The king became merely a stubborn, unhappy man. He retained his well-paid glamorous job, but was surrounded thenceforth by ministers who were unsympathetic to his royalist views, which never again prevailed.

4

The return of constitutional practices in Britain left the custom of kingship as the major difference between the English and American systems. There were grave fears in the new country lest the presidency as chief office of the state assume a monarchical tinge. It may be credited to Washington that his conduct of the office forever dispelled that possibility. He regarded the presidency as responsive to the public voice, republican in character and manner. At the outset, he addressed a letter to John Adams giving his thoughts as to the proper conduct of the office. Should he remain "equally distant" from "all kinds of company"? Or should he be wholly secluded. If the latter, "how is it to be done"? Again, how may any system which is adopted be brought "before the public and into use"?

He considered setting aside one day a week for receiving complimentary visits, and the possibility of giving audience to any business callers each morning at eight o'clock. He disapproved of lavish entertainments, and wondered "whether it would be satisfactory to the public" to limit the presidential levees to about four in a year.

He reviewed what he should do about calls in his private capacity, whether he might appear "rarely at tea parties." Further, might it not be "advantageous to the interests of the Union" for the president to make a tour of the United States during the recesses of Congress, to "become better acquainted with their people and internal circumstances"; also to be more accessible to "numbers of well-informed persons," who might give him useful information and advices on political subjects. (He later made several such tours.)

Some of the points might seem trivial, he granted, but they were not negligible at this stage. "Many things which appear of little importance in themselves and at the beginning," he wrote, "may have great and durable consequences from their having been established at the commencement of a new general government. It will be much easier to commence the administration, upon a well adjusted system, built on tenable grounds, than to correct errors or alter inconveniences after they have been formed by habit. The President in all matters of business and etiquette, can have no object but to demean himself in his public character, in such a manner as to maintain the dignity of Office, without subjecting himself to the imputation of superciliousness or unnecessary reserve." Such was the humble spirit of the man who nevertheless later was accused of "monarchical" tendencies.

Washington's simple manner [1] of conducting the office of president was significant of his concept of his duties. A lesser man might have become swollen with the powers which were his by Constitutional definition. The president was Commander-in-Chief of the Army and Navy, had the power to make treaties (by and with the consent of the Senate), and had control over a wide range of appointments. It was his duty to report to Congress periodically on the state of the nation and to recommend such legislation as he thought "necessary and expedient."

Within those elastic limits Washington might have stretched himself to be a Cromwell, though not king. In a superficial sense the presidency replaced both king and prime minister, since in America only the one man was

---

[1] Less simple than later practices, but primitive compared with royal courts.

chief of state. Actually, none of the functions of kingship were pertinent to the New World. The nation as such, not any ruling person, was the proper object of devotion and loyalty. Washington repeatedly, in his state papers, pleaded for ardent adherence to the union, not to himself.

The presidency, then, was broadly comparable to the post of prime minister. Washington deplored political parties, "or faction" as he called them, in the new country. He regarded himself as representative of the whole and not as a party man. Even so, he acted as a Federalist party man when he dismissed from office some three hundred anti-Federalists who were opposed to a strong central government. Even Washington, in spite of his non-partisan emphasis, was soon faced with an opposition in Congress. The distinction between party and national leadership does not seem significant to this writer, for either president or prime minister upon assuming office is the leader of the whole nation.

Whether Washington would have deplored a party system as it subsequently developed in America can be only a matter for speculation. His attitude must be considered in the light of the surrounding circumstances. America was an experiment in republican self-government. The eyes of the Old World were on the country, with doubt and skepticism. The nation, in Washington's opinion, was too new, too shaky, to afford dissensions; and the Hamilton-Jefferson rivalry was evidence of the potential dangers.

In August, 1792, the quarrel between the two men had reached such a pass that the President felt the need to step in. He wrote to each asking for "mutual forebearances, and temporizing yieldings *on all sides.*" To Jefferson he pleaded, "How unfortunate that internal dissensions should be . . . tearing at our vitals . . . If, instead of laying our shoulders to the machine after measures are decided on, one pulls this way and another that, before the utility of the thing is fairly tried, it must inevitably be torn asunder; and in my opinion the fairest prospect of happiness and prosperity, that was ever presented to man, will be lost perhaps *for ever.*"

The words temporarily had a pacifying effect, but Jefferson had become greatly alarmed over Hamilton's plan for the Bank of the United States. The majority of the bank's stock was held, and the majority of the directors were chosen, by private interests and only a minority of the directors were nominated by the government.

The bank had the benefit of government deposits and various other special privileges, in return for handling specific financial details for the Treasury. The bank's charter was comparable to systems which had worked in the Old World. The fact that it served like "assumption" to attach the financial groups to the government was no shock to Washington, and he proudly reported to Congress on the prompt subscription of the bank's stock.

There was, in fact, no coherent alternate system offered to the Hamilton plan, of which the bank was a part. The plan served the South as well as the

North. David Ramsay of South Carolina, urging the adoption of the Constitution by his fellow citizens, had pointed out that the meeting of foreign obligations was one of the chief advantages of the new union. Otherwise, he affirmed, steps undoubtedly would be taken to collect the debts, the first of which would be seizure of the ports—in which Charleston unquestionably would be a major sufferer. All things considered, the economic protection of the citizen had been assured through establishing the good credit of the government. Jefferson, however, saw added political prestige for Hamilton in the bank scheme, and he believed the establishment of the bank was an unconstitutional use of federal power.

The first serious challenge to the government's power oddly enough did not come from the South, but from Pennsylvania; not on an involved constitutional issue, but over the tax on whiskey. The tax had been voted legally by the people's representatives in Congress, but as the manufacture of whiskey was a sizable industry in western Pennsylvania, the burden fell particularly heavily there. Neither the producer nor the consumer was sympathetic to the excise. Many of the inhabitants of the western part of that state were hardy Scots who looked upon the beverage as one of the staples of daily life, and resented the tax.

Federal revenue agents were ignored, avoided, and ultimately resisted. Washington met the issue without hesitation. He had called upon the governor of Pennsylvania to collaborate in enforcement of the law, but the governor had remained passive. Washington realized that there would be opposition to federal enforcement, and described the situation in a letter to C. M. Thurston: "Actual rebellion against the laws of the United States exists at this moment . . . if the laws are to be so trampled on with impunity, and a minority (a small one, too) is to dictate to the majority, there is an end at one stroke to republican government. . . . Yet there will be found persons, I have no doubt, who . . . will nevertheless be opposed to coercion, even if the proclamation and the other temperate measures should fail. . . . It is not difficult by the concealment of some facts and the exaggeration of others . . . to bias a well-meaning mind."

A few hundred soldiers would have been fully sufficient to have enforced the law, but Washington took the opportunity to make a show of strength on the part of the new government. He called out the militia of several states, and assembled a force of fifteen thousand to put down the so-called rebellion. The ringleaders were readily apprehended, brought to trial and convicted. The federal authority had been asserted successfully, and all the culprits were pardoned.

The strength of the presidency was tested further by critical relationships with foreign countries. France and England were at war, and the sympathies of America were naturally on the side of her recent ally. Relying on this sympathy, the French emissary to the United States, Citizen Genêt, far exceeded his portfolio. He not only engaged in propaganda and in American politics, but he gave French commissions to American privateers, authorizing them to attack British shipping. Obviously such behavior was a violation of neutrality.

Washington's position in the matter was not easy, and made less so by the failure of Britain to carry out some of her agreements with America. The public would have supported a quiet ignoring of Genêt's activities, but Washington pursued his statecraft directly and honestly. He demanded, successfully, that France recall Genêt, and he sent John Jay as a special emissary to England for the purpose of making a satisfactory treaty there.

The Jay treaty proved to be anything but ideal from the American standpoint; but it was a treaty by the newest country in the world with the most powerful, a recognition of status among the society of nations, and for the nonce that was of indisputable value. Critics in Congress demanded that the President lay the confidential papers in the case before them, but Washington firmly declined, standing on his constitutional rights.

Washington was stalwart in asserting the powers of the established government, yet just as clearly he did not try to channel the power toward the aggrandizement of his office or on the behalf of an elite class of society. He could have won popularity again through a foreign war, but he strove successfully for peace.

As an eighteenth century Britisher, he had started with the principle that government derives its powers from the consent of the governed, and as president of the new country he set out to prove by his conduct of the office, that a people's government could manage its affairs as effectively and authoritatively as a royal state.

His desire to establish a strong financial structure for the country, his ability to enlist the support of the most eminent people, and his personal dignity, have served to give his administration an aristocratic cast, and to obscure the fact that Washington had moved a step further than the English doctrine of civil rights by visualizing a country which could provide happiness and prosperity for all.

In his brief First Inaugural he said, "Every valuable end of government is best answered by the enlightened confidence of the people, and by teaching the people themselves to know and value their own rights." To further the people's interest in their government, he proposed public aid to education, either through existing seminaries or "other expedients." He strengthened his belief in this project by providing in his will for the establishment of a national university, though the securities set aside for this purpose were in a company which ultimately became insolvent.

The impetus given to free education through Washington's influence was felt more in state and local circles than on a national scale; but free education became a characteristic of the American community, a cardinal part in its belief in self-rule. As others succeeded Washington in the presidency, the lack of free education had been supplied and hence the subject did not require as pointed presidential attention. In Washington's first administration, however, his emphasis on the value of popular education was not only pertinent but significant of his commitment to republican ideals.

For Washington's chief contribution to political philosophy, it is logical to turn to his Farewell Address which was directly intended as his testament for the nation. Several members of the Cabinet had a hand in it. Hamilton is said to have written parts of the final draft, but obviously it was Washington's philosophy through and through.

Here again was the doctrine of national unity and sovereignty which he had preached repeatedly to Jefferson and others. The people he held, had "an indissoluble community of interest as *one nation.*" He deplored foreign alliances and domestic party dissensions because they serve "to distract the public councils and enfeeble the public administration." In a country so new, a full unity of purpose was essential to survival. The greatest good would come through forgetting sectional rivalries and thinking in terms of mutual advantage. "The unity of government . . . is a main pillar in the edifice of real independence."

The fashions and yardsticks of liberalism, as has been noted, change from era to era. With Washington, liberty was something to be insisted upon, fought for, and upheld by a stalwart government responsive to the people. He believed in free education, but the issue of racial discrimination held little place in his consciousness.

All of the pre-Civil War presidents were imperialistic in the sense of intruding increasingly on Indian possessions, and Washington was no exception.

Self determination and home rule in the sense of separate state powers or any implication of the right of secession were abhorrent to him. He saw liberty protected by "the benign influence of good laws under a free government."

The broadest possible extent of free government, rather than the self-determination of localities was Washington's major contribution, in his acts and policies as president. Both Jackson and Lincoln rested on pure Washington doctrine in their concept of national sovereignty. Washington did not foresee an age, as did several presidents from Cleveland onward, when national advantage might be surrendered to a larger sovereignty on behalf of world freedom; but he did throughout the presidency affirm the importance of subordinating local interest to the greater good. In this respect, he stood for a principle which the future might expand to ever enlarging limits.

3
Decline of the National Ideal

During the contest of opinion through which we have passed the animation of discussions and of exertions has sometimes worn an aspect which might impose on strangers.

THOMAS JEFFERSON, *First Inaugural Address*

I

When Washington retired from office, Jefferson observed somewhat sourly, "The president is fortunate to get off just as the bubble is bursting, leaving others to hold the bag."

Jefferson was expecting an economic breakdown to result from Hamilton's financial policies. While he was wrong in that detail, he was correct in his intuition that Washington's retirement marked the final phase of an era.

All over the Western world there were changes in the political and philosophic accent. The positivism of Washington was out of style. His repeated pleas that a strong government was necessary, in order to maintain a free country over a large area, now smacked of authoritarianism. The younger generation who had grown up in the United States during or since the American Revolution had no sense of the vigilance and effort which had been required in the formation and perpetuating of the new nation. The new freedom had been handed to them on a platter.

The French Revolution, supposedly and avowedly bringing to mankind the blessings of liberty, equality, and fraternity, had also in practise been succeeded by the Reign of Terror and the dominating success of Napoleon's armies. This conflict between the ideal and the actual events had a profound influence on the American political scene. The philosophical democrats accepting the avowals of the French Revolution at their face value, assumed that France had carried further, along the path of freedom, what the American Revolution had begun. Conversely, the older American liberals, and the former supporters of America in England, such as Edmund Burke, looked upon the developments in France as a threat to the Constitutional liberty which had been established in America. The rejection of Lafayette by the French revolutionaries had strengthened that opinion. John Adams, Washington's successor, believed with Washington that the Union was the chief safeguard of liberty and made a sturdy effort to maintain the prestige of nationalism.

Adams had assumed office under peculiarly difficult circumstances. As stated, the tide was running against the federal principle. He replaced the towering Washington, and his dogged personality was ill-suited to the task. History has demonstrated that the presidency calls for a stature either heroic, or facile, or unassertive. Adams was burgherish, stubborn and aggressive; by no means mediocre, but poorly equipped to handle or evade opposition.

In a more established time, facing lesser antagonists, Adams might well have survived as an outstanding character, intelligent and statesmanlike. He would have shone in the age of Grant; but he was obliged to compete with such minds as Madison and Jefferson, and with the astute rivalry of Hamilton in his own party.

Party in America was an amorphous undefined idea. It applied primarily to factions in Congress and to theories of government rather than to organized masses of voters. Jefferson is supposed to have made the first mention of a formal opposition party when he wrote to Washington in May 1792, referring to "the Republican party who . . . are fewer in number than the monarchical federalists." Later this republican element became known as democratic-republican and finally, under Jackson, as a full-fledged Democratic Party. In Adams' time, however, the republicans were those who had opposed Washington's policies frequently in his second term, who disliked a strong central government, and who looked to Jefferson as a leader. The concept of a specific party system was still in embryo.

The manner of electing a president reflected the mental habit of the times. Each elector voted for two men, without designating which was the choice for president or vice-president. The man with the most votes was elected president, and the man with the second number became vice-president. When the nation was one unified party the electoral college was in effect a caucus. There might be rivalries of personality, but presumably any two men chosen held the same basic views. In the first two elections, the faults of the system were not apparent. Washington was the obvious unanimous choice, no one who opposed him could have won second place.

Adams had been second choice and hence vice-president for two terms. He was clearly destined to be the second president of the United States; but in this third national election, Hamilton pursued a course which divided national unity and accelerated the rise of parties.

Hamilton, born a West Indian, without adequate years of residence in the United States, was not eligible for the presidency. Under Washington he had been both a policy-maker and a Nestor for the administration, yet probably less a moulder of the president than he supposed. In any event, since he could not succeed to the office, his obvious bid for power now was to control the president, either directly or by making him dependent on Hamilton's support.

Adams was not a man to be controlled. He had little need of Hamilton's mental equipment, a fact which the latter realized. Had Adams been elected with a man of the Federalist faction in second place, his position as chief of government would have been indisputable.

Hamilton saw, however, that under the electorate system, if there were two strong factions, the two opposing leaders would be likely to capture the two first places. Hence he used his influence in the Federalist group to nominate Thomas Pinckney of South Carolina as a running mate for Adams, a candidate unlikely to poll a strong vote.[1] The scheme worked. Adams was chosen for first place, but found that he had the republican Jefferson as his vice-presidential bedfellow.

Adams, accordingly, stood alone. He not only had an opposition man as his chief colleague, but could command no loyalty from Hamilton, the leading influence in the Federalist camp. Possibly more than any other White House incumbent except Lincoln, he was obliged to carry on the presidency according to his personal policy.

While Adams would hardly be cataloged as a liberal president by any modern index, his sense of responsibility to the public was acute, and his determination to avoid war was carried out with agility and statesmanship. In fact, keeping the nation at peace was Adams' outstanding contribution to the tradition of his office, though many pressures were brought against him. Flamboyant France, still glowing with the excitement of her revolution, was alert to defy the world. She committed numerous hostile acts against the United States. Between the two countries there was undeclared but sizable naval warfare, but Adams stood fast for neutrality.

Hamilton was incensed. Strongly pro-British in sentiment, he endeavored to promote an alliance between the mother country and the United States and to wage war on France. Adams would have none of it, though French agents in America were agitating against him. He kept the peace with France through long and involved negotiations, in which he was hampered by opposition in both Cabinet and Senate.

The Senatorial obstructionism proved to be prophetic of similar future tussles with the executive on foreign affairs. The question frequently has been raised as to why the Senate, in this instance and on many occasions later, has blocked the pacific intentions of the presidency. Senators individually are responsible for their actions, in terms of the moment rather than of history. A jingoistic policy may be popular with their constituencies, whereas the burden of negotiations is not theirs. By no means can all senators be criticized on this score, but there have been frequent instances where the Senate seemed more concerned with its domestic quarrels than with national unity.

Adams' most unhappy experience oddly enough was on an issue not of his own choosing. The Alien and Sedition Laws were passed by Congress, not at the urging of Adams, but in imitation of similar acts adopted by Great Britain to resist the influence of the French Revolution. The French had sent agents both to Great Britain and to the United States to propagandize

---

[1] Hamilton pretended to believe that Pinckney could be elected president, but that attitude probably was political strategy.

against the established order. Genet had been the conspicuous forerunner of many more French agents, both open and surreptitious.

The Alien Laws extended the period of naturalization from five to fourteen years. Hence a foreigner would have a long seasoning before he could claim the protections of citizenship. Further, the law empowered the President to deport any undesirable aliens. While Adams did not exercise his powers of expulsion, many Frenchmen left the country after the enactment, thus giving support to those who had held that the measure was a patriotic necessity.

The Sedition Law had less excuse than the alien legislation and in certain sections was a clear violation of the Bill of Rights. While forbidding various clearly treasonable actions, the law also made it a misdemeanor to issue "a false or malicious writing against the President or Congress to stir up hatred against them." The penalty was a maximum of $2,000 fine and two years in prison. Scores were indicted under the act, ten brought to trial, and all ten convicted. Dr. Thomas Cooper, a Pennsylvania editor, was convicted of saying that Adams was incompetent and had as president interfered with the course of justice. Since the act was invoked primarily against opposition editors, its abuse of the right of free speech was doubly evident.

Jefferson and his followers seized upon the Alien and Sedition Laws as an opportunity to discredit the national authority. They logically could have challenged the acts on the ground of unconstitutionality. Only a few years later, in 1801, Chief Justice Marshall in *Marbury vs. Madison,* established that the Supreme Court could nullify an act of Congress which was unconstitutional (see Constitution, Article III, Section 1). That method of protest did not suit the Jeffersonians. It would be an appeal from the federal legislature to the federal court. Whatever the result, one branch of the federal authority would be strengthened.

Instead, Jefferson saw the opportunity to dramatize his states rights' doctrine, and thereby gave prestige to the future separatist leaders. Here, he enlisted the aid of Madison in drawing up a series of remonstrative resolutions for the use of state legislatures, rebuking the national government for usurpation of power.

The scheme was not immediately successful. Various of the states ignored, tabled, or merely debated the resolutions. Only Virginia and Kentucky adopted them; but their language was long remembered.

Jefferson and Madison in these documents affirmed the theory that the respective states had made a revocable compact in forming the national government, and that any state had the right to determine when the compact was broken. The Virginia draft of resolutions did not define the process of revocation or avoidance if she found certain federal laws inacceptable; but Kentucky did. Kentucky said: "Nullification is the rightful remedy." [2] That

[2] *Documents of American History,* edited by H. S. Commager, third edition, p. 184.

was new doctrine. The Declaration of Independence had affirmed the right of a people to secede when their consent had not been regarded; but here was the provocative theory that the states having once consented to a government of their own choice, under agreed terms, could repudiate the contract.

Madison in later years admitted that the resolutions were planned for political effect, and could not be sustained in historical fact.

Jefferson, however, had hereby strengthened the states' rights or state sovereignty theory which led to the nullification crisis under Jackson, later inspired John C. Calhoun and Jefferson Davis, and gave the South a cause for the Civil War.

The resolutions had no immediate effect on the Alien and Sedition Laws, which had been enacted for a two year period only. The creed of separatism had been stated, however, and was due to be re-iterated by a succession of anti-federalists, and to form the basis for a new concept of government, as contrasted with Washington's view of the national authority as the protector of public rights.

The advocates of separatism and of nationalism each claimed to speak for the public good and for individual liberty. Since the ideals were competitive, at points mutually exclusive, their application on specific issues was often confusing. For example, a believer in state sovereignty and local self-rule might use the doctrine to perpetuate the custom of slavery in his area. Or again, an advocate of nationalism, as the only bulwark of freedom strong enough to preserve human rights, might use that power to oppress certain areas or to build up a bureaucratic system. Each succeeding era in the presidency was torn between these two conflicting issues. Jefferson, as president, was so inconsistent that to follow a liberal course through his administration is like following Eliza across the ice.

2

Jefferson's influence on the presidency flows from two different sources. One is the Jefferson legend and the other is Jefferson as he was in his own time. Since legend has made him a great symbol of democracy, that was perhaps his greatest contribution to history, one which has continued, and doubtless will continue. There is no disposition here to dim the legend or to question the noble qualities of Jefferson as one of America's foremost statesmen, ranking certainly among the dozen top men in the nation's history. Some might even place him among the first three. On the other hand it would be misleading to affirm that the coming of Jefferson to the White House brought about any limiting anti-federal changes in the character of the presidency.

The legend of Jefferson as the nation's outstanding democrat arises primarily from his writings, few of which were published during his lifetime. The Declaration of Independence, of course, made him at once the nation's most eminent spokesman, but virtually everything else that he wrote in the cause of democracy is contained in his private correspondence or diaries and was not a part of his public testament.

Jefferson was a philosopher, a critic, a man hospitable to a variety of ideas, and he took pleasure in exploring new principles in a body of correspondence with persons all over the civilized world. During most of his lifetime he was essentially an opposition man. The radicals looked to him as a person of influence who could help their causes. Persons with utopian ideas found a sympathetic audience. Out of Jefferson's vast private writings, a bible of democratic thought could be compiled, and this has been done by Padover and others.

Conversely, the modern politician who swears that he abides by the principles of Thomas Jefferson would be shocked to learn of some phases of his commitment. He would be startled to know that Jefferson distrusted the city worker, that he made no effort to abolish slavery throughout the United States, that he doubted that the Negro had adequate capacity for citizenship, that he deplored the idea of a thriving industry in the United States, and that he believed the salvation of the country resided in decentralization and an essentially rural economy.

To understand Jefferson, his range of views, and his influences on national policy, it is advisable to consider briefly his origins, his character, his tastes, and the peculiar circumstances of his election to office.

Born in 1743 in a western section of Virginia, of well-to-do-parents, Jefferson had early opportunities for advancement. His father owned several thousand acres, and his mother was a Randolph. He had attended the College of William and Mary in Williamsburg, which was the capital city of Virginia. He had remained in that community to practice law and to be a member of the House of Burgesses during Virginia's Golden Age, when, as mentioned earlier, such men as Washington, Patrick Henry, George Wythe, George Mason, Madison, John Marshall and Monroe were familiar figures in Williamsburg.

In the Virginia legislature he had led a winning fight to abolish the customs of primogeniture and entail. The first provided for inheritance of estates by the oldest son, and the second allowed a testator to will the ownership of property beyond one generation. These provisions had tended to keep the huge Virginia plantations intact and would have perpetuated in the New World the undesirable English system of huge baronies, with the consequent impoverishment of younger sons and daughters. Jefferson also fought against the support of the Episcopal Church by state funds. In these measures, Jefferson was a valiant opponent of privilege, when restrictions and burdens hampered new and independent planters.

To wage such contests required imagination and courage, though in a limited economic area. Indeed, critics of Jefferson have complained that even during the Revolution and the early years of the new nation he was primarily interested in the affairs of Virginia. His *Notes on the State of Virginia* was his only public writing on the subject of government, except for his official state papers. The *Notes* reveal his distrust of white industrial labor and of the black man at the very period when he ardently was advocating his land reforms.

"While we have land to labour . . . ," he wrote, "let us never wish to see our citizens occupied at a work-bench or twirling a distaff . . . for the general operations of manufacture, let our work-shops remain in Europe. It is better to carry provisions and materials to workmen there, than bring them to the provisions and materials, and with them their manners and principles. The loss by the transportation of commodities across the Atlantic will be made up in happiness and permanence of government. The mobs of great cities add just so much to the support of pure government, as sores do to the strenth (*sic*) of the human body." [3]

Jefferson's fatalism and hopelessness on the Negro problem were characteristic of his fellow planters. He saw no possibility of assimilating the blacks in this country. In Virginia, he had advocated a plan for exporting the blacks under a foreign colonization, but the idea did not receive serious consideration.

As to the general capabilities of the colored people, section XIV of the *Notes* sets them low in the scale of humans, "in reason much inferior" to the whites. "Their inferiority is not the effect merely of their condition of life." He alleges that they have a different glandular structure giving them "a very strong and disagreeable odor."

After further disparagement of the black man's capacities in literature, the arts and sciences, Jefferson indulged in a typical self-protective clause, saying that he advanced these observations "as a suspicion only," and yet added that the "unfortunate difference of color, and perhaps of faculty, is a powerful obstacle to the emancipation of these people." [4]

Jefferson cherished the rights of individual man as a general principle; and on occasion deplored the fact that his social lot was thrown with the eminent rather than the humble, but he did not attempt to remedy the situation. Dumas Malone has affirmed that Jefferson "trusted the common man, if measurably enlightened, and kept in rural virtue," whereas Herbert Agar has said that Jefferson "never understood the implications of his own thoughts."

He was by temperament individualistic and withdrawn. To James Madison he had written in 1796, "From a very early period in my life, I had laid it down as a rule of conduct, never to write a word for the public papers." His pre-

[3] Thomas Jefferson, *Notes on the State of Virginia*, second American edition (Philadelphia: Printed for Mathew Carey, No. 118, Market Street, Nov. 12, 1794). Query XIX, 5.
[4] *Ibid.*, Query XIV.

ferred method was to inspire others to take the lead, to encourage the issu-ance of his views through other mouthpieces.

He cared primarily for the society of intellectuals. He was an avid reader, a student of literature, philosophy, architecture, government, mathematics, and applied science.

Shy as he was, he enjoyed contemplating the spacious terraces of the world of fashion and intellect. His long platonic devotion to Maria Cosway, whom he had met in Paris, gave his life a cosmopolitan tinge. She was the wife of a wealthy painter living in Paris at the time of Jefferson's stay there. They cor-responded for thirty-one years, in a tone of intellectual speculation.

Unquestionably he was inconsistent. Though plain in his dress and manner when in Washington, at home in Virginia he loved to live in the grand man-ner. At times he entertained eighty or more at dinner. At Monticello, guests swarmed upon him like locusts. His hospitality, coupled with the expense of developing his estate, and the signing of a worthless $20,000 note for a friend, finally impoverished him.

Henry Adams gave a searching criticism when he wrote that Jefferson "was superficial in his knowledge and a martyr to the disease of omniscience. Rid-icule of his opinions and of himself was an easy task, in which his Federalist opponents delighted, for his English was often confused, his assertions inac-curate, and at times of excitement he was apt to talk with indiscretion . . . Few men have dared to legislate as though eternal peace were at hand, in a world torn by wars and convulsions and drowned in blood; but this is what Jefferson aspired to do . . . He was sensitive, affectionate, and, in his own eyes, heroic. He yearned for love and praise as no other great American ever did."

Jefferson at times seemed to have been sicklied o'er with too much thought. His early struggles in the Virginia legislature appeared to have exhausted much of his zest or capacity for action.

Certain it is that Jefferson by nature had been more of a critic than a doer up to the time of his nomination for the presidency. He had been an ineffec-tive governor of Virginia, retiring amid considerable unpopularity. In Wash-ington's Cabinet, he had expended much of his energy in criticism of his col-leagues; and had resigned without making a conspicuous impression in State Department affairs.

His very election to the presidency resulted from a strange confluence of personal rivalries, which might be interpreted as the mysterious workings of Divine Providence. Adams was entitled to re-election and sought the office. His long-standing quarrel with Hamilton, however, had reached a crisis when he had dismissed two Hamilton men from the Cabinet. Adams found him-self without any organized support from the Federalist faction which still was controlled by Hamilton, and Adams was able to run no better than a close third in the electoral college vote. His total was sixty-five, while Jefferson at seventy-three was tied for first place with Aaron Burr. Never was there greater irony—Hamilton had punished Adams, but had promoted two of his bitterest personal rivals.

Jefferson's candidacy has been variously pictured as an influence from the West (because of his birth in Virginia frontier country), as the drive of rural interests and temperament against urban domination, and as the voice of the underprivileged. All three factors were present to some degree, yet as a leader of republican sentiment among the city masses, Jefferson was eclipsed by the dashing and reckless Aaron Burr.

Jefferson was tall, easy-going, awkward. He had ruddy hair, a prominent brow, large eyes which were heavy-lidded, a strong nose, and a long upper lip with a deep vertical furrow. His eyes were contemplative if he felt himself unobserved, but they were shifty when he addressed anyone directly. His voice was low, halting, and devoid of fire. Burr, on the other hand, was the glass of fashion, brisk, alert and plausible. He also had had a distinguished military career in the Revolution, when Jefferson had been a civilian.

Burr at this stage of his career was a figure of no small distinction. Well-born, brilliant, a successful New York lawyer, he had allied himself with Clinton in organizing an anti-Federalist faction, and he had served for several years in the United States Senate. In collaboration with Saint Tammany's Society in New York he had compiled a roll of the eligible voters of the city. This was followed by an organization campaign which was so successful that the Republicans had carried the state and thereby New York's electors were pledged to Burr.

Burr at the outset did not hope for more than the vice-presidency, perhaps nosing out Jefferson or Adams for second place. The tie vote now gave him a chance for the first office.

The contest, as the rules provided, was thrown into the House of Representatives. It required thirty-six ballots to secure the election for Jefferson, and he won by making certain compromises with the Federalists. Throughout the long deadlock Burr proved to be a purer Republican than Jefferson, as he steadily declined overtures from the Hamilton forces.

It is not suggested that Jefferson in giving assurances to the Federalists was being corrupted. His political record is blameless in that regard, but he was able to make clear to the Federalist managers that he would be a safe man on certain crucial issues. "I admit," Hamilton wrote, "that his politics are tinctured with fanaticism; that he is too much in earnest with his democracy; . . . but it is not true, as is alleged, that he is an enemy to the power of the Executive . . . While we were in the Administration together, he was generally for a large construction of the executive authority and not backward to act upon it in cases which coincided with his views . . . He is as likely as any man I know to temporize—to calculate what will be likely to promote his own reputation and advantage."

The theory of Burr as the purer Republican and of Jefferson as the compromiser is supported by the record, yet the issue actually may have been decided by the long-standing personal animosity between Hamilton and Burr. They were each egotists and opportunists who had been sharp rivals since their college days at Princeton. Perhaps Burr knew that any Federalist overture would be a trick, not to be considered under any circumstances. Possibly Hamilton rationalized that Jefferson was better to be endured than Adams whom he could not control, or Burr whom he hated.

An appraisal of the vote for Jefferson demonstrates that whatever influence he may have had because of his Virginia frontier origin was not a decisive element in his election. Without the twelve electoral votes of New York State, which he obtained in coalition with Burr, he would have had two fewer votes than John Adams. He also obtained the electoral vote of Pennsylvania. While it is true that the Western states of Kentucky and Tennessee supported him, their votes were too small to sway the result. The remainder of his political strength was in the South, where the mass of population was on the seaboard.

In the House of Representatives, where the vote was by states, Jefferson's strength still relied on northern support. He carried New York, New Jersey and Pennsylvania and won part of the vote in Vermont and Massachusetts.

3

Jefferson in later years referred to his election as "the revolution of 1800," but this was poetic license, as he himself suggested in his First Inaugural address, "Every difference of opinion is not a difference of principle," he said, ". . . we are all Republicans, we are all Federalists . . . During the contest of opinion through which we have passed the animation of discussions and of exertions has sometimes worn an aspect which might impose on strangers."

The campaign indeed did "impose on strangers" and on some future historians, for there was little in Jefferson's administration which was revolutionary.

Jefferson's First Inaugural has been hailed in some quarters as a masterpiece of statesmanship. In the sense of stating ideas so broadly that everyone could find an area of agreement, it was remarkable and conducive to unity. He advocated "the support of the State Governments in all their rights, as the most competent administrations for our domestic concerns and the surest bulwark against anti-republican tendencies." On the other hand, he called for "the preservation of the General Government in its whole constitutional vigor."

Other principles were also stated without specification as to their means of operation; "a jealous care of the right of election by the people . . . absolute acquiescence in the decisions of the majority . . . a well-disciplined militia . . . the supremacy of the civil over the military authority . . . econ-

omy in the public budget, that labor may be lightly burthened . . . encouragement of agriculture, and of commerce as its handmaid . . . the diffusion of
information . . . freedom of religion . . . freedom of the press . . . and
freedom of person under the protection of the *habeas corpus* and trial by
juries impartially selected."

That "absolute acquiescence in the decision of the majority" would seem
to impair the freedom of minorities, and to exclude local sovereignty or
nullification by a dissident state. Jefferson took care of that one, however,
in his First Message to Congress, "this Government is charged with the external and mutual relations only of the states; . . . the states themselves have
principal care of our persons, our property and our reputation." Consider
one phrase: "the external and mutual relations only of the states." Jefferson
in office violated that limitation, but the doctrine recurred to plague others.

Jefferson at the start of his administration was immensely popular and
remained so until the middle of his second term. The very equivocality of
his initial messages served to establish unity. Before his Inauguration he
resided at a boarding house and he walked from it to the Capitol to deliver
his First Inaugural, though later he sent his addresses by messenger because
of his poor speaking voice.

He abolished formality and protocol at the White House. Where Washington's moderate formality had been a marked change from court elegance,
Jefferson sought to do away with form and rank entirely. The fact that the
government was now fully established in the District of Columbia, which
was as raw in general appearance as a frontier town, enhanced the feeling of
democracy at work.

The new broom began to sweep quickly. There was no doubt that a party
government had come into power. The "outs" were in and the "ins" were
out. Jefferson removed judges in a wholesale manner, whenever expirations
of office or other conditions permitted. He excused the action on the ground
that Adams had made many "midnight" appointments, at the end of his
regime, aiming to forestall the new administration.

The judiciary was only one element to suffer. Jefferson dismissed hundreds
of officeholders in favor of his fellow-Republicans, exceeding even the record
of Jackson, usually considered to be the founder of the Spoils System.

In redeeming his campaign pledge to oppose continuation of the Alien
and Sedition laws, Jefferson asked the Congress, "shall we refuse to the unhappy fugitives from distress, that hospitality which the savages of the wilderness extended to our fathers?" Presumably, he was thinking not of the
Deerfield and other massacres, but of the gentleness of Pocahontas, from
whom he was descended. As mentioned previously, the laws expired auto-
matically, and were not renewed.

The President's belief in majority rule (states' rights excepted) collided
with the assumption that the Supreme Court had power to pass upon the

constitutionality of the Acts of Congress. Originally Jefferson had favored the system of judicial review. Later he feared that it would be a bulwark of the property interests, and in his post-presidential years he was eloquent on what he regarded as the usurpation of the Court.

In the presidency he chafed under the fact that the Supreme Court membership was Federalist in its composition, and constitutionally had life tenure during good behavior. Jefferson could have altered the situation by the appointment of more members. He might have sought to define and limit the powers of the federal bench through a constitutional amendment. Why he did neither has been a puzzle to his apologists, especially in view of his vigorous views in his later years.

In his First Message he merely said, "The judiciary system of the United States, and especially that portion of it recently erected, will of course present itself to the contemplation of Congress."

The contemplation resulted in the abolition of some lower court judgeships which had been established by Adams, but did not go to the heart of the issue. Again, in Jefferson's second term an attempt was made to impeach Justice Chase of the Supreme Court because of his political views. Whether Jefferson promoted the impeachment has been debated. In any event, it would have been a clumsy and ineffective means of control, and in this instance it failed. Impeachment thereby lost favor. Jefferson's very opposition to the court, because futile, strengthened the judiciary and its influence over congressional and presidential powers.

4

A strong court, while defining the limits of legislative or executive action, could expand the powers of the government by a broad construction of what the Constitution permitted. That may explain why Jefferson in office was not resourceful or diligent in curbing the court. In 1803 he needed all powers of government that the Constitution might allow, if not considerably more, for he wished to purchase Louisiana without delay. Such an action presupposed a national authority able to operate in the interest of a united people. A government concerned with "the external and mutual relations only of the States" could hardly take so drastic a step without consultation of its component parts, if limited to those powers expressly spelled out in the Constitution.

As long as Spain had had possession of Louisiana, the United States had been able to make agreements permitting free navigation of the Mississippi. Hence economic conflict was avoided; but unexpectedly Louisiana came into the hands of Napoleon, through his European victories; and if Napoleon became a force in the New World, the future of American rights in Mississippi commerce would be dubious.

Jefferson learned that Napoleon was willing to sell. The advantage to the

United States of buying the territory was overwhelmingly clear. French control of the Mississippi could readily threaten the entire development of the United States western frontier and even the very safety of the country. The asking price of $15,000,000 was negligible. But no delay was possible. The President had no specified powers to act under the Constitution, and the months which would be required for an enabling amendment were too hazardous to risk. Here was a fine dilemma for the strict constructionist Democrat-Republican.

Jefferson took the step which has been regarded ever since as one of his greatest contributions to the nation. He purchased Louisiana; but the action was completely inconsistent with his supposed theories of government. He considered going to the country with an appeal for a justifying amendment *after the fact,* but his advisers urged him to bluff it through. He adopted their view, writing to his supporters in Congress, "Whatever Congress shall think it necessary to do should be done with as little debate as possible and particularly so as regards the constitutional difficulty."

The Jefferson party guessed correctly that the measure was so universally popular that no one would raise the issue. From then on Jefferson could not consistently inveigh against those who believed that the Constitution implied broad powers, where no prohibitions were expressed. Never again could he be a strict constructionist.

Louisiana brought further embarrassments. The President set up therein a territorial government, having all the aspects of a crown colony, administered by federal offices and courts. Here was a "monarchical system" full blown, with Jefferson himself as the ruler.

5

In respect to Louisiana, Jefferson wisely allowed realistic good to triumph over his theories, but his tragic lost opportunity was his failure to find a solution for the slavery issue during his presidency, or even to seek a vigorous remedy when a mandate of the Constitution called upon him for some word on the subject.

Article I, Section 9 of the Constitution, provided that the importation of slaves should not be prohibited prior to the year 1808. The founders had deferred the issue until then, and Jefferson as president unavoidably found the issue in his lap.

Slavery was already discredited in much of the civilized world outside of the United States. Horace Walpole, as early as 1750, had written of "that horrid traffic of selling negroes—six and forty thousand of these wretches are sold every year to our plantations alone!—it chills one's blood." [5] The public conscience throughout the Anglo-Saxon world had been increasingly

[5] Horace Walpole to Horace Mann, February 25, 1750. *Toynbee Edition II,* p. 433. See Wilmarth S. Lewis, "Horace Walpole Reread," *Atlantic Monthly,* July, 1945, p. 48–51.

troubled over slavery in the latter part of the eighteenth century and into the nineteenth. Parliament abolished the slave trade in 1807. Eight of the United States had provided for abolition by 1804, though the Southern tier was stiffening in its demands for the protection and extension of slavery. The slaveholders were in the minority of white citizens and continued to be, but they controlled the political reins.

Slavery did not begin as an exclusively Southern institution. At the beginning of the republic, slavery was well entrenched in Delaware and was prevalent to a minor degree throughout the North. Some Northern sea captains prospered from the "black ivory" traffic. The climate and the plantation system of the South were economically favorable to Negro labor, though there were many phases of Southern economy in which slavery was a detriment, ethical considerations aside. Later, such Southern leaders as Robert E. Lee, J. E. Johnston, A. P. Hill, J. E. B. Stuart, Stonewall Jackson, voluntarily subsisted without slaves, before federal emancipation.

Jefferson as president, though a large slaveholder, had advanced some distance from his earlier views, as expressed in the Virginia *Notes*. On January 28, 1805, he wrote to W. A. Burwill prophetically, "we shall be forced after dreadful scenes and sufferings to release them in their own way, which, without such sufferings we might now model after our own convenience." Yet he would not force the issue. "I have long since given up the expectation of any provision for the extinguishment of slavery," he added, and evidently was determined to make no effort to forestall the disasters which he predicted for a later time.

When Jefferson came to address Congress on the slave trade on December 2, 1806, he merely said, "I congratulate you, fellow-citizens, on the approach of the period at which you may interpose your authority constitutionally to withdraw the citizens of the United States from all further participation in those violations of human rights which have been so long continued on the unoffending inhabitants of Africa, and which the morality, the reputation, and the best interests of our country have long been eager to proscribe."

Congress responded with the passage of a feeble law which had the merit of indicating the national right to be concerned with the slave trade. The act provided penalties on persons found guilty of "transportation," but it did not set free the transported Negroes, who were turned over to the authorities when a ship was condemned, to be dealt with according to state law. The principle of bondage was not impugned. The trade did diminish, however, under the weight of succeeding laws and public disapproval.

6

There was at least one principle, however, on which Jefferson had unqualified courage. Henry Adams in spite of his criticisms of Jefferson even on this point, said, "The essence and genius of Jefferson's statesmanship lay in peace . . . which was the clue to whatever seemed inconsistent, feeble or deceptive in his administration." [6]

In Jefferson's second term, his love of peace was to be sorely tested. He realized that war would not only be hazardous to the new country, but inevitably would consolidate federal power and would destroy the policy of economy and low taxes in which he had thus far been successful.

War, however, was rampant in Europe. France under Napoleon and England were in a titanic struggle. At the outset American commerce and shipping prospered enormously in supplying both belligerents. Each side in the conflict desired America as an ally, primarily because of her trade and shipping. Soon, each began the seizure of American vessels, on the excuse that America was helping the enemy. Shortly, this policy of seizure was adopted by both France and England as official Orders in Council.

Such measures were essentially acts of war. The United States had the choice of siding with France or England. Or, the nation could adopt a belligerent armed-neutrality policy, for which its ample fleet was substantially equipped, in vessels, men and spirit. There was a third and unpopular solution of keeping the American fleet at home and thus avoiding conflict with the warring powers.

The peace-loving Jefferson favored the last course. He fell into the error of believing that economic measures, without military force, would restrain nations desperately at war.

Jefferson proclaimed an embargo on all shipping from American ports. He assumed that this would choke off the supplies to France and Britain, and that the consequent embarrassment would bring them to terms. He was able to win the support of Congress for his policy; but his assumptions proved to be unfounded.

Such a policy was, of course, an exercise of federal powers which vitally affected the domestic economy of the several states, and was inconsistent with earlier Jeffersonian dogma. Further, the attempts to enforce it required an extensive use of federal police powers, more far-reaching than Washington's suppression of the Whiskey Rebellion.

The embargo was a failure in many respects. The New England states fairly successfully defied it. Their clippers ran the gantlet and made fortunes, whereas the Southern states suffered in lack of free markets for their tobacco and cotton, and had to pay excessive tolls on their clandestine shipments. Jefferson prevailed upon Congress to put more teeth into the law through successive revisions. Finally, a Non-Intercourse Act was passed forbidding all commerce with France, Great Britain or their colonies.

France and England were not moved by whatever economic inconveniences they may have suffered. The United States ministers to each country were

[6] Henry Adams, *History of the United States under the Administration of Thomas Jefferson*, p. 445 (A & C Boni, 1930).

instructed by Jefferson to offer to withdraw these measures if the belligerents would cancel their hostilities toward American shipping; but these proposals were rejected. Cotton mills and workers in England had been deprived of work, but other phases of Empire economy had prospered. The English government sarcastically pointed out that the policy of American vessels being kept at home was beneficial to the free course of British trade in the rest of the world, where British vessels could now proceed without their usual competition.

Jefferson was forced to the realization that his foreign policy had not developed according to his hopes. In his Seventh Annual Message to Congress, October 17, 1807, he said, "the love of peace so much cherished . . . may not insure our continuance in the quiet pursuits of industry." He reported the efforts and failures of the American ministers. After a rather gloomy recital of the state of the nation (including reference to alleged plots against the government by former vice-president Aaron Burr), Jefferson was able to point cheerfully to a Treasury balance of $8,500,000.

He suggested that Congress decide how this money might be usefully expended, unless the situation should be "superseded by a change in our public relations now awaiting the determination of others." The delicacy of this wording has never been surpassed by any other tight-rope walker in diplomatic language. The determination of others, the "others" being France and England, was to ignore the rights of the United States as long as its nonresistant, nonbelligerent policy continued. The "public relations" soon made war unavoidable, though not until Jefferson had retired.

7

With American economy disrupted and foreign policy an obvious failure, Jefferson came to the end of his administration at the lowest point in his political and personal reputation. Several state legislatures nevertheless urged that he serve for a third term. He replied that eight years of one president was all that the Constitution would bear and that repeated re-elections might lead to an hereditary succession. Thus he strengthened the tradition initiated by Washington against a third term, though there is considerable doubt that he could have been re-elected, had he chosen to run.

Jefferson's relationship to the liberal tradition in the presidency is a provocative phenomenon in American history. It reaffirms how strongly any tradition is determined by the "shifting channels of individual minds," that manners of government are swayed by personalities.

Jefferson's intrinsic character and good will made him an enduring part of the American tradition. His inconsistencies have been emphasized here because they were a part of his nature and his administration, and typical of the contradictions in the American temperament.

His advocacy of states' rights, carrying the weight of his prestige, encouraged the activities of separatist leaders, and undid much of what Washington tried to accomplish in building loyalty to the national ideal.

His purchase of Louisiana, on the other hand, was a strong precedent in favor of national authority. Since the Louisiana deal was imperialism by purchase rather than by conquest it was free from the usual criticisms of imperialistic policy, yet it extended the national responsibility.

His economic outlook was exclusively rural, and, as C. A. Beard has said not too generously, it implied "the possession of the federal Government by the agrarian masses led by an aristocracy of slave-holding planters," with accompanying opposition to urban types of wealth and activity.

His tepid position on slavery encouraged the weakness of the presidency on that crucial topic.

His courageous peace policies set an example for the presidency; with few exceptions, the presidents of the United States, in sharp contrast to many foreign rulers, have steadfastly tried to avoid war.

His democratic attitude and his sincere if vague devotion to the common man served to reaffirm the presidency as a leader and servant of the people.

Population was growing toward the West. By 1830, Tennessee had 682,000 persons, more than South Carolina, or Georgia, and more than double that of New Jersey. Ohio had more than 900,000, Indiana 343,000.

The cities still were negligible, representing less than 9 per cent of the nation's population; though including 31 per cent of the total in Massachusetts and Rhode Island; and 15 per cent in New York and Pennsylvania.

The United States was growing speedily. It had nearly 13,000,000 in 1830, compared with 5,300,000 when Jefferson came to office. Twenty-four states voted for Jackson in 1828, as against 16 for Jefferson in 1800.

The war of 1812 had been succeeded by a brief deflation and then a boom era. During Jefferson's embargo, American manufactures, which he dreaded, had necessarily thrived. In 1807, there were only 8,000 cotton spindles in the country, by 1809, there were 80,000. The tariff henceforth became a national topic in the sense that it affected many sections of the country.

The nation from 1815 to 1828 basked in calm, confident optimism. The South American republics, one after another, rejected European domination. At the instance of John Quincy Adams, then Secretary of State, President Monroe in 1823 proclaimed that the United States would not tolerate interference by Europe in the Western Hemisphere.

Slavery had become a secondary issue. The slave trade had been a national subject; but in 1820, slavery within a particular state came to national notice. Maine, hitherto a part of Massachusetts, and Missouri sought admission to the Union. The Missouri Compromise adopted by Congress admitted Maine as a free state and Missouri as a slave state. It further provided that all future states in the area north of the southern boundry of Missouri would be "forever free."

That issue had seemed settled, and the country was moving forward in undisturbed expansion, except for repetitive troubles with the Indians (Custer's last stand was in 1876). In general, the new nation was feeling the benefits of expansion. Ohio had become a state in 1803 under Jefferson. Louisiana had followed in 1812, then Indiana, Mississippi, Illinois, Alabama, Maine and Missouri, all for Jackson except Maine.

4

The Rise of Saints and Sinners

*As soon as the multitude begins to take an interest in
the labors of the mind, it finds out that to excel in some
of them is a powerful method of acquiring fame, power
or wealth.*

DE TOCQUEVILLE

I

The era in which Jackson came to the presidency was a time of utopias,
not only in the sense of bizarre social communities, but in many avenues of
thought. Man had achieved a new sense of freedom, and with it a confidence
that the mastering of his destiny was just around the corner.

In the United States, by 1828, the fear of any interference from Europe had
been dispelled through the fall of Napoleon and the peace treaty with Great
Britain in 1812. The stability of the national government had been assured
by experience. Madison, Monroe, and John Quincy Adams had been conservative up-builders, and Monroe's famous Doctrine had given the country
a pride in its world-wide influence.

There had been signs of change in the economic scene. The industrial
revolution, although in embryo, had given rise to workingmen's societies
who had eloquent leaders and trenchant pamphleteers. They were still a
small minority voice, for more than 90 per cent of the population lived in rural
sections, and even in "the industrial North" less than 12 per cent of the people lived in communities having more than twenty-five hundred persons. The
spread of cotton-ginning in the South had increased the population and wealth
of the cotton-belt states, and augmented the usefulness of Negro labor.

The demand for change which was in the air, however, was a broad spiritual tide which was manifested in many forms of human activity. Robert
Owen had founded his community at New Harmony, Indiana, which failed in
1827. Joseph Smith in 1830 proclaimed his Book of Mormon. John Humphrey
Noyes in 1834 was to affirm his doctrine of perfectionism and his assertion
of personal sinlessness, which resulted in the forming of the Oneida Community. In Boston, William Ellery Channing was preaching a new theology
known as Unitarianism, which affirmed the essential divinity of man, and
that God was revealed through man. The implications of the doctrine were
revolutionary; and the religious bodies of New England, which comprised
most of the people, were cloven by this issue. Unitarianism at its outset had
the awakening gleam of a new revelation, though in time many of its followers regarded its implications passively and politely.

Suffrage had been extended to most of the free males by all the states except

South Carolina. The political prestige of property-holders was thereby diminished, and masses of men had new hopes of progress through their newly acquired franchise. The growth of the scientific method had promoted the impression that the mysteries of the universe would be rapidly revealed, and such philosophers as Bentham had encouraged the idea that all truth was discoverable and measurable in the material world.

The bursts of energy in the New World were not limited to the utopians and the reformers. It was an age of get-rich-quick, vast speculation, visions of huge development. Land speculation, wildcat financing, gambling, lotteries, all forms of greed ran rampant. The army of sinners was as conspicuous as the saints, nor did they consider themselves sinners. Had not everyone come to America to make a fortune, so the attitude ran.

Henry Clay gave expression to the commercial enthusiasms of the country in his advocacy of "the American system" in which he called for a high protective tariff and substantial internal improvements by the government. "Are we doomed to behold our industry languish and decay yet more and more?" said Clay. "But there is a remedy, and that remedy consists in modifying our former policy, and in adopting a genuine American system. . . . This is to be accomplished only by the establishment of a protective tariff." Government protection and government funds were to be provided, not to entrench old wealth, but to create wider commercial opportunities.

America must be made industrial, Clay held, or become a dependency on Great Britain who was supplying the greater part of the manufactured goods for the United States. He deplored "a continuation" of what he called "the British colonial system" and urged that the resources of the country be developed. The program in part was similar to the early Hamiltonian ideas. Hamilton had not been able to establish his protective tariff system, but a start had been made by the Tariff Act of 1816 under a democratic administration. Now, however, the Southern states had veered back to a low tariff policy, and Northern New England because of its shipping interests opposed the tariff. Yet despite the coolness in those two important sections, the Tariff Act of 1824 passed with a comfortable majority in both House and Senate, indicating the vigor of the expansionism sentiment.

In short, freedom of a new type was in the air. Not loyalty to the national government, not zeal for state or local ways, but a generation which rejected earlier men and earlier views. The individual might seek a new theology, new society, or a new fortune. The emergence of such a man as Jackson, not associated with the old guard of any camp, was logical.

Jackson ultimately may be moved down several niches in the liberal Hall of Fame by the claims of F. D. Roosevelt or Woodrow Wilson, each far more liberal than Jackson, in the modern sense of the term, but to date the Jackson Day dinners perpetuate his name as a popular symbol. In recent years he has come to overshadow Thomas Jefferson, hitherto regarded as chief examplar of the Democratic Party. The toga has been placed the more securely on his shoulders by Arthur M. Schlesinger, Jr.'s, *The Age of Jackson,* which ably establishes that the early working class movements supported Jackson and provided philosophies of government which sound familiar to modern ears.

In his own time, however, Jackson's rise to office may be attributed chiefly to his extrovert active nature, to the color of his career, rather than to the content of his doctrine. In the presidency, too, the manner of his fighting often had more popular appeal than the details of his cause. In the liberal tradition, Jackson was always a fresh breeze whether or not, as the historian Abernethy affirms, he was essentially conservative. The cut of his jib was liberal.

When Jackson was elected president in 1828, he was an old stager, without being handicapped by old affiliations. He had served as the first representative from the new state of Tennessee as early as 1796. In 1798 he had been a U. S. senator and again in 1823. He had been one of the superior judges of Tennessee, and for more than thirty years he had been intermittently in political affairs, gathering a wide knowledge of the frontier needs and attitudes, as his career had gradually taken him westward. He furthermore continuously had alleged that he preferred private life, usually convinced persons including himself that this was so, and, hence, was not embarrassed by compromises and deals on his way toward the highest office.

"Old Hickory" he was called by his soldiers early in his military career. Hickory brooms were emblems of his political campaigns. The repute for a self-reliant toughness was his mainstay with the people more than any particular measures. "With all his hickory characteristics, I suspect he has good stuff in him," said Washington Irving; and the "hickory characteristics" were more associated with his general fame than whatever "good stuff" Irving had in mind.

Andrew Jackson during his presidency became known as a champion of the people, an opponent of financial power, and an advocate of federal union as opposed to states' rights. He was, however, violently anti-British, isolationist, a slaveholder, and an imperialist as to this continent. He not only fought the Indians, but broke treaties which peaceful tribes had made and kept in good faith. He championed states' rights when they did not run counter to his immediate purposes. In fact, he could support both sides of many questions with vigor and aplomb. His career was close to being a Horatio Alger story, for he was the first president to have spent most of his life on the frontier area, and the only one to have made most of his fortune in commerce. Though both a lawyer and a soldier, he prospered chiefly through trading and land deals.

2

Jackson was born in the Waxhaw section of South Carolina on March 15, 1767, the son of Irish Protestant parents who were among the leading citizens of that pioneer community.

Andrew was an ambitious youngster, with reddish brown hair and blazing small blue eyes. He seized upon schooling with avidity. By the age of nine he was a "reader" for the settlement, reading aloud the newspapers and letters for those members of the community who had not had the rudiments of education.

He was in his early teens at the start of the Revolutionary War. The British forces swept victoriously through South Carolina, and young Andrew was taken prisoner. An officer demanded that the boy black his boots, whereupon Andrew raised his left hand in protest, claiming the courtesies of a prisoner of war. The officer struck him with the sword, cutting deep into the boy's left wrist and gashing his forehead, leaving a facial scar which remained the rest of Jackson's life. It was an unwise blow from Mother England, for from then on Jackson was constantly opposed to any move on behalf of the British interest.

Jackson's father had died shortly before the boy's birth and his mother had passed away when Andrew was fourteen, while she was nursing Revolutionary soldiers in Charleston. Jackson thereupon was supported by well-to-do relatives who sent him to a good school, where he applied himself industriously. At the age of sixteen, however, a short cut to riches and fame seemed to be at hand. An uncle in Ireland, a prosperous weaver and merchant, left him approximately $1,500. This was a substantial capital for the times, and in prudent hands could have become the basis for a lifetime of security. The funds from this bequest had been sent to Charleston, and Jackson went there to claim his estate.

He suddenly became a gentleman of the South Carolina seaport, then one of the most metropolitan cities of the New World. Andrew bought himself fancy clothes, played at dice games and the horses, and within nine months was penniless. In fact, only a lucky throw of the dice enabled him to leave Charleston with bills paid and in possession of a single horse.

The young Jackson, however, was evidently possessed of extraordinary personality and alert wits. He journeyed to Salisbury, N.C., where he studied law in the office of Spruce Macay. While there he attracted the favorable attention of William Blount, one of the political wheelhorses of the State. In 1788, through the Blount influence, Jackson at the age of 21 was established in law practice in the western territory of North Carolina. The territory was admitted to the Union as the State of Tennessee in 1796, which gave Jackson an unusual opportunity to get into national politics, for the young state was in need of capable men.

Shortly after coming to Nashville, Jackson became involved in a love affair which influenced the remainder of his life, both public and private. He boarded with a family named Donelson, wealthy and influential people. The daughter of the house, Rachel, was a vivacious girl, with an ample comely body, large dark eyes, dark hair, and olive complexion. She already was married but living with her parents, being separated from her husband, Louis Robards.

Her husband came to claim her and take her to Kentucky, and a brief reconciliation followed. Rachel soon wrote her family asking to be brought back home, and Jackson undertook the task as an emissary for the parents. Robards sued for divorce, and Jackson married Rachel in 1791. It developed two years later that the divorce decree had not been final at the time of the Jacksons' original marriage and a repetition of the service was necessary. Jackson fought against a second ceremony as a mark of humiliation and confession, but his friends pointed out that it was unavoidable.

Rachel Donelson Robards was the great romance of Jackson's life. After meeting her he had no interest in any other women. The cloud of scandal cast over their marriage, which was revived repeatedly by political opponents, sobered and hardened him. Rachel herself according to contemporary accounts became fatter and more bucolic through the years, but Jackson's devotion was undiminished.

Jackson's early career took place during the formative days of the republic. His term in the House of Representatives was under Washington, and his first term in the Senate was under the presidency of John Adams. After that almost twenty years were spent in the military and business affairs of the frontier. Leadership on the western frontier required more than political or legal sagacity. A man needed to be able to fight, to fight the Indians in their frequent outbreaks, and to use a gun if need be in the enforcement or supplementing of local law.

Jackson was appointed major general of the Tennessee Militia in 1802. He became potentially the General Washington of that area, both as first citizen and lord of the manor. He and fellow settlers had acquired vast acreages of land which gave promise of great fortune. Jackson's land deals in Tennessee and Mississippi were conspicuous throughout his life, at times making him wealthy, and again placing him dangerously in debt. "The Hermitage," near Nashville, an estate of 640 acres, was the nucleus of his holdings and was his home for most of his life. At times he owned other lands and houses as well as costly furnishings and livery. Profit-making was one of his major pursuits.

Jackson's successful campaign against the Indians finally brought him a commission as major general in the United States Army. The regular army high command were scornful of militia officers and the old guard in Washington were cool to Jackson. They sensed a threat to their own stability and eminence in the prominence of a militia officer. Hence, when the second war with Britain began in 1812, Jackson's services were not desired. He wished to lead an army for the capture of Quebec, but his offer was denied. Even when the regular army met repeated failures to the North, when Washington itself was sacked by the British, Jackson was still on the outside of the inner circle.

When he won a rousing victory against the Indians at Horseshoe Bend on March 27, 1814, and when word came that the British had an expedition destined for the capture of New Orleans, the government could no longer afford to ignore him and he was commissioned to undertake the defense of that area.

Jackson found the city full of intrigue. The self-interest of New Orleans as a port had kept her ears open to attractive propositions, notably from Spain. Jackson, therefore, had the job of keeping the natives friendly at his back, while he prepared to meet the invading British.

His overwhelming defeat of the British on January 8, 1815, in the battle of New Orleans, a slaughter in which two of the enemy's generals and thousands of his troops were killed, served to make Jackson a national hero.

As the peace treaty had been signed with Great Britain prior to the battle of New Orleans, Jackson's triumph obviously had no influence on the treaty terms. Without that victory, however, the prestige of the United States would have been painfully dimmed. The Navy had been the country's only conspicuous strength. The sacking of the country's capital by the enemy and the frequent land defeats had given the impression of a nation weak, poorly organized, incapable of self defense, a nation which might be easy prey for the next aggression. The battle of New Orleans, on the other hand, gave every European chancellory reason to wonder if Great Britain had not been fortunate to make peace when she did.

Jackson was not through with his conquests. The control of Florida by Spain impaired the freedom of traffic from the Mississippi to Atlantic waters and jeopardized the security of Louisiana. The acquisition of Florida in some manner had been a matter of contemplation by the government for a considerable time. When the Seminole Indians from Florida made an attack on the Alabama-Georgia border, Jackson was dispatched to deal with them. He chased them back into Florida, seized forts in which they had taken refuge, captured Pensacola, and took possession of Florida in the name of the United States. He also hanged two British agents whom he found engaged in plots against this country, and executed a brace of Indian chiefs without trial.

Jackson claimed that his actions were responsive to government orders, which was denied in some quarters in Washington. A Senate Committee reprimanded him, but his success was so popular throughout the country that the government needed to handle the issue delicately. Spain naturally protested, but was persuaded in 1819 to settle for a cash sale: As a vindication, Jackson, was named first governor of the new territory of Florida, though he soon withdrew from that politically unpromising, and presumably dull, post.

The conquest of Florida, coupled with the victorious defense of New Orleans, obviously made Jackson a presidential possibility, though it was twelve years after New Orleans before he reached that goal.

Many commentators have suggested that Henry Clay, John C. Calhoun, Daniel Webster and other brilliant lights could have graced the presidency more effectively than the certain less known persons who occupied the White House from Monroe to Lincoln. The superiority of the un-elected, however, is open to debate, and the temper of the times made most of them ineligible. The prominent statesmen of the day had harangued the Congress for so long on so many issues that the public was weary of them. Jackson was clearly the favorite popular candidate. If he had been unavailable, it is probable that some figure other than the familiar ones would have emerged.

The politicians in office were well aware of the danger, and the violence of their efforts to discredit Jackson pushed him into the liberal camp and surrounded him with the halo of the persecuted. The campaign to ruin Jackson converging from various sources, was vicious in the extreme. The opposition again exhumed the story of Jackson's premature marriage to Rachel, a matter now many years old.

The General had more than once fought duels on this subject, and now his opponents doubtless hoped to goad him to similar combats, from which his friends dissuaded him with difficulty.

Nothing could hold back the popular demand, however. Tennessee sent Jackson to the Senate in 1823, and initiated his candidacy for the presidency in 1824. He had the largest number of votes among the four candidates, but since no candidate had sufficient votes for a choice the contest was thrown into the House. Jackson had had about 153,000 popular votes to 108,000 for Adams, while Clay and Crawford had about 47,000 each.[1] In the voting by states in the House, Jackson and Adams each had seven states, whereas Clay had only four. It soon became apparent that Clay would be able to swing the election, as he wished. Henry Clay was the only candidate aside from Jackson to represent the West. His program of high tariffs, encouragement of business, and expansion coincided with the general feeling of the western area at that time. Furthermore, since Clay came from Kentucky and would have given the West a new interest in the White House had he been elected, it was assumed in many quarters that he would be loyal to his section of the country, and would support Jackson who had so large a share of the popular vote. Clay, however, in his long political career had become essen-

[1] These often quoted figures are incomplete and subject to qualifications. For detailed comment see Edward Stanwood, *A History of Presidential Elections,* p. 70–75.

tially a Washingtonian, and he doubtless judged that the election of Adams would not stand in the way of his own future ambitions, whereas Jackson was a more popular rival.

At any rate Clay threw his strength to John Quincy Adams, assuring him of election, and subsequently was made secretary of state. Jackson then, and the West in general, clamored that a bargain had been made against the wishes of the electorate, and when Adams ran for re-election in 1828, Jackson defeated him handily.

In the election of 1828 Jackson had 178 electoral votes to 83 for John Quincy Adams, who was running for a second term; yet in the popular vote Jackson fared moderately, as he had slightly under 56 per cent of the total. Nevertheless as presidential elections go in this evenly balanced country, it was a famous victory.

Any impression that Jackson was elected by the revolt of the West alone, or by a working-class movement alone, is untenable. Separately or together, these elements were a minority. Jackson did carry the new western states and the solid South; but it was the margin of independent votes which swung the larger states his way. In this 1828 election he needed 132 electoral votes. The South gave him a nest egg of 97, possibly because he was one of them and a slaveholder, though a kind one. Ohio and states West added 27 votes, making 124. That left a debit of 6 votes to carry. Maryland gave him 5 (out of 11) and Maine 1 (out of 9). Pennsylvania's total of 28 and New York's 20 (out of 36) magnified the result, though they were unneeded. Nevertheless the urban societies naturally climbed aboard the bandwagon, and their leaders regarded him as their man.

3

An unfamiliar lot of characters now swarmed upon Washington. At the President's first reception at the White House, hordes of persons from all over the countryside tramped through the rooms, ruined chairs with their muddy boots and crowded the President against the mantelpiece, from which he had to be extricated by his friends. The social life of the capital was turned upside down. Jackson bought twenty spittoons for the East Room.[2] New faces, more than new ideas, frightened the old inhabitants, for Jackson had not yet given any sign of holding radical views.

The old man was a hero, but he was old, tired, and ill. The ruddy hair had turned to an upstanding white brush. His long narrow face was seamed. The small blue eyes still blazed in their sockets, but the tall thin frame was worn. Had Jackson met kindliness and co-operation in the White House, it is reasonable to conjecture that he would have died in peace and inconspicuousness, but his enemies gave him just the tonic that he needed, violent opposition.

[2] Charles Hurd, *Washington Cavalcade.*

His principles, supported by other popular leaders of the day, were hard money, limited paper currency, little government spending, and a balanced budget. In later times these principles were the bulwark of the most conservative elements, illustrating that the liberal point of view is defined not by constant measures, but by issues of the times which can shift to diametrically opposite sides. A firm metallic standard of money, no lavish public expenditures, and a balanced budget, Coolidge was a Jacksonian!

Many of the monied people at this time held views that modern Wall Street would consider financially radical. Like Henry Clay, they desired tariffs and government spending to encourage new manufacturers and land speculation. The pay-off could come at a later date. The construction of vast public improvements would mean fat contracts. If paying off the federal debt meant a constriction of public money, that would be bad for the speculators.

At the earliest stages of his administration Jackson was so prostrated by personal tragedy that not even opposition could arouse him to interest. On the way to Washington for the inauguration, Mrs. Jackson had again heard gossip attacking her character, based on the old story; had suffered a stroke; and had died. The General was inconsolable and had little zest for his new duties, but was prevailed upon by his intimates that it was his duty to carry on.

Only his close associates realized the depth of his sorrow, knew of his ill health, his violent headaches. To the world at large he continued to be the doughty general, and an early incident in the Cabinet circle enhanced the impression. Jackson had named Senator Eaton of Tennessee as secretary of war. Eaton had become infatuated with Peggy O'Neale Timberlake, the daughter of a Washington tavernkeeper, and the widow of a naval officer. Jackson advised Eaton to marry Mrs. Timberlake promptly, which was done.

Official Washington, however, refused to countenance the match, and most of the Cabinet ladies failed to call upon their colleague's new wife. Jackson, who for a lifetime had suffered from an unjust breath of scandal, regarded this as a personal affront, and directed that his Cabinet ministers instruct their wives to recognize the Eatons or their portfolios would be withdrawn.

Whatever the merits of the issue, this first official battle of Jackson was of immense popular interest, understandable by everyone, far more absorbing than tariffs or finance. Whatever Mrs. Eaton's conduct might have been, she was a tavernkeeper's daughter whose presence would have been resented by the Washington die-hards anyhow, and now the Cabinet ladies had been told they could pay their respects or leave town. What a man, this new President!

4

New faces were numerous. Senator William L. Marcy of New York had said gloatingly "to the victors belong the spoils." A politer term for the practice was "rotation in office." Jackson apologists have pointed out that he did not dispense with more office holders than Jefferson had, and turned out fewer than some later Presidents. To the extent this is true Jackson by his own lights was the lesser man.

He held that men who remain long in office are "apt to acquire a habit of looking with indifference upon the public interests." Officeholders come to regard their jobs as "a species of property." Nor did Jackson believe that any extensive training or experience were requisite. "The duties of all public officers are . . . so plain and simple that men of intelligence may readily qualify themselves for their performance."

He warmed to his subject in his initial message to Congress, affirming that no one man had any more "intrinsic right" to official station than another. He favored limiting appointments to four years, pointing out that the government employee removed from office would have the same opportunities of obtaining a livelihood as the millions who never held office and that, therefore, those dismissed could have no cause for complaint. Indeed the President added that "rotation constitutes a leading principle in the republican creed."

It was this forthright advocacy of rotation more than the number of dismissals which gave Jackson the reputation of fathering the spoils system. He carried his idea logically to the recommendation that the presidential office be limited to a single term of four or six years.

5

The warfare between Jackson and his regular Cabinet, his need for friendly advice from those who would not be political rivals, and the eagerness of the liberal wing to capture the President for their cause gave rise to Jackson's famed "Kitchen Cabinet" who were his private advisers. Their influence marked a new phase in the conduct of the presidency.

Jackson's "Kitchen Cabinet" was not a clearly defined or static group. Amos Kendall and Francis P. Blair, newspaper editors, were steadfast members. The former was given a government post as auditor, but primarily served as an ideaman for the administration and a writer of many of its documents. Blair was made editor of the Washington *Globe,* the official organ of the Jacksonians. George Bancroft, historian, was a trusted adviser who drafted Jackson's First Inaugural. Martin Van Buren, the only one of the official Cabinet to become an intimate, was the chief political councillor of the inner circle.

Under the ministrations of these men Jackson became a social philosopher. Schlesinger Jr. observes "Kendall's supreme skill in interpreting, verbalizing and documenting Jackson's intuitions made him indispensable." Undoubtedly the Kitchen Cabinet were responsible for making Jackson articulate, though to what extent they governed his ideas will always be debatable ground.

Despite a good education in his youth, Jackson was uncouth and awkward in expressing himself, as his personally written letters indicate. Equally, he was abrupt and terse in his thinking, yet his public messages are smooth, clear, well-elaborated. Most, perhaps all, of the presidents have had literary assistance in the preparation of their state papers though several of them had superior writing talents in their own right. In Jackson's case the gap between the native man and the synthetic president of the official papers is striking. It is ironic that Jefferson, who was capable of exalted prose, often chose to be dry and equivocal in his presidential papers, while the rough-hewn Jackson's messages in the main are characterized by literary grace and clarity.

6

Jackson earmarked himself as a dangerous man in the eyes of the financial fraternity by hinting in his First Message to Congress, December 8, 1829, that the charter of the second Bank of the United States, due to expire some six years hence, would not be renewed.

The charter was similar to that of the first bank, established by Hamilton. It specified five government representatives on its board of twenty-five directors; also one-fifth of its capital was subscribed by the government. It was the repository of public funds, the transfer agent for the funds, and made public payments without charge; but the government had little control over the bank's policy, either in detail or in its major practices, beyond the fact that the secretary of the treasury could remove government deposits if he presented the reasons to Congress.

The first bank had been founded in 1791 under a twenty-year charter. In 1811 when the charter expired an effort was made to renew it, but the Republicans were against it and the project was allowed to lapse. The war of 1812, however, created a situation in national affairs which required some centralized banking facilities, and in 1816 the second Bank of the United States had been chartered, again for a twenty-year period.

Jackson had been on both sides of the national bank question before he came to the presidency. In 1817, he had opposed the bank because of its potential interference with states' rights. During his governorship of Florida in 1821 he had favored the establishment of a branch there on the grounds that the local people desired it.

The Bank of the United States had served well in its early days and its current president, Nicholas Biddle, in his initial years had been a man of exceptional brilliance and probity. The extensive powers and prestige of the bank, however, had inflated him. Most financial historians of today hold that the Bank was soundly conceived, but deplore Biddle's political folly.

As long as the bank had issued notes only against its resources, the flexibility of credit had been kept within reasonable bounds, and its paper could always be redeemed in specie. In time, however, the bank established numerous branches and issued notes against them printed to look like the drafts of the parent bank, with the result that Biddle was able to create or withdraw vast funds of credit at will.

Jackson on July 10, 1832, vetoed a premature bill to recharter the bank ahead of its expiration date, and later demanded the withdrawal of government deposits.

Jackson's initial criticisms of the bill to renew the charter were tolerant, calm and wise. He agreed that a central bank of some sort was desirable, but doubted that the present bank could be justified under the Constitution, because it gave exclusive privileges to a group of private citizens over whom the government had inadequate control. He pointed out that bank stock in value of $28,000,000 was now privately subscribed and affirmed that "the door of competition" should be opened in the re-establishment of the charter, which might give the government much more favorable terms.

Jackson affirmed that the current bill proposes that "the bounty of our government is . . . to be again bestowed on the few who have been fortunate enough to secure the stock and at this moment wield the power of the existing institution . . ." Jackson obviously was unmoved by the Hamiltonian theory that it was advisable to have the most powerful financial interests closely tied in with the government; and he was advised chiefly by men who deplored financial power without knowing how to regulate it in the public interest. In European countries, notably England and France, the state banks were owned chiefly by the large capitalists, but that argument carried no weight with Jackson.

The conservative elements, not surprisingly, feared a government bank, under the control of the inexperienced Jackson. The President, alienated from his Cabinet, unsympathetic to the elder statesmen, swayed by unofficial advisers, commanded little financial confidence. The Biddle group, however, seemed not to realize that their arbitrary demand for renewal under the old terms was untenable. They refused compromise. Worse, Biddle used all the banks powers of credit, favors and bribery in the effort to force renewal. By so doing, he played into Jackson's hands.

"It is to be regretted," Jackson's message continued, "that the rich and powerful too often bend the acts of government to their selfish purposes . . . every man is equally entitled to protection by law; but when the laws undertake to add to these natural and just advantages artificial distinctions, to grant titles, gratuities, and exclusive privileges, to make the rich richer and the potent more powerful, the humble members of society—the farmers, mechanics, and laborers—who have neither the time nor the means of securing like favors to themselves, have a right to complain of the injustice of their government . . . In the act before me there seems to be a wide and unnecessary departure from these just principles."

Such a diatribe, obviously not in Jackson's diction but bearing his authority, was a new note in government. For the first time the Executive had sounded the note of class distinction. Biddle had started the fight, and his methods were questionable, but now to the Jacksonians he became the archtype of wicked wealth.

Biddle in desperation set out to punish the President and the country by a nation-wide contraction of credits in 1833, which produced the panic of that year. Delegations throughout the land called upon the President to relieve the situation, but his continuous answer was, "Go to Nicholas Biddle!" The storm which Biddle had hoped to center upon the President devolved upon himself, and even earlier supporters of the bank realized that its restoration and recharter were unlikely.

Biddle financed newspapers and bought editors. Jackson countered with such a wooing of the press through government favors, using the government purse, that the independent press became alarmed. Pollard's *The Presidents and the Press* gives a lively account of the contest for the favor of public opinion.

The Richmond *Enquirer* which had fought for the election of Jackson said:

We wish the Executive would let the Press alone. We cannot any more approve of the appointment of so many of its conductors to office, although they be required to give up their papers, than we approved of the great pains which were taken by Mr. Clay to turn obnoxious Editors out . . . and to put in his devoted Partizans.— We know that General Jackson solemnly disclaims all intentions to reward his supporters or to bribe the Press to support his measures. And we believe him— we know also, the reasons by which he justifies these appointments . . . But we are better satisfied with his motives than his reasons—with the integrity than with the expediency of the appointment.

The *Enquirer* was but one of many voices to this effect. The *National Journal* of Washington listed forty-two editors who had been placed on the public payroll, and observed: "Our liberties are in danger the moment the government begins to tamper with the press; but the danger becomes more imminent when so large a number of individuals who constitute the public press have been openly and opulently rewarded out of the public treasury."

The charter was not renewed, and Jackson's victory served to solidify his reputation as a popular leader.

7

The bank issue was made to order for any politician; but Jackson was faced with a far graver question, namely a test of the authority of the national government. When Congress enacted new tariff schedules in 1828, the South Carolina legislature passed a resolution affirming its right to nullify the act of the federal government. "Nullification" immediately became a national issue. Again, like the "Whiskey Rebellion" and the Kentucky Resolutions, it challenged the fundamental authority of the federal government.

What Jackson's position would be was not clear to the country. He had used the states' rights argument in opposing the bank. "Nor is our government to be maintained or our Union preserved by invasions of the rights and powers of the several states," he had said in his veto message. "In thus attempting to make our General Government strong we make it weak. Its true strength consists in leaving individuals and states as much as possible to themselves." These sentiments were not conclusive. Jackson, like many another home-rule advocate who has come to federal office, was capable of reinterpreting his principles in the light of new occasions.

That was what he did in respect to the resolution of South Carolina. He bristled with defense of federal authority. In proclamation and message, Jackson expounded the sovereignty of the federal government and of the Constitution, with all of the zeal of President Washington and using substantially the same reasoning. "It is the acknowledged attribute of free institutions that under them the empire of reason and law is substituted for the power of the sword," he said. As to the argument that the original states had entered into a compact and for that reason could secede, Jackson held, "It is precisely because it is a compact that they cannot. A compact is an agreement or binding obligation."

He affirmed that he had the highest reverence for the "reserved rights" of the states, but that "in becoming parts of a nation, not members of a league, they surrendered many of their essential parts of sovereignty."

He pointed out that at every stage in the history of the Revolution, the united colonies had considered themselves as forming one nation and that "in this sense the states are not sovereign."

The firmness of the president on this issue was a surprise in some quarters. At first there was even some doubt as to how seriously he meant his proclamations. The doctrine of reserved rights had been preached so frequently, had been given so much impetus by Jeffersonian arguments that it had come to be regarded as both Southern and Democratic gospel, and Jackson was a Southern Democrat, ex-Carolinian, slaveholder and planter.

While the issue was at the crisis, Jackson attended a Jefferson birthday dinner on April 15, 1830. Many nullificationists were on hand. A score of speeches and toasts supported the position of states' rights. When the President was called upon for a toast, he gave the single sentence, "Our Union, it must be preserved!" He followed this up later by commanding the armed forces to be ready to enforce the law and he promised to hang any opponents. In South Carolina itself there were many sympathizers with Jackson's view. They as he, saw the impracticability of a southern confederacy. The nullification resolution was repealed and the federal Union took on a new vigor.

8

Though the charge of inconsistency can be leveled at Jackson and his associates on many counts, their record on public economy was both unassailable and courageous. The spoils system saw to it that a sizable share of the available jobs were given to the faithful, but it did not extend to creating contracts for them at government expense. The necessary government contracts, notably on printing, were earmarked for the friends of the administration, but the creation of public works was frowned upon as an unpardonable extravagance. If there were a surplus in the government treasury that was a sign that taxes should and could be reduced.

Jackson's position in respect to public works was positive and adroit. In Tennessee where the speculative fever was high, government expansion was favored. Jackson in his first campaign had been able to avoid committing himself on the public works issue. By 1830, .however, after he had served for two years, the pressure, by western constituents particularly, for improvements in their areas was growing.

Jackson and Van Buren concocted a scheme to dramatize the president's opposition to government spending. Van Buren was to watch the "pork-barrel" bills as they were introduced, and pick out a vulnerable one on which to hang the issue.[3] In April, 1830, Van Buren was able to report that the so-called Maysville Act would pass the Senate. This was a bill to build a turnpike from Maysville to Lexington, Kentucky, in the heart of the Jackson stronghold. A veto of a measure benefiting that area would demonstrate to the country the sincerity of Jackson's convictions. Van Buren and Kendall drew up the final form of the veto which, of course, was delivered in Jackson's name, and defeated the measure.

Jackson opposed the Maysville road bill on several counts. He believed that if the federal government should have a surplus it should be returned to the states. Again, he held federal taxes should not be used for any local project unless it were national in character; and that yardstick, he affirmed, would be very difficult to apply, as the opinion of successive Congresses might well differ in respect to the national worth of any particular project. He had grave doubts as to the constitutionality of spending federal money on extensive improvements and suggested that if it were the will of the people to do so the method should be through an amendment to the Constitution. Finally, he observed, "In the best view of these appropriations, the abuses to which they lead far exceed the good which they are capable of promoting. They may be resorted to as artful expedients to shift upon the government the losses of unsuccessful private speculation, and thus, by ministering to personal ambition and self-aggrandizement, tend to sap the foundations of public virtue and taint the administration of the government with a demoralizing influence."

9

Andrew Jackson on the Indian question presented an extraordinary picture of the liberal temperament struggling in the coils of reality. Jackson's

[3] Marquis James, *The Life of Andrew Jackson*.

democracy did not extend to the color of red or black. Yet officially his advisers made him consistently the champion of the underdog. Aside from Jackson's presidential addresses, there was no evidence to indicate that he had any regard for the Indian as a fellowman or any respect for his rights. Left to his own devices, it seems probable that the President would have made no attempt to rationalize the policy of the government toward the Indian, but since he allowed himself to be presented as a notable humanitarian on this subject, the course of his reasoning deserves consideration here.

In his Second Message to Congress, December 6, 1830, Jackson said, "Humanity has often wept over the fate of the aborigines of this country." He pointed out sadly that one tribe after another was disappearing from the earth, but said that "true philanthropy reconciles the mind" to such matters just as in life one generation gives way to another.

The extinction of the red man, he indicated, was all in the course of progress. "Philanthropy could not wish to see this continent restored to the condition in which it was found by our forefathers." He asked what "good man" would prefer a country covered with forests and ranged by a few thousand savages to the current republic occupied by more than twelve million people endowed with "all the blessings of liberty, civilization, and religion."

These pious remarks were a preamble to saying that the government proposed to acquire extensive lands occupied by the red men of the South and the West "by a fair exchange" and to send them to reservations where "their existence may be prolonged and perhaps made perpetual."

The President conceded that the Indians might find it painful to leave the graves of their fathers; but he pointed out that the white inhabitants of the United States obviously had left the land of their birth to seek new homes. In fact, the Indian might well consider himself fortunate over this new offer of the government. "How many thousands of our own people would gladly embrace the opportunity of removing to the West on such conditions!"

Jackson doubted whether the wandering savage had a stronger attachment to his home than the white man. Besides, since the Indian did not get along satisfactorily with his white neighbors in the same area something needed to be done about it. "Rightly considered," said Jackson, "the policy of the General Government toward the red man is not only liberal, but generous."

And a year later, on December 6, 1831, Jackson reported further on the condition of the Indians under the new government policy. He pointed out that the savage on his reservation was not "beyond the reach of philanthropic aid and Christian instruction." In fact, he noted that those who were missionaries to the Indians now had wider scope "subject to no control but the superintending agency of the General Government," and therefore they could proceed more readily than in a general community to advance the Indians "from barbarism to the habits and enjoyments of civilized life."

Unfortunately for this cheerful prospect, the missionary efforts seemingly did not work out to Jackson's satisfaction. For in his message to Congress on December 7, 1835 the president reached a startling degree of pessimism. "All preceding experiments for the improvement of the Indians have failed," he said. "It seems now to be an established fact that they can not live in contact with a civilized community and prosper."

10

The liberal tradition in the presidency, as channeled through Jackson's mind, has been presented here as a series of lantern slides—the new type in the White House, rotation in office, Kitchen Cabinet administration, the bank issue, cultivation of the press, reassertion of federal authority, opposition to spending for public work, singular attempt to justify the extinction of the Indian. Many of the issues were concurrent and re-current throughout Jackson's eight years in office. All took place in the atmosphere of new times, with a new group of men controlling the government.

As has been seen, the administration was unpredictable. In the closing days of Jackson's rule, a new issue arose which turned him back to the states' rights theory, while at the same time forging a new weapon of federal control. The controversy stemmed from the activity of the Abolitionists. Impatient at the indifference in Washington, alarmed over the spread of slavery in new territories, the anti-slavery forces had embarked on a campaign of "education." They imported speakers from England. They wrote pamphlets and letters to the editor. They had the support of many newspapers.

Moreover, and this caused the chief uproar, they carried their mission into the South. They mailed their literature to whites, and allegedly to blacks, in the slave states. No considerable number of blacks could have been reached by the Post Office, but the principle enraged the Southern slaveholders. The pamphlets were inevitably inflammatory, some inciting directly to servile insurrection.

The question raised here of free speech and free press obviously was a delicate one. The Abolitionists cited Tom Paine and other pamphleteers of freedom in justification of their procedure, but Jackson seemingly had no hesitancy suppressing the campaign as far as he could. In his Seventh Message to Congress, December 7, 1835, he denounced the Abolitionists' conduct. Internal peace, he held, depended on noninterference with slavery in the South, on "the maintenance in good faith of those compromises of the Constitution upon which the Union is founded." He inveighed against "the emissaries from foreign parts who have dared to interfere in this matter" and characterized the anti-slavery activities as "unconstitutional and wicked attempts" by "misguided persons."

Not content to leave the matter of suppression to the state authorities, Jackson called upon Congress "to take such measures as will prevent the Post-Office Department, which was designed to foster an amicable intercourse and correspondence between all members of the Confederacy, from being used as an instrument of an opposite character."

A singular touch, that use of the word "Confederacy," rather than "Union." Jackson had used Union doctrine and had threatened force to block nullification of the tariff laws, yet he invoked states' rights and the federal authority to suppress agitation against slavery. "Confederacy," the term was a harkback to the Articles of Confederation, which the Constitution had superseded. Jackson went a long distance in his conciliatory language, and the concept was to be revived later to divide the Union.

Jackson's stand on the limits of free speech, his attitude on noninterference with slavery, his use of the Post Office as a means of federal enforcement, and his concessive language for the sake of harmony, are again examples of how policy is influenced by the background of the Executive, and the exigencies of the moment.

Jackson brought about a few changes in the liberal tradition of the presidency, though the changes were not as drastic or fundamental as some might suppose. On the surface, the change of personalities throughout the top branches of the executive was the most conspicuous new note. The decline of the Virginia statesmen and other eastern notables has been lamented, but the shift demonstrated that the government was not to remain in the hands of a virtually self-perpetuating oligarchy, however able.

The charter of the United States Bank had lapsed before and its second demise left a financial vacuum and created new political issues. Jackson had sounded a prophetic note in popular appeal. Jefferson had attacked "monarchical government"; it remained for Jackson to cry out against the abuses of wealth.

The pose of perfectionism in office was another new fashion introduced by Jackson, after his first inaugural, an attitude which has become familiar in public life. Possibly this mien was foisted on Jackson by his over-zealous literary aides. Washington, Jefferson, most of the elder statesmen were wont to deplore their inadequacies, either from conviction or good manners. Jackson publicly admitted to no qualms. Whether on the extinction of the Indian or on noninterference with slavery, his tone was high minded.

With all its pros and cons, Jackson's was an invigorating administration, active not passive, giving prestige to the office. His nullification battle was his severest test. In it, he held the country together until the crisis faced by Lincoln. He retired in a wave of prosperity induced by state bank inflation. Courageously he had tried to put on the brakes through curtailment of credits, but that issue did not come to a head until the time of his successor, Martin Van Buren.

5

Liberal in Depression

All communities are apt to look to government for too much.

MARTIN VAN BUREN, *Special Message to Congress,*
September 4, 1837

I

One of the most gracious, and on occasion most courageous, of men ever to occupy the White House was Martin Van Buren. For years, virtually to the present time, he has been the subject of controversy. He served but one term and his early detractors tried to dismiss him as a nonentity, a dissembler, a politician of no moral stature.

Yet the interest in this supposedly inconsequential fellow still burns quietly like a perpetual candle. He is the subject of a biography by Denis Tilden Lynch, published as late as 1929. Schlesinger, Jr., devotes much space to him in *The Age of Jackson.* Gerald Johnson in *American Heroes and Hero Worship* must needs include him, even if somewhat satirically. Look in the publishers' catalogs where most one-term presidents are noted with only one book or two devoted to their fame, and there are a half-dozen or more biographies on Van Buren, including that of the eminent historian George Bancroft, who wrote a glowing eulogy.

There were several causes which served to bury the reputation of Martin Van Buren. Some say that he was the victim of the forces of reaction. Unquestionably the conservatives libeled Van Buren, but he was not without support from the Democratic press, which was fully as skilled as the conservatives in the art of vituperation. More importantly, the financial panics during his administration produced a popular revulsion against him that was completely damning for years to come. Finally, for forty years after his term the nation was occupied with a series of new issues—territorial expansion, slavery, civil war, and the reconstruction era. There was little occasion in those times to remember Van Buren, whatever his merits; yet he made impressive contributions to the liberal tradition of the White House.

As in the case of Jackson, moreover, surprise has been expressed that Van Buren was chosen for the presidency at a time when such men as Daniel Webster, Henry Clay and John C. Calhoun were available. There is no need to discuss further the relative merits of those gentlemen, but it is important to emphasize that Van Buren in his own period was as considerable a figure as most of his contemporaries. Monroe thought highly enough of Van Buren to offer him a place on the Supreme Bench, but he preferred a more active life.

Van Buren had been Jackson's secretary of state, his mentor, his constant companion, a force for harmony in the administration, willing to resign his Cabinet office in order to remove dissension. At the end of Jackson's eight years, he was the logical heir-apparent, and was nominated at Jackson's behest.

Yet if Jackson helped to make Van Buren, the reverse was equally true, for "The Flying Dutchman" had brought to the service of the choleric western general an experience and knowledge of political ways which are vital to the success of any administration. He brought also an established reputation which had survived many political battles. He had been state senator in New York, state political leader, United States senator, and governor. Moreover, like Jackson, he represented a new sector of the population, as distinguished from the elite who had supplied the popular leadership in the early years of the Republic.

Van Buren was born in Kinderhook, near Albany, N.Y., on December 5, 1782. His parents were truck farmers. They were also keepers of a tavern, and owned a few slaves. Their status obviously was prosperous, but a far cry from the wealth and position of the patroon families of the Hudson, the merchant-smugglers of Massachusetts, or the Virginia aristocracy.

The young Martin was brilliant and ambitious. After a village school education, he entered a law office at the age of fourteen, where he supplemented his lack of schooling by intensive and systematic reading.

From the outset, he was marked for eminence. Golden-haired, dapper, with alert eyes, fastidious in dress, and having an engaging manner, his talents were soon recognized by his fellows. He campaigned for Jefferson in 1800, and at the early age of eighteen was sent as a delegate to a state congressional caucus. By the time he was twenty-five, he could afford to marry his childhood sweetheart, Hannah Hoes. Four sons were born to them, but the mother died after only twelve years of marriage. During this time he acquired a high reputation at the bar and amassed a fortune which made him financially independent.

Van Buren, a widower before he was forty, thenceforth devoted virtually all of his time to political activity and brought new techniques to popular government. He organized mass meetings, county committees, political clubs. He has been credited, or demerited, with being the first American political boss. He was certainly the first to engineer politics on such a scale, though Aaron Burr had been a pioneer in the art. While the "spoils system" was the outgrowth of Van Buren's New York political machine, he himself never used it for purposes of graft.

He was steadily on the side of the underprivileged, in part for political reasons; yet steadfastly, even when it meant his own downfall. The progressive extension of manhood suffrage in the various states presented an opportunity for leadership, or bossism, which was inevitable. The very size of the new vote called for some systematic method of organization, which gave rise to the party system in its modern form.

Van Buren basked in the atmosphere of Washington. As secretary of state under Jackson, he was the *beau ideal* of a diplomatic figure, suave, politic, entertaining, civilized. His hospitality was of the best in delicacies and service. He capered gracefully in the ballroom, and his lace cuffs were of notable elegance. His once dapper figure became comfortably rotund.

In the *affaire Eaton,* his conduct was impeccable. She was sponsored by his chief, and he treated her with all the protocol she rated as a Cabinet wife. She was sneered at as a tavernkeeper's daughter. He, a tavernkeeper's son, addressed her with courtliness and consideration. Though Peggy O'Neal‑ Eaton's character was debatable and her manners flamboyant, Van Buren like a calm, unobtrusive tugboat, guided her through the choppy social seas. Silly as the issue seems in retrospect, Van Buren's aplomb in this matter commanded admiration in many quarters and strengthened his ties with Jackson.

Those ties, of course, had far more substantial strength than a single incident. One phase of Van Buren's political sagacity suggests that "Saki" heroine of whom the author said, "She kept in her armoury the weapon which can be so mightily effective if used sparingly by a really sincere individual—the knowledge of when to be a humbug." [1] The Little Fox of Kinderhook could feint and conceal the direction of his intent when such procedures served his purpose. He tempered and smoothed the rough tactlessness of the Old Hickory. Yet Jackson, who was completely intolerant of fraud, said of Van Buren that he was "one of the most frank men . . . a *true man* with no guile." [2]

By the time Van Buren had resigned from the Cabinet to promote peace in the official family, had been blocked from an ambassadorship by machinations of Calhoun, and had served in Jackson's second term as vice-president, the public were fully aware of his essential principles. William H. Seward, later in Lincoln's Cabinet, said at this time, in 1835, "It is utterly impossible, I am convinced, to defeat Van Buren. The People are for him. Not so much for him as for the principle they suppose he represents. That principle is Democracy . . . It is with them the poor against the rich; and it is not to be disguised that since the last election [i.e. of Jackson], the array of parties has very strongly taken that character."

Seward was right. In the election of 1836, Van Buren had a larger popular vote than the combined totals of his opponents, Daniel Webster, Hugh L. White, and William Henry Harrison. (Willie P. Mangum received South Carolina's electoral vote, where the electors were chosen by the Legislature, and no popular vote was held.)

That Van Buren would succeed Jackson had been generally expected, abroad as well as at home. Tyrone Power, the British actor, in a memoir of a three-years' tour of the United States shortly prior to the election, had pub-

---

[1] Saki (H. H. Munro), *When William Came,* p. 5 (John Lane, The Bodley Head, 1926).
[2] *Correspondence of Andrew Jackson,* V, IV, p. 260.

lished ·a series of shrewd and observant comments on American places and persons. Of Van Buren he said: [3]

Mr. Van Buren's manner I thought highly characteristic of his political character, —cool, courteous; with a tone quiet but persuasive, a voice low-pitched, but singularly effective from the clearness of his enunciation and well-chosen emphasis. He bestows an undivided attention to the matter before the house becoming his situation.

As vice-president, this gentleman is chairman of the senate; a situation at this time of peculiar delicacy, considering his position as the proclaimed director of the measures of General Jackson's cabinet, and heir to his party and his power. His filling this chair with so little reproach under assaults and provocations which it required the greatest good temper and good sense to encounter or turn aside, I consider no slight evidence of that wisdom and political sagacity for which his party give him credit, and which have acquired for him amongst his admirers the familiar cognomen of the Little Magician.

Van Buren's administration began serenely on March 4, 1837. His inaugural address confidently urged the preservation of American democracy as a world experiment. The country had been enjoying a boom throughout the Jackson era, and prosperity still reigned. The population of the country had grown from 10,000,000 in 1821 to 16,000,000. All sections had gained, and notably the West. Michigan at the start of the Van Buren term had 200,000 inhabitants, compared with 10,000 in 1821. Illinois had 400,000 compared with 60,000 at the earlier date. Pittsburgh, to quote Power again, was already "smoky . . . upon the manufacture of iron, glass, pottery, etc." [4] Everywhere expansion was observed. Town and country were lavish with new houses, or with old houses embellished with new scroll work and balconies.

Washington, itself, however, bore a dingy appearance. Most of its roads were deep in black mud. Pennsylvania Avenue had been covered with a macadam surface, but Congress had declined to vote the few hundred dollars which would have been necessary for water-carts to dampen the road from the near-by Potomac. Consequently, except in the rainy season, the surface gave rise to clouds of dust. The deplorable condition of Pennsylvania Avenue was much talked of, but no relief was in sight, for Congressmen dared not appropriate funds to make the national capital more agreeable, as long as they were denying incessant clamors from their own constituents for local appropriations. Congress had been encouraged in this economy by the constant refusal of both Jackson and Van Buren to favor public improvements wholly or partly aided by federal funds.

It must be remembered that the federal government, still under fifty years

[3] *Impressions of America,* by Tyrone Power, Esq.; Philadelphia: Carey, Lea & Blanchard, 1836, vol. I, p. 164. Mr. Power was a leading actor of his time, highly regarded as a person and as an artist on both sides of the Atlantic. His *Impressions* give a remarkably dispassionate appraisal of both sides of a contentious American scene. He was the great-grandfather of the present American actor, Tyrone Power.

[4] *Ibid.,* vol. I, p. 195.

of age, was the subject of suspicion by the states. Federal taxes were unwelcome and must be kept at a minimum. Prosperity was rampant, and as long as the government at Washington did nothing to interfere, criticism would be relatively mild; but the nullification crisis and the failure of Clay to arouse wide public enthusiasm for his "American system" had discouraged initiative by the federal government.

When Van Buren came into office, all outward signs were favorable for his enjoying a popularity of long duration. The critics of Jackson and his followers could get little serious attention as long as boom conditions prevailed. The Jackson era, however, had been supported by a wave of speculation which, as we have noted, the General had seen with foreboding. Consequently, Van Buren had inherited two Jackson measures, each aimed to be corrective, but each explosive.

When Jackson had decided, in concert with his advisers, that the Bank of the United States was evil, he had been right in resisting improper financial influence, but had been ineffective in providing a satisfactory banking substitute. His victory, however, had left him in a popular but embarrassing vacuum, because as a practical matter some repository had to be found for government funds and government surplus. Van Buren saw that an independent national Treasury was necessary. This was one of his first aims while in the White House, and an outstanding contribution of his administration.

Before Van Buren was able to take that step, which required action by Congress, he was faced with the immediate consequences of the removal of the deposits from the Bank of the United States to local institutions. The surplus at the time of his accession had amounted to $37,000,000. Jackson had favored placing surpluses, nominally as demand deposits, with some twenty leading state banks, though about fifty in all enjoyed some deposits. Webster and Clay had approved this policy, whereas Van Buren had originally opposed it, though later he was somewhat persuaded to it by Amos Kendall, the eloquent editor of the Jackson regime.

Unfortunately and not surprisingly, the state banks in general had been less conservative than Biddle. These unearned and unanticipated funds in the state bank resources had led to a wave of credit expansion. Jackson, as has been seen, was well aware of the risks of speculation, having lost and made fortunes in that fashion. He had aimed to curtail inflation, by his issue of the Specie Circular which was promulgated on July 11, 1836. This required that federal lands, open to public purchase at $1.25 per acre, must be paid for in gold or silver. Up to that time land speculation was almost limitless, as the purchaser could pay in whatever currency the states provided.

When Van Buren came into office in March, 1837, fiscal reform was long overdue. With his independent Treasury already in mind, he declined to issue the last of the federal payments which the state banks were expecting. The banks protested violently, as credits were over-extended and the need for further support was critical. Further, the effects of the Specie Circular, which Van Buren declined to withdraw, were already being felt. Within six weeks after his inauguration, a delegation of merchants from New York appealed to him, saying that some federal relief was necessary or many financial houses would have to go to the wall.

Van Buren in his Inaugural had stated that American democracy was on trial. The trial was perhaps nearer at hand than he realized. By May, 1837, most of the banks of the country were closed, and the industrial and financial classes were prostrated. The nation had not been in such a fix since the days of Jefferson's embargo. The crisis was more frightening than the embargo because its causes were little understood by those unfamiliar with finance. Most sections of the country, which were rural and largely self-sustaining, were not seriously affected; but the cities, the merchants, the newly rich and the press were damaged and were vocal. Above all, there was a sense of shock that such a thing could happen to the American paradise.

In a special message dealing with the conditions Van Buren truthfully said, "The difficulties and distresses of the times, though unquestionably great, are limited in their extent, and can not be regarded as affecting the permanent prosperity of the nation. Arising in a great degree from the transactions of foreign and domestic commerce, it is upon them that they have chiefly fallen. The great agricultural interest has in many parts of the country suffered comparatively little."

Van Buren's calmness and immobility under fire were infuriating to those who sought relief. When pressed to call an extra session of Congress to do something about the crisis, he yielded by setting a date three and one-half months hence.

He was unmoved by outcries against the Specie Circular. Public lands had been made available to settlers at a fixed price in specie. Those who had traded in the national resources with inflated dollars, had only themselves to blame. When he finally addressed the assembled Congress, his advice was that individuals should put their own houses in order, that the panic was due to over-activity in business and over-expansion in credit. He reiterated that the next installment of the surplus for the state banks should be withheld, that an independent Treasury should be established, but he conceded that Treasury notes might be issued temporarily to meet the needs of the government.

Those who may have expected that Van Buren would try to cure the situation by an extensive government relief were due to be disappointed. "All communities are apt to look to government for too much," he said. "Even in our own country, where its powers and duties are so strictly limited, we are prone to do so, especially at periods of sudden embarrassment and distress. But this ought not to be. The framers of our excellent Constitution and the people who approve it with calm and sagacious deliberation acted at the time on a sounder principle. They wisely judged that the less government interferes with private pursuits the better for the general prosperity. It is not its legitimate object to make men rich or to repair, by direct grants of money or legislation in favor of particular pursuits, losses not incurred in the public service. This would be substantially to use the property of some for the benefit of others. But its real duty—that duty the performance of which makes a good government the most precious of human blessings—is to enact and enforce a system of general laws commensurate with, but not exceeding, the objects of its establishment, and to leave every citizen and every interest to reap under its benign protection the rewards of virtue, industry, and prudence."

The country, or all of those involved in its financial and industrial interests, including thousands of land purchasers, speculators or otherwise, were forced to accept this policy which led to a general deflation. The ultimate wisdom of the policy was evident in the continued prosperity of America from 1840 to the Civil War.

In fact, the readjustment in credits came about so rapidly that under normal circumstances Van Buren's first term might well have witnessed the beginning of the new prosperity; but in 1839 there came disastrous crop failures. They hit the country a severe blow, more far-reaching than the earlier depression. Here was an actual destruction of real values affecting the great majority of the population. It is doubtful if any president could survive two such disasters.

Certain critics of Van Buren have emphasized that he was skilled politically on behalf of Jackson, but not for himself. The charge seems well-founded and is a credit to him, because in certain situations where principle was involved Van Buren followed his conscience rather than taking the political course.

Notably that was so in his attitude toward the annexation of Texas. Texas had been settled by colonies from the United States, had revolted from Mexico, and had sought annexation with this country. The massacre at the Alamo had taken place in 1836 and public feeling had remained high against Mexican rule. The situation could have been a godsend for any president who desired to use it to divert public attention from panic and crop failure; but Van Buren opposed annexation, for in it he saw seeds of trouble for the country.

Annexation, first of all, would presumably mean war with Mexico, and consequent additions to public spending and public debt to which he was opposed. Annexation would mean expansion of territory which would be slave territory. The President regarded the institution of slavery as one of the most dangerous political issues. While personally deploring slavery, he held that it was a matter to be determined by the states. In his Inaugural he had announced opposition to any attempt on the part of Congress to abolish slavery in the District of Columbia, and also said that he was "equally decided to resist the slightest interference with it in the states where it exists."

But where the Constitution, in his opinion, permitted, Van Buren was against slavery. "The suppression of the African slave trade has received the continuous attention of the government," he reported in his Fourth Annual Message to Congress, December 5, 1840. . . . "I submit to your judgments whether this government, having been the first to prohibit by adequate penalties the slave trade, the first to declare its piracy, should not be the first also to forbid to its citizens all trade with the slave factories on the coast of Africa, giving an example to all nations in this respect which if fairly followed can not fail to produce the most effective results in breaking up those dens of iniquity." [5]

The President's reluctance to annex Texas not only thwarted those elements of the South that favored slave extension; but also disappointed the expansionists and the mass of the people who thrilled at the idea of adding so much land to the nation's possessions. As a president during panic times Van Buren's chance of re-election to a second term would have been slight, and his stand on Texas further dimmed his chances.

Van Buren, indeed, was abused because of his courageous adherence to the democratic-republican theory of limiting federal powers. He put the finances of the government on a sound basis. In his message to Congress on December 5, 1840, he opposed "grants of public money for works of internal improvement." He advocated "simple, unostentatious, and economical administration of public affairs." The government expenses should be defrayed wholly by the customs' receipts and the sale of public lands. "Under no pretense whatsoever" should the taxes exceed the amount "actually necessary to the public service."

As to the new Treasury system, he said: [6]

The new system established by Congress for the safekeeping of the public money, prescribing the kind of currency to be received for the public revenue and providing additional guards and securities against losses, has now been several months in operation. Although it might be premature upon an experience of such limited duration to form a definite opinion in regard to the extent of its influences in correcting many evils under which the Federal Government and the country have hitherto suffered, especially those that have grown out of banking expansions, a depreciated currency, and official defalcations, yet it is but right to say that nothing has occurred in the practical operation of the system to weaken in the slightest degree, but much to strengthen, the confident anticipations of its friends.

Despite his conscientious conduct of the office, the fates seemed against Van Buren. During his term, Canada revolted against British rule. There was strong sympathy for the movement in the United States, especially in

---

[5] The statement was noble in intent, but somewhat inaccurate. The penalties were not adequate and the United States was not the first country to prohibit the Slave Trade.

[6] In the revulsion against Van Buren, the Treasury Act was repealed in 1841, but it was re-established in 1846 and has continued in service of the public ever since, a monument to its founder.

the North. Many volunteers crossed the border to aid the insurrectionists. Here was an opportunity for expansion to the North, such as the South envisioned in the Texas prospect; but Van Buren refused to be drawn into war. He issued proclamations of neutrality, disavowed and denounced the Yankee volunteers, and thereby became criticized as a tool of Great Britain.

His frequent unpopular positions coupled with the double depression were more than could be sustained at the polls. Van Buren lost re-election by 170,-000 votes, a slight margin but so distributed as to be costly. He even lost New York state.

His significance, however, obviously lies in his conduct in the presidency. Even more than Jackson he had come to office through democratic processes. No military repute had aided his rise, which was due to plain but astute politics. Like Jackson, he was identified with the commonalty rather than the privileged, and had a humbler origin than his predecessor.

As a commoner and a liberal in depression he was a notable example of the capacity of the plain people to produce their own leaders. In his judgment, government expenditure to relieve the financial distress was unsound, and he refused to be stampeded. No man in peacetime faced greater pressures to act or greater opportunities for increase of personal power through the distribution of government favors; but he remained calm and self-possessed.

In foreign affairs he enhanced the pacific tradition, declining the temptations of imperialism. In the independent Treasury, he aimed to provide the government with a self-sustaining financial apparatus. Van Buren as well as Jackson proved that neither recklessness nor dangerous ambition need be characteristic of an avowed leader of the masses.

When Van Buren went out of office, popular reform was at an end for many years. The romance of untrammeled expansion was in the air. The roster elected up to Lincoln's time, in the main, were temporizers, letting events take their course; for the most part, they were presiding officers rather than policy-makers; but ultimately the time came when new issues had to be faced.

Between Van Buren and Lincoln came twenty years of further expansion, and of political inertia.

The country continued to grow apace, and few were willing to come to grips with the unresolved disputes of nationalism and slavery.

Through war with Mexico, purchase from Mexico and treaty with England, more than 1,200,000 square miles were added to the nation, bringing it to the present area of the continental United States. By the time of Lincoln's first election there were thirty-three states in the Union.

The creation of new states and territories inevitably revived disputes on slavery and states rights, sharpening the zeal of the Abolitionists and leading to notable debates in Congress by Clay, Webster and Calhoun, all three of whom passed from the scene before the 50's were over.

Yet the public was lulled by a long prosperity lasting until 1857. President Pierce assured the country in 1853 that agitation over slavery had ceased; and in 1856 the nation let itself be distracted by transient issues. In 1856, for example, the native American Party, rousing prejudice against the great influx of German and Irish immigrants polled 874,000 votes.

Meanwhile the South, bewildered and alarmed at the growth of the country, seeing itself becoming a minority voice, seemingly unable to grasp its potentialities in the new areas and new markets, offended by the Abolitionists of the North, drifted toward secession. By no means all Southerners were thus affected, not even all the leaders, but the fear psychosis was potently at work.

6

Lincoln and the Modern World

The dogmas of the quiet past are inadequate to the stormy present. The occasion is piled high with difficulty, and we must rise with the occasion. As our case is new, so must we think and act anew. We must disenthrall ourselves, and then we shall save our country.
ABRAHAM LINCOLN, *Second Annual Message,*
December 1, 1862

I

The personal life of Abraham Lincoln, his general political career and the dramatic events of the Civil War are so familiar to the American public that they do not require detailed repetition here.

Any character as spacious, as protean, as Lincoln, however, lives again for each generation. He has something new to say for each generation, and for each turn of world crisis.

If the South had a lost cause, so even more did Lincoln. The successful trial by arms ultimately saved the Union, abolished slavery and hallowed Lincoln in the brilliant light of victory. But the cause which he lost, namely his attempt to settle the differences peaceably through the appeal for economic freedom for all, has an arresting significance for our time; and each main step in his efforts may help a modern world to find the solution of its future through peaceful means.

Lincoln aimed to preserve the Union without resorting to war. He repeatedly proposed various plans for the freeing of the slaves, peacefully and with compensation to the slaveholding states. In the midst of complete victory of arms, he advocated a restoration of the seceding states on terms of full amnesty, self-government and without malice.

In all three projects he failed, but that was not the end. The League of Nations failed; but it laid a ground-work of international thinking on which the United Nations could be erected without the need for new preliminary foundations. Similarly, with the benefit of hindsight and in the light of Lincoln's prestige as a man of the ages, it is easy to see that his desired and unrealized program might have saved untold grief then and for generations to come.

The cynic might say that only when Lincoln's doctrines of Union and emancipation were written on a drumhead did they prevail. Yet that would be an unhistoric half-truth. His lost cause, namely his attempts to reach a peaceable solution, and his tolerance toward the secession States, emphasized a repudiation of force as a final principle. Today, Lincoln's philosophy and action suggest anew that in a modern world strong differences of economics and ideology can be resolved through patient understanding; and that the alternative of war is intolerably costly. He also accepted the hard final fact that liberty must be fought for if need be.

To the liberal of the open mind, wherever the opening may lead, Lincoln will seem a kindred spirit. In the sense of being an experimentalist by temperament, Abraham Lincoln was not a liberal. If the term refers to championing the cause of minorities, as such, against the powers of a centralized state, he was not a liberal. He said "These politicians are subtle and profound on the right of minorities." [1] If the term liberal suggests that he would form a beneficent planned society and force it upon minority groups for their own good, Lincoln was not a liberal. While he insisted on Union, he equally favored self-government of the states in domestic affairs.

Currently, all shades of thinking claim him. J. G. Randall, one of his most recent biographers, has said, "In the shortest list of American liberal leaders he takes eminent place: liberalism with him was no garment; it was of the fiber of his mind." [2] Randall, however, also refers to the active opposition to Lincoln within his own party because of his conservatism. The Abolitionists and various other professional liberals of Lincoln's time regarded him as unsatisfactory.

As late as 1897 Henry Villard, a liberal journalist of note, made the following patronizing comment on the martyred president: "When he entered the White House, he was certainly ready, as the record shows, for a compromise on the slavery question and remained so until the next year. He was also a believer in the doctrines of the spoilsmen and practiced them in the distribution of offices. Yet I am convinced that, had he lived long enough, he would have become a sincere and determined civil service reformer." [3] Poor Lincoln!

Today, to persons who believe in moderation and mutual tolerance, Lincoln's fundamental principles of government appear obvious and incontrovertible. To save the Union, to free the slaves, and even to be good to your enemies seem hardly debatable; but it is necessary to revert briefly to the history of the times to understand how exhaustively Lincoln wrought the new framework of opinion out of the sincerely diverse and vehement views which existed in both North and South. The famed Gettysburg address and the Second Inaugural were not documents of sudden inspiration, but rather the climactic statement of philosophy and action which had been evolving throughout the long struggle.

Most of the Southern leaders throughout the history of the Republic until 1860 had affirmed their loyalty to the Union and to the Constitution. Robert

[1] Message of July 4, 1861.
[2] *Dictionary of American Biography,* vol. XI, p. 258.
[3] Henry Villard, *Lincoln on the Eve of '61,* p. 101.

E. Lee wrote as late as 1866, "All that the South has ever desired was that the Union as established by our forefathers, should be preserved, and that the government as originally organized should be administered in purity and truth." There had been affirmations of state sovereignty, to be sure—in the Virginia and Kentucky Resolutions during John Adams' time; in an opinion by Mr. Justice Chase in 1796; in the Hartford Convention of 1814; yet South Carolina's failure to achieve nullification had given pause to state sovereignty advocates.

The threat of separation was still dormant in May, 1860, when Lincoln was nominated on the Republican ticket; but in the gap since Van Buren there had been no President who would face bravely the economic issues, particularly slavery, which were increasingly dividing the country. The presidents of those intervening years were, except Fillmore, either Southerners, Democrats, or both, and hence unsympathetic with the demands of Northern opinion. Nevertheless secession spirit was being formed in the deep South. As early as 1851 the Camden, S. C. *Southern Republic* editorialized: "We will secede. The first assault will be made upon us by the federal government by the act of retaining the forts about Charleston. *This will be war.*"

The Democratic platform of 1856, on which Buchanan was elected, had affirmed loyalty to the Union, past, present, and future, but issued warnings. It stated that attempts to interfere with questions of slavery would "endanger the stability and permanence of the Union." It also said that any attempts to interfere with domestic slavery "as consummated, must end in civil war and dis-union."

The sharpness of the issue was further emphasized by the third plank of the platform affirming "that the Democratic Party will resist all attempts at renewing, in Congress or out of it, the agitation of the slavery question, under whatever shape or color the attempt may be made."

Several incidents in the administration of Buchanan brought public temper to a high pitch. A federal boat dispatched to supply Fort Sumter in the harbor of Charleston, S.C., was fired upon by the shore batteries of the state, and turned back. Guerilla warfare broke out in bloody Kansas where slavery was the issue. John Brown of Ossawatomie on October 16, 1859, made his raid on Harper's Ferry, Va., with the intent to free the slaves.

Meanwhile Lincoln had been one of many Northern politicians who were agitating the slavery question. The school books have recited various of his early pronouncements on the subject. On June 16, 1858, he had said, "A house divided against itself cannot stand. I believe this government cannot endure permanently, half slave and half free. I do not expect the Union to be dissolved—I do not expect the house to fall—but I do expect it will cease to be divided. It will become all one thing, or all the other."

While these words did not exclude his later peaceable approaches to the issue, they were regarded as incendiary. They helped to win the support of the Radical Republicans [4] for his nomination in 1860. The Democratic platform of the same year reaffirmed the planks already quoted from the 1856 platform, and the election was fought out intrinsically on the slavery issue. There were ten Southern states in which not a single popular vote was cast for Lincoln.

Actually, the Republicans with a possible victory in sight were holding out the olive branch. The party platform recognized the rights of the states to determine their own policies, and by inference repudiated the Kansas affair, saying "The maintenance inviolate of the rights of the states, and especially the right of each state to order and control its own domestic institutions according to its own judgment exclusively, is essential to that balance of power on which the perfection and endurance of our political fabric depend; and we denounce the lawless invasion by armed force of the soil of any state or territory, no matter under what pretext, as among the gravest of crimes."

The platform condemned the reopening of the African slave trade, opposed the theory that the Constitution "carries slavery" into the territories of the United States; but in general it was conciliatory.

To the disgust of the Radical Republicans, Lincoln was even less vigorous than his platform. He was biding his time, avoiding commitments, and evolving his first plan for peaceful settlement. The addresses of his 1860 campaign were deliberately non-committal to the point where supporters became alarmed. Samuel Bowles said, "Lincoln is a simple Susan, and the men who fought a week at Chicago to nominate him have probably got their labor for their pains." Charles Francis Adams referred to Lincoln as "saying whatever comes into his head" and "perambulating the country kissing the girls and growing whiskers."

Henry Villard, who was covering Lincoln's campaign for the New York Herald, was vaguely impressed by the candidate's sincerity and his way with the plain people, but Villard's enthusiasm was guarded. "I dare say that there are dormant qualities in 'Old Abe' which occasion will draw forth, develop and remind people to a certain degree of the characteristics of 'Old Hickory.'"

Between the time of Lincoln's election in November, 1860, and the inauguration on March 4, 1861, secession had come.

In December, 1860, South Carolina seceded because of the election. Her leaders placed no faith in the assurances of the Republican platform. Her "Declaration of the Causes of Secession" recited that Lincoln had declared

---

[4] Radical as well as Republican is capitalized here because the Radical Republicans were a self-styled and cohesive element in the party. They sought more drastic and immediate action than the moderates.

that "government cannot endure permanently half slave and half free." South Carolina therefore declared that she "resumed her separate and equal place among nations."

In contrast to the later official position of the Confederacy, the South Carolina Declaration affirmed that slavery was the heart of the matter. It referred to Article 4 of the Constitution requiring that fugitive slaves should be returned to their owners. "This stipulation," said the South Carolina declaration, "was so material to the compact that without it that compact would not have been made."

The Declaration then went on to cite that the laws of certain Northern states had abrogated Article 4, that servile insurrection had been stirred up and constant agitation carried on. "Thus the Constitutional compact has been deliberately broken and . . . South Carolina is released from her obligation." By February, 1861, the Confederacy had been formed. Jefferson Davis, in his Inaugural, asserted that the Confederacy was in the spirit of the Constitution of the United States. Said he:

Governments rest on the consent of the governed. . . . It is the right of the people to alter or abolish them at will whenever they become destructive of the ends for which they were established . . .

The right solemnly proclaimed at the birth of the United States, and which has been solemnly affirmed and reaffirmed in the Bills of Rights . . . undeniably recognizes in the people the power to resume the authority delegated for the purposes of government. Thus the sovereign States here represented have proceeded to form this Confederacy; and it is by abuse of language that their act has been denominated a revolution . . .

We have changed the constituent parts, but not the system of government. The Constitution framed by our fathers is that of these Confederate States.

A piece of comic relief was introduced into the situation some months later (though it was seriously meant), when Mayor Fernando Wood of New York recommended to the Common Council a peaceful secession by that municipality. He predicted that the federal government would be dissolved; and he observed with more emotion than grammar, "It behooves every distinct community as well as every individual to take care of themselves."

2

President Buchanan did nothing between November, 1860, and March, 1861, to remedy the situation, and it is doubtful that there was anything that he could have done. Lincoln in his First Inaugural offered a program which could have been accepted with saving of face by all parties. He chose to assume that the issue was one which still could be settled by peaceful discussion. He overestimated the persuasiveness of reasonableness and good will in the circumstances, and underestimated the emotional sectional loyalty of the South. Or, at any rate, he felt that the effort should be made toward peace.

Lincoln began by assuring "the people of the Southern States" that there was no reasonable cause for the apprehension which "seems to exist" that the accession of a Republican administration would endanger their interests. He quoted from one of his public speeches. "I have no purpose, directly or indirectly, to interfere with the institution of slavery in the states where it exists. I believe I have no lawful right to do so, and I have no inclination to do so."

The President-elect referred to the clause in the Republican platform recognizing the rights of the states, and he added, "I now reiterate these sentiments, and in doing so I only press upon the public attention the most conclusive evidence of which the case is susceptible that the property, peace, and security of no section are to be in any wise endangered by the now incoming Administration."

He also pledged that the Constitutional provision for the return of fugitive slaves would be enforced and that "there will be no invasion, no using of force against or among the people anywhere."

"I take the official oath today with no mental reservation, and with no purpose to construe the Constitution or laws by any hypercritical rules."

Obviously, there was to be no action by the government, no beginning of the war, no inflammatory incident, if he could avoid it. "There needs to be no bloodshed or violence, and there shall be none unless it be forced upon the national authority."

Even the normal function of the government in occupying its properties and collecting duties would not be enforced in localities where hostility would not permit competent resident citizens to officiate. "There will be no attempt to force obnoxious strangers upon the people for that object." Rather than enforce the strict legal rights under irritating circumstances, he said, "I deem it better to forego for the time the uses of such offices." There would not even be any insistence on the delivery of the mails. The mails would be delivered "unless repelled."

He discussed the theory of Union and constitutional rights at some length, appealed to "a patient confidence in the ultimate justice of the people," asserted that "nothing valuable can be lost by taking time," and pointed to the impracticability of war as a procedure for reaching a settlement. "Suppose you go to war, you can not fight always; and when, after much loss on both sides and no gain on either, you cease fighting, the identical old questions, as to terms of intercourse, are again upon you . . . We are not enemies, but friends. We must not be enemies. Though passion may have strained it must not break our bonds of affection."

This degree of conciliation to states which had already announced the formation of a separate and avowedly permanent confederacy, this willingness to suspend the normal operation of the federal offices where they were opposed, was dangerously close to being an abdication of the federal authority.

Lincoln was taking a desperate chance, for his position could be construed as weakness both by the South and by foreign governments. He intended, however, to preserve the symbol of authority by the retention of Fort Sumter in the harbor of Charleston, S.C., or of Fort Pickens, off the coast of Florida. Either one would be a visible stronghold of federal authority in the Southern area.

Relief could have been sent to Pickens, but confusion arose in the dispatching of the orders, so that that project failed. Sumter, already highlighted by the attack which had previously been made upon a relief boat, was the logical and dramatic symbol. Lincoln had been assured by General Scott that the fort had enough supplies to maintain the garrison for a year and a half. That would give Lincoln considerable time to conduct peaceful negotiations. The fort could remain quietly manned by federal troops, and it seemed improbable that an unprovoked attack on it would be made by the South. Lincoln counted heavily on Sumter as the key to his strategy.[5]

Shortly after the inauguration, however, Lincoln learned that Scott had been in error. Word came that the fort had only enough supplies to hold out for a few weeks. That changed the whole balance of the carefully wrought plan. Lincoln must now either abandon Fort Sumter or take the risk of sending reinforcements.

He chose the latter course, and hoped to avoid hostile incidents by limiting the relief to supplies of food. As a further precaution, Lincoln dispatched a messenger to the governor of South Carolina to inform him that the government was sending food supplies, and only food supplies, to Sumter and that the relief ship was accordingly pacific in its purposes. The mission was not successful. General Beauregard in charge of the local Confederate troops called upon Major Anderson, the fort's commandant, to surrender. This was refused. Beauregard began bombardment of the fort and two days later Anderson was obliged to evacuate, sailing north with his garrison. The war had begun.

Fort Sumter was evacuated by the Union forces on April 14, 1861; and on the following day Lincoln called for 75,000 militia to suppress the Confederacy and "to cause the laws to be duly executed." The peaceful moratorium was over. The threat of force, however, accomplished no more than the olive branch had done. In fact, the proclamation rallied to the secession cause those Southern states which had hitherto been indecisive.

3

Lincoln, while moving to enforce the authority of the government, still left the door open for reconciliation, without retribution. In any modern totalitarian state, Lee, "Stonewall" Jackson, Beauregard, and most of the other

---

[5] For exhaustive presentation of this strategy see David M. Potter, *Lincoln and His Party in the Secession Crisis* (1942).

Southern generals would have been eligible for execution. Perhaps in any modern state, totalitarian or not, for they were graduates of West Point who had sworn to protect the federal government. It is significant of the tone of Lincoln's policy that the generals of the Confederacy have come down to us in a tradition of honor, even romance, not tarred by vilification.

Congress was called into special session on July 4, 1861. Lincoln's message formulated his outstanding reasons for pursuing the war: "This issue embraces more than the fate of these United States. It presents to the whole family of man the question whether a constitutional republic, or democracy —a government of the people by the same people—can or can not maintain its territorial integrity against its own domestic foes. . . . It forces us to ask, Is there in all republics this inherent and fatal weakness? Must a government of necessity be too *strong* for the liberties of its own people, or too *weak* to maintain its own existence?"

He went at length into the history of the forming of the Constitution and the Republic, affirming that the states and their rights were creatures of the Constitution and that the state sovereignty idea was invalid. His reasoning followed closely that of Washington when the latter had pleaded for loyalty to the Union.

Lincoln affirmed that "this is essentially a people's contest . . . for maintaining in the world that form and substance of government whose leading object is to elevate the condition of men." He referred to the internal disorders and said that "ballots are the rightful and peaceful successors of bullets," and that the only appeal from an election which had been held constitutionally and fairly was to wait for the next election. Under a republican form of government "what men cannot take by an election neither can they take by a war."

This address though reasonable in tone was clouded by the turmoil of the occasion, and by the fact that it was not too clear what the ballots had decided, for Lincoln had won but 40 per cent of the popular vote against the Northern and the Southern Democratic candidates. The president had assumed his war powers as Commander-in-Chief. He had suspended *habeas corpus* proceedings between Philadelphia and Washington. He was *de facto* a dictator, even though temporarily and regretfully. Some of his own party viewed his actions with surprise and alarm, whereas the Radical wing chafed at his continued efforts toward conciliation.

Lincoln himself at this point apparently had some doubts about his policies, for he continued, "Lest there be some uneasiness in the minds of candid men as to what is to be the course of the government toward the Southern states *after* the rebellion shall have been suppressed, the Executive deems it proper to say it will be his purpose then, as ever, to be guided by the Constitution and the laws, and that he probably will have no different understanding of the powers and duties of the federal government relatively to the rights of the states and the people under the Constitution than that expressed in the inaugural address."

"Probably." This may have been a hint that the secessionists could go so far that those states might lose their Constitutional rights. That was the position soon eagerly embraced by the Radical Republicans. Or, more likely, he was forecasting that the opportunity for the Confederates to return to the Union as slave-owning states would not continue indefinitely.

4

In fact, six months later, in his Second Message to Congress, Lincoln enlarged the Union issue to emphasize specifically the basic right of economic freedom; and by inference that spelled the abolition of slavery throughout the nation. The South Carolina Declaration gave him this opportunity. So did the Confederate Constitution. While the latter's preamble did not mention slavery, its detailed provisions endorsed the protection of the slavery system in perpetuity. Thus property, especially property in human beings, was avowed as a foundation stone of the Confederate cause.

If the Southerners who were not slaveholders could be brought to see that their best economic future lay with the Union cause, the war could be promptly ended. Tradition to the contrary notwithstanding, the great bulk of the Southerners were not slaveholders. The owners of huge plantations, most of the wealthy class, nearly all the political leaders had slaves; but these men were a small part of the population. The majority were small farmers, shopkeepers, and wage earners. Their best opportunity resided in a free economy.

The economic as well as the political freedom of the individual was the crux of the matter. The President in his message held that the slavery argument was placing the rights of property above that of human beings, that it assumed a fixed relationship between labor and capital. "Labor is prior to and independent of capital," said the President, and there are no fixed rules governing their relationship. He pointed out that in most of the Southern states a majority of the whole people were neither slaves nor masters, and that in the North at that time most men worked for themselves and were neither employers nor hired hands. The point was an important one. The bulk of the people were farmers using their own labor. Families were large. Wives, sons and daughters as well as the father of the family tilled the soil. Single-family enterprises were the norm, "asking no favors of capital on the one hand nor of hired laborers or slaves on the other." He pointed out, too, that in the main those who were now employers had in their earlier days relied on their own labor or worked for another.

Lincoln knew whereof he spoke. In a later age the freedom to conduct one's own business is less available for the average man, where more capital is needed and more risks involved. But the path was not always easy then. Lincoln himself had failed as a storekeeper, but had gone on to other goals.

He understood the procedures and the intrinsic liberty which were provided in a republic freed from privilege.

"This is the just and generous and prosperous system," he concluded, "which opens the way to all, gives hope to all, and consequent energy and progress and improvement of condition to all. No men living are more worthy to be trusted than those who toil up from poverty; none less inclined to take or touch aught which they have not honestly earned. Let them beware of surrendering a political power which they already possess, and which if surrendered will surely be used to close the door of advancement against such as they and to fix new disabilities and burdens upon them till all of liberty shall be lost."

Lincoln's plea, for all immediate practical purposes, was a failure. The failure was not necessarily in the way the philosophy was presented, nor in the responsiveness or unresponsiveness of the Southern populace. The initial fault was in the lack of means of communication.

5

The South lived, if not behind an iron curtain, certainly behind a curtain of mist through which there was little penetration. The papers equipped to handle out-of-state news were now often without telegraphic service and without regular correspondence from Washington. The presidential documents, of course, were transmitted to Southern officials, but even when they reached the Southern press they were meagerly reported and were received in an editorial atmosphere which was generally hostile. At best, there were great physical handicaps to the dissemination of news. In the rural sections—and the country was predominantly rural—the situation was naturally worse than in the cities.

Lincoln had an acute sense of the importance of the press to any man in public life. He had corresponded for newspapers in his early days, and as president was always greatly concerned regarding newspaper comment. He carried on personal correspondence with Horace Greeley of the New York *Tribune,* Henry Raymond of the New York *Times,* and other editors. In general, Lincoln was given an unusually full press coverage by New England, the middle Atlantic and the Midwest newspapers.[6] Some of his state papers such as the First and the Second Inaugural were printed in full in many newspapers; yet the coverage was pitifully inadequate compared to modern times.

The general shortage of space made it impracticable to give a full report of Washington news. But further, the era of objective reporting had not yet arrived. Most of the great papers were the projections of interesting personalities such as Greeley, and Samuel Bowles of Springfield, Massachusetts. The editorial comment was likely to have more prominence than the thing

[6] See excellent summary by James E. Pollard in *The Presidents and the Press.*

commented on. The Associated Press, born in 1848, was still a struggling young outfit. Hence it was that Lincoln's policies did not and could not have a thorough and continuing presentation to the public.

His brief proposal to free the slaves by compensating the owners for financial loss incurred, was commented upon in the Northern press on its first mention in March and July, 1862, but his great exposition on the subject in December was almost wholly ignored. In the Southern press, understandably, even where news from the White House might have been available, the inclination was not to treat it objectively, but as enemy propaganda.

Lincoln believed that if the mass of the Southerners had access to the facts, if they had the opportunity for self-expression, they would embrace the Union cause. "It may well be questioned whether there is today a majority of the legally qualified voters of any State, except, perhaps, South Carolina, in favor of disunion," he had said in his message of July 4, 1861, affirming that the voters had been coerced.

The degree of actual or potential Union sentiment in the South, however, could be only a matter of speculation. The appeal to the self-interest of the plain people in the causes of Union and emancipation, even if it had been widely heard throughout the South, might not have evoked a general response.

Traditionally the Southerners had not thought of themselves as plain people. Their habit of mind was colored by the plantation. The population of the South was composed mainly of large kin-groups. Nearly every clan had its notable and wealthy leaders and the less prosperous of the group had the pride of the old blood tie. It will be recalled that Andrew Jackson in his South Carolina young manhood was hoisted up the ladder by an influential relative, and basked in the role of an aristocratic dandy. He donned his democratic vestments much, much later.

Therefore, one can only guess as to the possibilities of Lincoln's immediate persuasiveness had he been able to project his words to all the people; yet this lack of communication was unquestionably a handicap in his efforts toward freeing the slaves gradually through payments to their owners, and in seeking a healthy reconstruction. Economic freedom for the colored man and the white laborer was not to be purchased by the impoverishment of others.

6

Lincoln's purpose from the early days of his presidency was to compensate the owners of the emancipated slaves. He was convinced that compensation was an important part of the procedure. The idea was not a new one. Other countries had recognized the principle of payment, and the gradual abolition of slavery under such a method gave an opportunity for a more orderly transition. Great Britain in 1833 had voted twenty million pounds to free the slaves of the British colonial planters. The program included a seven-year apprenticeship to prepare both the economic system and the slave for the transition to a free wage pattern. In Mexico, Argentina and Colombia slavery had been ended under plans which provided for gradual change to the new order. Lincoln's move toward a general freeing of the blacks was initiated in his special message to Congress of March 6, 1862, in which he requested that they adopt the following joint resolution:*

Resolved, that the United States ought to cooperate with any State which may adopt gradual abolishment of slavery, giving to such State pecuniary aid, to be used by such State, in its discretion, to compensate for the inconvenience, public and private, produced by such change of system.

Lincoln in this message emphasized that the plan was voluntary. He felt that one or more states would respond to the offer and that would "initiate" emancipation. He was willing to start with that. "In my judgment gradual and not sudden emancipation is better for all." Once a start was made on this principle the main economic quarrel, namely slavery, would be near settlement. Then "practical reacknowledgment of the national authority would render the war unnecessary, and it would at once cease."

Congress passed the resolution. It attracted no "practical" response from the Confederate states. Indeed, the disasters and ineptitudes of the Union armies, who suffered defeat after defeat in the first three years of the war, discounted any proposals that might come from Washington. Meanwhile, of course, the Radical Republicans were urging a blanket emancipation at once without any nonsense about compensation.

Lincoln was not ready for forced emancipation. In May of '62, Major General David Hunter had taken it upon himself under martial law to declare the slaves in Georgia, Florida, and South Carolina "forever free." Lincoln promptly repudiated this action in a public proclamation; and he urged the slave states to respond to his purchase offer:

I beseech you to make the arguments for yourselves. . . . I beg of you a calm and enlarged consideration of them . . . This proposal makes common sense for a common object, casting no reproaches upon any. It acts not the Pharisee. The change it contemplates would come gently as the dews of heaven, not rending or wrecking anything.

This presentation also produced no response. The resolution adopted by Congress had not specified any terms of compensation. On July 14, Lincoln sought to make the proposal more definite by recommending a bill which provided that the government would pay for the slaves in bonds bearing 6 per cent interest. Congress did not act on this suggestion; and on September 22, 1862, Lincoln signed what became known as the preliminary Emancipation Proclamation. It was issued on September 22, 1862, several days after the battle of Antietam when Lee's forces had been driven back. Before that the Union armies had been so unsuccessful that any such proclamation would have been theoretical if not ridiculous.

Here he stated that on January 1, 1863, one hundred days hence, he would proclaim as free all the slaves held in those states still in rebellion. Even now, he added that before final action "upon the next meeting of Congress," in December, 1862, he would "again recommend the adoption of a measure tendering pecuniary aid" to all states "not then in rebellion against the United States" who would "voluntarily adopt immediate or gradual abolishment of slavery."

Lincoln's second annual message to Congress on December 2, 1862, redeemed that promise. He renewed his proposal that the freedom of the slaves be accomplished through payment of interest-bearing bonds. He began by saying that there were already many opinions in respect to the best way of dealing with slavery. Some would perpetuate it. Some would abolish it suddenly. Some would end it gradually and with compensation for the slave owners, and still others would try to export the slaves through colonization, and there were other minor diversities. Hence, it was foolish to waste strength in trying to establish any particular system as being the ideal one. Mutual concessions to reach a harmonious end were obviously to be desired.

He agreed that his long term proposal would not suit those who were in a hurry to abolish slavery, but on the other hand it would give an opportunity for the nation to prepare both the colored people and the social scene for a gradual absorption of the freed men.

The system would give each state an opportunity for considerable discretion on its own part as to how rapidly it would free the colored people within their borders. In a conciliatory tone he affirmed that "the people of the South are not more responsible for the original introduction of this property than are the people of the North," and allowed that the North had profited in its commerce with the Southern economy. Hence, he again disavowed any self-righteous tone.

Lincoln argued that the financial burden of paying for the slaves would be continuously lighter for the taxpayer, as the increase in population would reduce the average per capita cost. In 1862 the population was thirty-one million, and Lincoln estimated that it would be one hundred million by 1900, a prophecy which proved to be twenty-four million too high. In any event, compared with the cost and the agony of the war, the expenditure would be negligible.

He was willing to take the humblest tone to Congress if he could win them to this scheme: "Nor do I forget that some of you are my seniors, nor that many of you have more experience than I."

He urged Congress to shake loose from the fetters of traditional thinking: "The dogmas of the quiet past are inadequate to the stormy present. The occasion is piled high with difficulty, and we must rise with the occasion. As our case is new, so must we think and act anew. We must disenthrall ourselves, and then we shall save our country."

"Fellow citizens," he concluded, "*we* cannot escape history . . . We, even *we here* hold the power and bear the responsibility. In *giving* freedom to the *slave* we *assure* freedom to the *free* . . . We shall nobly save or meanly lose the last best hope of earth. Other means may succeed; this could not fail. The way is plain, peaceful, generous, just—a way which if followed the world will forever applaud and God must forever bless."

Only a month remained before the final Emancipation Proclamation. That procedure was the one desired by the Abolitionists. Why coddle the rebels, welcoming them back into the Union and paying them for their property!

Lincoln, though rebuffed, though the war continued and the slaves were set free, did not yet abandon hope for his plan. As late as February 5, 1865, he renewed the proposal before his Cabinet, seeking support for again presenting the subject to Congress, but not one would vote for it.[7]

7

Lincoln had failed in his effort to settle differences without warfare. He had also failed to establish the freedom of the slaves by an equitable system which would be just to their former owners. Above all, however, as he wrote to Horace Greeley, August 22, 1862, his "paramount object" was "to save the Union."

If I could save the Union without freeing any slave, I would do it—if I could save it by freeing all the slaves, I would do it—and if I could do it by freeing some and leaving others alone, I would also do that . . . I have here stated my purpose according to my views of official duty, and I intend no modification of my oft-expressed personal wish that all men everywhere could be free.

As the war continued, even the objective of Union began to seem unattainable. Lincoln proclaimed a general amnesty, with certain exceptions, to all secessionists who would return and take the oath of allegiance. He fostered the forming of pro-Union governments in the Southern states, promising to recognize any who would affirm their loyalty, abolish slavery, and establish the fact that they were elected by at least 10 per cent of those citizens who were qualified to vote in 1860. Several Southern state governments were recognized by Lincoln on this basis; but his program was violently opposed within his own party.

There was some doubt of renominating Lincoln in 1864, but the Republicans felt too insecure to drop him. In fact, the convention at Baltimore named Andrew Johnson, the war-governor Democrat from Tennessee, as vice-presidential candidate, and decided to run their ticket under the name of the National Union Party. The Radical Republicans did not bolt, as staying in office was their first desire; but they were chafing increasingly at the President's policies. A tide of victories for the Union armies, late in 1864, gave the Lincoln ticket a sizable majority, which nevertheless did little to placate the self-styled radicals.

[7] *Lincoln's "Complete Works,"* edited by John A. Nicolay and John Hay, Gettysburg edition, vol. XI, pp. 1–3.

The Second Inaugural with its "let us judge not, that we be not judged" and its "with malice toward none and charity for all" only infuriated many of the Republican leaders in Congress. Their displeasure continued as Lincoln dealt respectfully and conciliatingly with the Confederate states in their ultimate defeat in 1865.

Lincoln's course has been presented here as that of a liberal mind. Many additional instances could have been cited. Conversely, in numerous instances he stretched the executive power to a dangerous degree, though never for personal aggrandizement. His purposes throughout, as modern generations view them, were humanitarian; but Lincoln in the eyes of the left wing of his party was an arch-Conservative, if not worse. Now that victory was safe, they began to speak out louder and louder.

Representative George W. Julian of Indiana, a founder of the Republican party, in a lengthy and typical address, blamed Lincoln's policies for the long duration of the war. "A little wholesome severity, summarily administered, would have been a most sovereign panacea." He referred to Lincoln's attitude of toleration as "the horrid infatuation that so long shaped the policy of the government in resisting this slaveholders' rebellion." He observed that "a system of retaliation, which would have been a measure of real mercy, has not yet been adopted . . . The times of brotherly love toward rebels in arms have gone by forever" and predicted that Congress would "provide for parceling out the forfeited and confiscated lands of rebels in small homesteads among the soldiers and seamen of the war."

Regarding the critics of the government, such as himself, Julian said, "the moral appeals and persistent criticism of these men saved our cause from the complete control of Conservatism and thus saved the country itself from destruction." [8] Julian purported to believe that Lincoln had recanted from his earlier principles, as evidenced by the fact that his Second Inaugural stated that slavery "was somehow a cause of the war." Lincoln, in fact, had said this in his December, 1862, message on compensation. Julian failed to note that the Second Inaugural mentioned both North and South as "those by whom the offense came."

The President had not changed in his basic attitude. To the day when he was assassinated on April 14, 1865, he continued in his effort "to finish the work we are in, to bind up the nation's wounds."

The Julian "system of retaliation" was close at hand. Many years passed before Lincoln's dream of a spiritually reunited nation came into being; but his words, what he wished to do, his counsel on how to treat our fellowman even if he has been our enemy, have become more and more an exalting scripture for the nation's conscience.

[8] Louis M. Hacker, *The Shaping of the American Tradition*, pp. 620–627.

7
The Liberal Battleline Shifts

*The single vote by which Andrew Johnson escaped
conviction marks the narrow margin by which the
Presidential element in our system escaped destruction.*
W. A. DUNNING, *Essays on the
Civil War and Reconstruction*

I

The fact of the American internal war, whatever it may be named, its
length, the triumph of the North and the prostration of the South brought
about a new orientation of liberal issues.

Fortunately the passions of the day centered around Andrew Johnson as
a lightning rod. He was strong enough and stubborn enough to make the
presidency the focus of contending views. Fortunately, indeed, because the
confusion and anger of the times well might have been diffused in a number of inconclusive separate vicious squabbles, prolonging issues indefinitely.
Conceive, for example, the chaos which might have surrounded a temporizing Buchanan. Johnson chose to take his stand firmly and unafraid, even at
times tactlessly and combatively and for that the nation owes him thanks.
He made the presidency rather than the nation the battleground.

The personal struggle of Andrew Johnson in the presidency is one of the
most inspiring sagas in the American tradition, and it shall not be omitted
here. A strong "channel," that mind! But first let us see what had happened
to American issues. The "consent of the governed" doctrine had been settled
through force of arms to mean that the nation, nothing smaller, was that
unit of consent. Lincoln had pleaded for toleration and brotherhood in victory, but the fact of force was there. The doctrine of state sovereignty was
forever laid to rest. The authority of the federal government was no longer
to be challenged. Henceforth the main issue would be as to how wisely it
might exercise that authority.

Justice as between sections should theoretically no longer be an issue, for
all sections were with equal right a part of the whole, though Johnson's main
battle was to establish that premise.

The idea of Constitutional liberty for the free citizen faced a new test,
with slavery abolished forever and the new status of the colored people to be
determined. The Indians were long since doomed to be a dependent people.
From the standpoint of the presidency they receded into a minor problem.

Imperialism was virtually extinct. The contest to acquire territory for
economic or political purposes was at an end and the nation now had far
more land than its population could utilize for many years hence.

Peace with foreign nations also was no longer an issue. There was no urgency to fight for new territory, every reason to avoid combat. Alaska could be acquired by purchase not by the route of conquest. No European country, in turn, was disposed to invade a nation hardened, if battered, in the practices of warfare.

Even domestic commercial differences were dormant in the North. Those who were able to return to the simple agricultural economy of the farm and village were happy to do so. They were the vast majority of the population. The war's end was marked by sharp declines in industrial activity and prices.

The chief issue of the day was internal and political—what should be done about the conquered South? Who would control it, what would be its new pattern? The Radical reformers and the carpetbaggers fought for dominion over the South, together and separately. Some of the former believed that all reforms could and should be effected at once. The latter claimed the spoils of victory. Johnson stood for the self-determination of the South, and thus laid the cornerstone of a new national unity.

Held within bounds by the war and by the prestige of Lincoln, the Radical Republicans hitherto had chafed and seethed. Now that he was gone they saw their chance, and felt that they were righteously entitled to it. Vengeance upon the South, martial law below the District of Columbia, enfranchisement of the Negroes through elections policed by federal agents—these were among the aims of the group led by Ben Wade of Ohio, George W. Julian of Indiana, Thaddeus Stevens of Pennsylvania, and Charles Sumner of Massachusetts, a group which now virtually controlled Congress. They needed to secure their positions promptly, for if the representatives of the Southern States were re-admitted to Congress under such conditions as Lincoln had proposed, the narrow margin of control now held by the extremists would be wiped out. Much depended on how fully the Radicals could influence, or would need to influence, the new President. If the Southern whites were not kept under control, Stevens said "they, with their kindred copperheads of the North, would always elect the President and control Congress." Johnson's decision—whether to follow Lincoln or heed the Radical Republicans, would be a determining factor.

Andrew Johnson was one of the strongest of the American presidents in point of character, humaneness and vision. He came to office well-equipped for his task, a man of broad political experience. He had served ten years in the House of Representatives, two terms as governor of Tennessee,[1] and a part-term in the United States Senate. He had been the only Southern senator to remain loyal to the Union. In 1862 he had been appointed military governor of Tennessee.

He understood fully the needs and desires of the common people, for he

[1] Several years previous to being the appointed military governor during the Civil War.

had the humblest origin of any man who has occupied the White House. Some presidents have been wealthy, some were born in log cabins, but in virtually every case the man has had a homestead, some inheritance, or well-to-do relatives or patrons to help him on his career. Johnson was born the son of a tavern porter and a maid,[2] in Raleigh, North Carolina, on December 29, 1808. His parents had only their meager wages and their quarters in the inn wherewith to subsist. When Andrew was three years old, his father died, and at the age of ten the boy was apprenticed to a tailor. Johnson's mother remarried and in 1826 she, Andrew and his stepfather moved to Greenville, Tennessee.

Johnson became a skillful tailor, but was at an early age interested in politics. While he had almost no formal schooling, he steeped himself in the writings of the elder Pitt, Charles James Fox, Edmund Burke, and other protagonists of the common man. At the age of nineteen he married Eliza McCardle, the daughter of a shoemaker. She was a school teacher who devoted the rest of her days to his education, for he was continuously conscious of his lack of learning and pursued his studies throughout his mature life.

He had a stalwart physique. He was five feet nine inches in height, had piercing black eyes, a strong, mellow voice, and a self-possessed manner. Moreover, possibly because of his tailoring experience, he was always well-dressed and presented a fine appearance. The impression of Johnson as an uncouth ruffian was invented by his opponents and fostered for years by partisan or lazy historians. This view is contrary to contemporary evidence and has been corrected by such careful modern biographers as Robert E. Winston, Lloyd Paul Stryker, and St. George L. Sioussat.

Johnson had been elected to Congress in 1843, at the age of thirty-five. Before that, he had served in the Tennessee legislature as a Jacksonian Democrat, and had campaigned for Van Buren. In Congress he had become noted particularly as an advocate of the Homestead Law, which gave an opportunity for poor men to establish themselves as farmers. As governor of Tennessee he campaigned for better schools and libraries.

Such was the character of the man to whom the nation was entrusted by the assassination of Abraham Lincoln. Unlike many of the President's colleagues, Johnson was true to his chief and was among the first to recognize his stature. "Mr. Lincoln is the greatest American that has ever lived," Johnson wrote to a friend. "I do not mean by this to detract from the name of Washington; but Washington was an Englishman, you know, after all." On another occasion he said, "I am only trying to carry out the measures toward the South that Mr. Lincoln would have done had he lived."

The task Johnson faced was obviously one of great complexity. The Radicals desired to confer the ballot on all the freedmen at once, to police the

[2] R. H. Battle, *Library of Southern Literature*, vol. VI, p. 2719.

white vote by distinguishing between the "loyal" and "disloyal," to seize the large plantations and divide them into small holdings. Some, like Julian, would turn over these lands to the Union veterans, others would give them to the blacks and the poor whites. The Radicals were also projecting a large program of education, health and general improvement for the colored race and the loyal whites. Louis M. Hacker, in *The Shaping of the American Tradition* (pp. 593–596), presents the Radicals' case sympathetically. He concedes that in carrying out parts of the program there were abuses and instances of self-interests, but clears them on intent—"They sought to make the idea of equality work."

Against this project of imposed equality were many considerations. Did the unlanded or non-plantation whites desire salvation or enlightenment through the means of Northern force? Apparently they did not. Further, would the black man benefit by sudden full citizenship?

Had there been complete good will on all sides, the difficulties would have been great enough. The freedmen numbered around four million. Most of them were unlettered, although some knew trades, and all by the misfortune of their slavery had no knowledge of self-rule.

They were freed, it is true, but landless and jobless in an impoverished countryside. Lincoln's plan of compensation could have provided the initial "pump-priming" capital to stimulate production and employment. As it stood, the colored people were the victims of each side. Various Southern states moved toward restrictive laws concerning the blacks, while the Radical Republicans sought to give them the vote, and to keep that vote under Northern manipulation.

In following Lincoln's pattern Johnson had pitiably small support in the official ranks. In the Cabinet, Gideon Welles and William H. Seward, secretaries of navy and state respectively, were the only men strongly in favor of continuing with Lincoln's policies. Edwin M. Stanton, Lincoln's war secretary, pretended to support the administration, but was actually a tale-bearer to Stevens *et al,* advising them of his chief's programs so that the measures might be anticipated and opposed.

Johnson's leading critics may have been of good intent, but they were as bizarre a group of humans as ever occupied the public stage. Thaddeus Stevens bore a grudge against society. He had been born with a club foot. His father had deserted the family. Urged on by his mother, Stevens had succeeded despite the severest misfortunes. By 1865, as a member of Congress, he was a grim and seasoned fighter with both ancient and recent grudges to be served. He had finally acquired considerable properties in southern Pennsylvania, only to have them destroyed by Lee's troops in their march on Gettysburg.

Charles Sumner, born to the purple, brilliant and fluent, was a United States senator from Massachusetts. His talent for invective had brought him a brutal beating from a Southern opponent from which he had not fully recovered. A single man in his fifties, inadequately appreciated, having borne no arms in the war, he too had scores to pay which allied him with Stevens.

Ben Wade, senator from Ohio, was made of cheerier stuff. He was a rough and ready politician, sixty-five by now. He thought that Johnson's tolerant attitude toward the South was "political suicide." He was being groomed by Stevens for leadership of the Senate, and perhaps for higher office. He approved of Stevens.

Outside of Congress also there was eloquent opposition to Johnson, including Wendell Phillips and Horace Greeley. Greeley, who had often deplored Lincoln's firmness for the Union, now was against amnesty and reconciliation. Of him Johnson said astutely and humorously:

I always considered Greeley a good enough editor before the war, although I never agreed with him, but in all other matters he seemed to me like a whale ashore. He nearly bothered Mr. Lincoln's life out of him, and it was difficult to tell whether he wanted Union or separation, war or peace. Greeley is all heart and no head. He is the most vacillating man in the country or was during the war. He runs to goodness of heart so much as to produce infirmity of mind . . . Greeley was a sublime old child.

Johnson, Welles, and Seward did not wholly back public support. Henry Ward Beecher, pastor of Plymouth Church, Brooklyn, N.Y., who had been a stalwart supporter of Lincoln at first endorsed Johnson's policies. So did General Sherman. So did Grant.

In general, the military leaders who had actually borne arms on the battlefield were the most tolerant. General Sherman said:

I perceive the politicians are determined to drive the Confederates into guerilla bands, a thing more to be feared than open organized war . . . we could settle the war in three weeks by giving shape to the present disordered elements, but they may play out their game . . . I do not favor the scheme of declaring the negroes . . . to be loyal voters, whereby politicians may manufacture just so much more pliable electioneering material . . . they are no friends of the negro who seek to complicate him with new prejudices.

2

Johnson, at the outset, was fortunate that Congress was not in session. On the day before he died, Lincoln had said, "I think it providential that this great rebellion is crushed out just as Congress has adjourned and there are none of the disturbing elements of that body to embarrass us. If we are wise and discreet we shall reanimate the states and get their governments in successful operation, with order prevailing and the Union re-established before Congress comes together in December."

Johnson hastened to bring about restoration on the Lincoln pattern. As early as the twenty-ninth of May, 1865, he issued a Reconstruction Proclamation granting "amnesty and pardon, with restoration of all rights of property except as to slaves," to all but a few classifications, and the exceptions were permitted to apply for clemency.

Johnson then proceeded to appoint provisional governors, or recognize governors already chosen, for the purpose of getting state governments re-established. Loyalty to the Union and acceptance of the Thirteenth Amendment which abolished slavery, were the only conditions required. The public in general was gratified, and Johnson was acclaimed in many quarters. The President himself said, "We are making very rapid progress—so rapid I sometimes cannot realize it. It appears like a dream!"

Thaddeus Stevens wrote to Sumner, "If something is not done, the President will be crowned king before Congress meets. . . . The danger is that so much success will reconcile the people to almost everything." Ben Wade said, "To me all appears gloomy," and Wendell Phillips alleged that President Johnson's plan of reconstruction was a practical fraud upon the North.

As Congress was about to convene in December, all the Southern states, except Texas, had formed governments and chosen their senators and representatives. No wonder Johnson felt that the breach was healing rapidly.

From the Radical point of view, however, this was throwing away the fruits of victory. No social revolution was involved in the Johnson program. The same leaders and interests as before the war were coming back into power. Slavery was abolished, but otherwise little was changed. The opportunity radically to reform the South would be lost if the present new governments continued.

At the very start of Congress, the issue was joined. Thaddeus Stevens called a caucus which proposed appointing a committee of fifteen to pass upon the qualifications of states for readmission to the Union. This was wholly inconsistent with the Lincoln-Johnson theory. The states were in the Union already, and as Gideon Welles wrote, the committee was "in conflict with the spirit and letter of the Constitution."

Johnson, according to Welles, did not expect the Stevens caucus to prevail. The President's message to the Congress was already prepared and should do much to clarify the purposes of the administration. The document had been drafted by the historian, George Bancroft, and reviewed by Seward. It unequivocally met the issues of the hour. Following a long exposition of the indestructibility of any state under the Constitution, Johnson reviewed the existing situation:

The United States had recovered possession of all its forts and arsenals in the South. Resistance to the General Government was at an end. The existence of military rule by the North if continued "would have divided the people into the vanquishers and the vanquished and would have envenomed hatred rather than have restored affection."

He took the position that, if it was to be affirmed that the states could not legally secede, which had been the contention of the Union party, then the states had not seceded legally and their intrinsic status remained unimpaired. Hence, as soon as it was possible to restore the legislative procedures in the Southern states, they had the right to resume their part in the nation, and he, Johnson, had been using the facilities of the federal government to bring about these local restorations as rapidly as possible.

He agreed that the effort of the federal government to bring about these provisional state governments was "attended with some risk . . . for its success it requires at least the acquiescence of the states which it concerns." Nevertheless, in the interest of order and the restoration of a peaceful society, he felt that the risk of setting up a disloyal government, or one which might represent only a faction in the given state, was less than to leave things in the unsettled situation of a military rule.

Johnson on the day after Lincoln's death had told a Congressional committee, including Ben Wade, that treason "should be made infamous." This had encouraged the Radicals momentarily to think that Johnson would favor their policies of punishment and reform. Now he qualified that statement.

"It is manifest that treason, most flagrant in character, has been committed," he said. "Persons who are charged with its commission should have fair and impartial trials in the highest civil tribunals of the country, in order that the Constitution and the laws may be fully vindicated, the truth clearly established and affirmed that treason is a crime, that traitors should be punished and the offense made infamous, and, at the same time, that the question may be judicially settled, finally and forever, that no State of its own will has the right to renounce its place in the Union."

The indestructibility of the states, the legal dealings with treason—one other cardinal issue remained—whether freedom from slavery should be accompanied by the right to vote. Universal suffrage was a new idea, not only in the world, but in the United States. Negroes and all persons without property were excluded from voting in some Northern states. Massachusetts Abolitionists, such as Sumner and Phillips, who wished all male Negroes to be given the vote, denied the privilege to all women, white or black. Not until 1920 were there a sufficient number of states in favor of woman suffrage to enact it by Constitutional amendment.

Johnson appealed first for economic justice for the freedmen. "While I have no doubt that now, after the close of the war, it is not competent for the General Government to extend the elective franchise in the several States," he said, "it is equally clear that good faith requires the security of the freedmen in their liberty and their property, the right to labor, and their right to claim the just return of their labor." He affirmed that industry must be freely opened to them, but that the franchise should be reserved to the decision of each state.

Johnson's program as set forth in his message seemed so reasonable to him, so much in accord with the Constitution, so close to Lincoln's ideas, that he did not anticipate the violence of opposition which followed. The message of the President of the United States was normally the first order of business before the Congress, and Johnson hoped that his carefully reasoned appeal would satisfy all but the extremists. Congressional endorsement could solidify the gains he had made to date and inaugurate a new era of amity.

The committee of fifteen, however, delayed the reading of the message. The Clerk of the House under Stevens' direction omitted the names of Southern representatives when calling the roll, and the issue of whether or not the Southern states were members of the Union was thereby precipitated at once before the presidential message was even heard.

3

In the many months which followed, a succession of bills on Reconstruction according to Radical Republican ideas were passed, sent to the White House and vetoed. They all had the goal of keeping the South under military control.

The essential details may be briefly stated. There were two attempts to pass a new Freedmen's Bureau Bill. The Bureau had been established under Lincoln as a temporary measure to assist the freed slaves in becoming adjusted to civilian life. The first measure greatly extended the powers originally contemplated and used the desirable purposes of the Bureau as an excuse for military occupation. In his veto measure of February 19, 1866, Johnson outlined the dangers:

The proposed bill, he affirmed, would extend the existing temporary jurisdiction of the Freedman's Bureau with greatly enlarged powers. The bureau was to be governed nominally by the president of the United States, but acting through the War Department and a commissioner for the bureau. Agents were to be selected from the army or from civil life. The country was to be divided into sub-districts and districts with an army of salaried agents.

In eleven states it was proposed to give the bureau jurisdiction over all cases affecting freedmen and refugees allegedly discriminated against by "local law, custom or prejudice."

Any white person charged with depriving a freedman, namely a former slave, of any civil rights might be subject to imprisonment or fine or both. Yet the bill did not define what those civil rights were.

An agent appointed by the bill would exercise the office of a military judge. He might be a stranger entirely ignorant of the laws of the place. No provision was made for any general legal supervision of the fitness of such agents or of the way in which they performed their office.

No provision was made for jury trial or any fixed rules of law or evidence under the operation of the bureau. Trials could proceed without any previous charges or indictment; and the punishment would be fixed not by statute, but by a court-martial. From the tribunals there was no provision made for appeal nor any writ of error which might be made to the courts of the United States. Johnson concluded "I cannot reconcile a system of military jurisdiction of this kind with the words of the Constitution."

While the presidential veto prevailed in this instance, a second similar bill was soon introduced having enough supporters to carry over Johnson's opposition. The actual functioning of the bureau had its meritorious side. It became a vast relief organization aiding thousands of families including whites as well as blacks. There are numerous cheerful accounts of it in contemporary Northern sources; but the price of these benefits was rule by martial law, and many abuses.

Similarly, the so-called Civil Rights Bill aimed to enforce the immediate enfranchisement of the Negro through drastic interference with the rights of the states as outlined in the Constitution. Here again Johnson protested in a vigorous veto message:

In all our history, in all our experience as a people living under Federal and State law, no such system as that contemplated by the details of this bill has ever before been proposed or adopted.

They establish for the security of the colored race safeguards which go infinitely beyond any that the General Government has ever provided for the white race. In fact, the distinction of race and color is by the bill made to operate in favor of the colored and against the white race.

It interfered with the state legislation, he affirmed, and would tend to break down the whole system of relationship between federal and state law. He held that it would only serve to reawaken the spirit of rebellion and to delay the return of a true spirit of union and peace.

This and a series of other Reconstruction Acts were obviously, as Johnson said, something new "in all our history." The more vicious phases of military occupation and denial of self-government were abandoned even by the younger Radical Republicans after several years. Yet the war had brought one fundamental change in national structure and policy which endured. The Fourteenth Amendment of the Constitution declared that all persons born or naturalized in this country are "citizens of the United States" and of the state in which they reside. The states were by this amendment no longer the sole custodians of citizenship.

The Fourteenth Amendment also limited state representation in Congress in proportion to the number of citizens actually qualified to vote. In other words, either let the black man vote or else don't claim him as part of your population for representation purposes. Johnson agreed that this was a fair limitation. He desired no color discrimination, as such, and recommended a progressive franchise based on education and moderate property qualifications.

The amendment also forbade any possibility of a compensation measure such as Lincoln had suggested. Federal authority was hereby affirmed forever and state "sovereignty" liquidated. Nationalism was the new rule of the country. Had this been established under circumstances tolerable to the Southern whites, a new era of amity might have followed.

Unfortunately, federal authority, federal oppression and Negro enfranchisement were all tied together, to the ultimate disadvantage of the freedman's cause. The Southern states, as well as the slaveholding state of Delaware, rejected the Fourteenth Amendment at the outset; but the governments set up under the Lincoln-Johnson plan were turned out by Reconstruction and the new regimes accepted the amendment.

Throughout the differences between the White House and the Legislature, the opposition naturally made every effort to make the President appear as a stubborn unreasonable man, trying to block the popular will. Actually, Johnson vetoed but twenty-one acts out of scores which were passed by the Congress. Indeed, he avoided collisions on all points but the central policy of Reconstruction. On this he was adamant.

Johnson encountered so much turmoil in his contest with the Radical Republicans on reconstruction and the powers of the presidency, that much of his day to day constructive work has been forgotten.

Johnson worked for international peace in a ticklish situation. France, England and Spain had formed a loose-knit alliance to protect their subjects and properties in Mexico. A succession of rulers in Mexico had resisted foreigners. There was no stability in government and many "outrages" were committed, as Europe regarded them. Protection, rather than invasion, had been contemplated by the European powers at the outset; but Napoleon III of France, after a dubious plebiscite in Mexico, had named the Archduke Ferdinand Maximilian of Austria as Emperor Maximilian the First of Mexico. These events had occurred during the Civil War under Lincoln and became a Johnson legacy.

General Grant in June 1865 affirmed to Johnson that Napoleon III had committed "an act of hostility to the United States." Johnson desired no more war. As mentioned previously, the nation wished no more fighting and Europe had no zeal to engage America on this side of the Atlantic. Johnson, with the advice of Seward, his secretary of state, and other members of the Cabinet, realized that time was on his side. True to the liberal tradition in the presidency, Johnson did not seek military grandeur when it might have served him personally. He decided to wait the issue out. A French-ruled empire on the American continent would be intolerable, against the Monroe Doctrine, but there was no need for a trial of arms at once. Actually, a local revolution occurred and Maximilian was executed, without the United States government becoming involved.

Then came Alaska. The circumstances were remarkably similar to those which Jefferson had encountered in the purchase of Louisiana. Russia, as

Napoleon I had in the earlier case, made the initial approach. Her ambassador made the proposal to William H. Seward, formerly in Lincoln's Cabinet, now secretary of state under Johnson. Seward deserves the credit for prompt receptivity and action, for bargaining over the terms until the price was $7,200,000 for 500,000 square miles of territory, including four thousand miles of coastline replete with bays and harbors.

With Johnson's warm approval the Senate ratified the agreement on April 9, 1867, though the reconstruction controversy was continuing. The House, however, refused to vote the money, and the opposition forces jeered at the project. The territory was referred to as "Walrussia" and as "Johnson's polar bear garden." Johnson did not wait for the House to approve funds and took possession in October 1867, when the United States flag was unfurled at Sitka and the U. S. Army took over from the Russian troops. Meanwhile a growing public opinion approved the action, and in July 1868 the House voted the appropriation 113 to 43.

4

Johnson's courage on Alaska was all the more notable since he had already "gone to the country" on the reconstruction issue in the fall of 1866, at the mid-term Congressional elections. He believed earnestly that he expressed the popular will in pursuing the Lincoln policy of toleration. He denounced the Radical leaders by name, and that may have lost him some votes, as the president is held by some to be above the strife. The disfranchised South obviously had no voice at the polls. Hence the president had to look wholly to the North for support. At any rate, the Radical Republicans won, and forthwith determined to get rid of the president by the process of impeachment and conviction.

The impeachment of a president was not a popular step. It had not been attempted hitherto in the history of the republic and it was discussed for some months in Congress before the Radical Republicans completed their plan.

The plan took shape in the passage of the Tenure-of-Office Act in March 1867, which provided that a president might not remove an appointee who had been approved by the Senate without the consent of the Senate. Johnson was advised that the act was unconstitutional, and many years later this was held to be the case, though at the time the Supreme Court avoided ruling on it.

Stanton, the secretary of war, as noted previously, had been secretly an informer for the Radical Republicans though pretending to be a supporter of the President. Now, he came out in his true colors. The President dismissed him and appointed General Grant in his place. Stanton refused to retire and Grant, who had promised Johnson to take the office despite any obstacles in the way, changed his mind. Johnson then appointed a man named Thomas. Stanton still refused to yield, and the Radicals had their issue.

They succeeded in obtaining a vote to impeach the President at the bar of the Senate. The vote was in March 1868, a year after the first step in the program. The President was accused on eleven points, including the heinous crime of criticizing Congress; but the trial centered on the power-of-removal issue.

The term *impeachment* is confusing, as it is an accusation not a conviction. As in the case of an indictment, the accused is innocent until proved otherwise, but the mere fact that the impeachment had been brought against the President was, of course, a national scandal.

At this point Johnson became the victim of his own attorneys. He had stated to the press that there were previous examples in which a president had removed an appointee without the consent of the Senate, and without being challenged therefor. The point was well taken; but it was going to be used in the case by Johnson's lawyers and they became greatly perturbed over his attempt at public self-defense. At the close of a Cabinet meeting the attorney-general said to the President: "You are now, Mr. President, in the hands of your lawyers, who will speak and act for you, and I must begin by requesting that no further disclosures be made to newspaper correspondents. There was in the papers yesterday, or this morning, what purported to be a conversation between the President and a correspondent, in which the Pickering correspondence was brought out and made public. This is all wrong, and I have to request that these talks or conversations be stopped. They injure your case and embarrass your counsel."

His attorneys conducted the case with skill, erudition and good temper; but the impeachment trial obviously was not comparable to an ordinary court case. Johnson had spent a lifetime amid the various issues involved. His real trial was before the bar of public opinion. The contest was intrinsically political rather than legal. Nevertheless he, the chief figure, was kept by his counsel hidden from the stage and silent while his accusers week after week held the limelight.

On May 16, 1868, the Chief Justice, presiding over the trial held by the Senate, held that Andrew Johnson, President of the United States, "stood acquitted" on the charge relating to the Tenure of Office Act, and acquittal on all other points followed shortly. He had won a technical victory. By one vote his accusers had failed to muster the necessary two-thirds for conviction; but Johnson's prestige and reputation were severely damaged.

In his fourth and last message to the Congress on December 9, 1868, Johnson made a final appeal for his concept of a liberal policy. He pointed out that the reconstruction had failed—that the attempt to place the Southern whites "under the domination of persons of color" had destroyed good relationships and prevented co-operation in industrial enterprise. In vain, he urged upon Congress a "timely revocation of injurious and oppressive measures."

Johnson's chance of renomination under any circumstances would have been slight. The National Union Party had been a wartime coalition. The Democratic Party at this stage was composed mostly of Northerners who had no sympathy with the man from Tennessee. Robert E. Lee said, "Everyone approves of the policy of President Johnson, gives him his cordial support, and would, I believe, confer on him the presidency for another term if it was in his power." This presumably meant every one of Lee's acquaintance, and was hardly politically helpful to Johnson at this period.

Johnson was not an active candidate. The Democrats nominated Horatio Seymour of New York, a Tammany man, and the Republicans nominated Grant.

Johnson's commentary on the man destined to be his successor is touching in its clarity and lack of rancor. Said Johnson of Grant, "He was the strongest man of all in the support of my policy for a long while, and did the best he could for nearly two years in strengthening my hands against the adversaries of constitutional government. But Grant saw the Radical handwriting on the wall, and heeded it. I did not see it, or if seeing it did not heed it. Grant did the proper thing to save Grant, but it pretty nearly ruined me. I might have done the same thing under the same circumstances. At any rate, most men would."

Johnson's term in the presidency was a tortuous period in the history of liberalism. Measured by ideal standards, the nation had failed miserably in its approach to re-union and the solution of the Negro's status. Whether a more tactful president could have done what Johnson tried to do is a matter of speculation. Presumably Congress would have pursued the same course under a weak president, and without rebuke. Johnson at least asserted a steadfast moral leadership. His attempt to re-establish the Southern states at the least kept that aim before the public consciousness and assured the South that it had a friend at the head of government, that there was some element of hope for their future.

On the race problem, Johnson's advocacy of moderation seemingly fell on deaf ears everywhere. A program of equality in economic opportunity for the colored people, of education and gradual enfranchisement was sound in theory. Johnson blamed the Radicals for destroying that plan. Perhaps it was unworkable anyhow. An embittered South turned against the Negro, and a more tolerant policy was delayed for generations. At best, the size of the colored population in relation to white created racial tensions which were difficult to relieve.

As Dunning has indicated, the impeachment trial was a supreme test of the presidential office. Had Johnson lost, it may be assumed that the Executive powers would have been seriously impaired. No president would have dared defy Congressional leaders. As it was, the trial strengthened the office and gave future presidents a precedent for bold independent action.

A sodden era succeeded the end of Johnson's term, eight years of moral and financial turmoil.

The nation gained nearly a third in population despite war losses, but the aftermath of battle was woe to the victors as well as to the vanquished.

Manufactures throve for a time, but wages and prices began a long decline. The whole nation was exhausted, the health and pride of the young free nation had been blackened with gunpowder. The country walked in an evil trance. never had it been more barren of literature, enterprise, character.

The cities for the first time knew poverty and beggary on a large scale. The farmers were the least unfortunate class, having a roof and foodstuffs, but their lands and equipment still suffered from the neglect of war years.

In the White House, Ulysses S. Grant needed a better brand of whiskey than had served him on the camp ground.

8

Hayes and the Moral Reformation

Not until the advent of President Hayes, his irre-
proachable cabinet and the Puritanical tone which Lucy
Hayes gave to administration entertainments, did the
social atmosphere improve.

ALLAN NEVINS [1]

I

A notable liberal rector of a fashionable Episcopal church in Brooklyn, N.Y., addressed his congregation perplexedly on the occasion of his twenty-fifth anniversary in the parish. During that long ministry, he explained, he had endeavored to arouse his wealthy morning congregation to the social obligations of their Christianity. In the same period, he had attempted to impress on the socialistic audiences who attended his Sunday evening forums that no social planning can serve humanity unless its agents and the individuals of society are imbued with the need for personal salvation. Each class of zealots, the well-to-do religious and the ardently planning socialists, continued resistant to their full obligations, the rector observed regretfully.

The issue is one which has been long extant in reform and liberalism, and is frequently divisive. Cromwell was able to incite a middle-class religious revolt against the usurpations of Charles I and thereby promote a program of social reforms. Franklin Roosevelt in his first term repeatedly described himself as a reformer and a liberal, campaigning against personal wickednesses as well as advocating new social measures; but the reformer and the liberal in any given era, are often far apart. The liberal in today's connotation may be inclined to assume an effortless native goodness in all individuals and to concentrate on improving the pattern of the state. As a natural corollary, he may tend to appraise the liberal leaders of the past by the extent to which they changed the structure of the social order.

As we have seen, the first sixty years of the Republic witnessed recurrent debates on the meaning of the Constitution. The statesmen and the reformers treated it as the chief social instrument, orientating most of their arguments around the relative powers of the states and the general government. For nearly forty years following the Civil War, however, most of the liberal drive by political reformers, educators, newspapermen, magazine writers, was against governmental corruption, a fight for integrity in public office. With few exceptions, social change by law was negligible. For more than thirty years there was no amendment to the Constitution, between the fif-

[1] Allan Nevins, "The Emergence of Modern America," *A History of American Life,* vol. VIII, p. 96.

teenth (equal rights for white and colored) finally proclaimed in 1870 and the sixteenth (income tax) proclaimed in 1913.

Rutherford Birchard Hayes, nineteenth President, was destined to be the leader of a long overdue moral reformation. He became the cleaner and the restorer of the nation's conscience. His four years in office have been well-nigh forgotten; perhaps because of an assumption that a one-term president must have failed to retain public endorsement. Hayes, however, was the one president to advocate one term of office and adhere to that view once in power. James K. Polk had also declined renomination, but not on the grounds of general principle.

Hayes was unpopular with most of the leaders in both parties, yet but for this courageous house-cleaning during four brief momentous years, the United States might well have become as corrupt as many an Old World dynasty, with as dire results. Not seeking re-election, he needed to give hostages to no man.

In 1877, the prestige of the United States government was at low ebb. After the defeat of Johnson's efforts the worst elements in public life had had full sway. Grant, sadly incompetent as a civil administrator, headed an eight-year administration which was notorious for customs thefts, stockjobbing, every type of favoritism and peculation. Grant desired to run again, but public gratitude for his military successes had become exhausted. There was a wave of public repentance and a seeking after personal salvation.

The postwar inflation, followed by depression, the cynicism in high places, homes broken through loss of loved-ones, the continued oppression of the South, made a mockery of national pride and shook the people's confidence in their one-time glorious democracy. The people turned to soul-searching and a quest for the meaning of God. In the 1870's came Dwight L. Moody and Ira D. Sankey in a series of religious revivals which swept through the country. R. A. Torrey, B. Fay Mills and a score of other evangelists were hardly less influential. The Protestant churches, which embraced the vast majority of the population, were crowded by converts and former backsliders who pledged themselves to lead a Christian life, every day of the week. There was no doubt of the sincerity of the movement. Worldly things had failed, military glory, government, material success. The church which was already the social center of the community offered a way of life. Colleges and schools were founded by the score.[2] The missionary movement went forward with revived impetus. And in the first office of the land the public desired a good man, good in the righteous, characterful sense.

Hayes was a good man. His life story had almost a copybook rightness. He was born in 1822 in Delaware County, Ohio, the posthumous son of a farmer. An uncle provided him with an education at Kenyon College and Harvard

[2] Sixty universities and colleges were founded in the United States in the decade 1870–1880.

Law School. He married a childhood sweetheart in 1852. In 1860 he campaigned for Lincoln. He enlisted in the war and was wounded at South Mountain. He was in the House of Representatives in 1864, then served two terms as governor of Ohio, 1867–1871, and was elected governor for the third time in 1875. In the governor's chair he was known for his liberalism, his reform tendencies and his freedom from party control.

Hayes was a solid citizen. As a young man he had joined the Sons of Temperance. His wife, Lucy Hayes, was a pillar of Temperance and of Methodism. She was also a graduate of Wesleyan Female Seminary and attended classes at Ohio Wesleyan University (she could not enroll, as it was then a men's college).[3] Mr. and Mrs. Hayes were educated, substantial family people. By the time of Hayes' nomination in 1876, they had several children.

Hayes was a churchman. Some sources refer to him as a Methodist, others as an Episcopalian, and still others say that he was not a communicant anywhere (though he quoted from the Prayer Book in his First Inaugural).

Since he was conspicuously a representative of the church people and their belief in moral reformation, the point is worth pursuing. Hayes did ultimately unite with the Methodist Church in Fremont, Ohio, after he had retired from the presidency. He apparently did not attach much significance to denominationalism. According to William Dean Howells,[4] who wrote a campaign biography, he was raised in the Presbyterian Church and was later a regular attendant with his wife at Methodist services.

During his days at Harvard Law School, he sampled various churches in Boston, writing home rather critical reports on the sermons.

In Fremont (named Lower Sandusky in the days of Hayes' young manhood), where he first practiced law, he oscillated between the Episcopal and Presbyterian followings, who were apparently having a rather lively time. In October, 1847 he wrote to his mother, "Our Episcopal church has shut up shop, so I have turned coat and come out Presbyterian. I presume you will not feel dissatisfied with the change." And then a month later he wrote to his sister, "Our Church (the Episcopal) goes off finely now, as the Presbyterian minister (who was a great knave) nearly broke down his congregation."[5]

Hayes went on to say that the vestry was made up of six of the finest men in town who were all "rowdies" before marriage, and quoted someone as saying that most of the officeholders in Washington were Episcopalians.

---

[3] Mary M. Ramsey, editor, *Ohio Wesleyan Magazine.*

[4] William D. Howells, *Life and Character of Rutherford B. Hayes* (Riverside Press, Cambridge, 1876).

[5] *Diary and Letters of Rutherford Birchard Hayes,* edited by Charles Richard Williams, and published by the Ohio State Archaeological and Historical Society, 1922–1926, five volumes. References by courtesy of Miss Mary M. Ramsey, Ohio Wesleyan University, Delaware, Ohio.

"It is a favorite church of party leaders who want to be genteel one day in seven." Hayes, however, continued to attend the Episcopal Church when he moved to Cincinnati until through Mrs. Hayes' influence he became a regular attendant in the Methodist fold. In modern times this breadth of religious thought, the facility of feeling at home in various churches, is not uncommon; but in the sectarianism of nineteenth century America it bespoke an unusual flexibility.

2

Rutherford B. Hayes was the logical candidate for the Republicans in 1876. The regulars had been tarred by past associations. Hayes had a clear record and the support of such notable reformers as Richard H. Dana, Carl Schurz and G. W. Curtis.

Samuel J. Tilden of New York, his Democratic opponent, was also a man of merit. Each party was sensible of the popular demand for personal virtue in the White House.

Tilden won the larger popular vote in the election, but its distribution was such that the vote in the electoral college was determined by which of two rival electoral groups should be seated from three of the Southern delegations. Here both Tilden and Hayes showed their stature. Tilden agreed to abide by the result, even though he knew that the Republicans could control the seating of electors. Hayes in turn obtained unchallenged endorsement of the electors in dispute by promising the Southern democrats that military surveillance from the North would be withdrawn.

This agreement, known as "the Bargain," was possible through a fortunate confluence of events which Hayes used to the full. The old-line Republicans, who might have preferred to see "Reconstruction" continued, were in the nutcracker. On the one hand a Tilden victory would throw them out of any federal patronage in the South or elsewhere. On the other side, they were forced to support Hayes who recognized the bargaining position of the South, and welcomed the chance to offer it (with the commitment of his colleagues) terms which he himself favored.

Hayes in office immediately assured the country that he would be nonpartisan. "The President of the United States," he said in his Inaugural, ". . . should strive to be always mindful of the fact that he serves his party best who serves the country best."

Then followed a shocking recommendation, shocking to the politicos: that there be an amendment to the Constitution limiting the presidential term to six years and forbidding re-election. This was unwelcome doctrine,[6] from a party standpoint. It struck at the very roots of self-perpetuation. But even more alarming in the Inaugural Address were these words:

"I call the attention of the public to the paramount necessity of reform in

[6] Jackson had advised it, but not to the extent of declining a second term.

our civil service—a reform not merely as to certain abuses and practices of so-called official patronage which have come to have the sanction of usage in the several Departments of our Government, but a change in the system of appointment itself; a reform that shall be thorough, radical and complete."

Hayes went to work with vigor. He divorced himself from the men who had surrounded Grant. His nominations for the Cabinet were chiefly men who had distinguished themselves in public service, without regard to party regularity. Secretary of State Evarts and Secretary of the Interior Schurz were instructed to draft rules governing appointments. Applicants seeking clerical jobs could no longer rely on political preferment, but were required to apply directly to the head of a department who would be held responsible for his selections.

The Customs' office patronage was exposed. In an Executive Order of May 26, 1877, Hayes directed that the collection of the revenues should be "on a strictly business basis." A striking commentary on the existing situation! He demanded that party leaders should have no more influence in appointments "than other equally respectable citizens," and declared that government employees should not be assessed for party funds, compelled to work in party affairs, or be deprived of expressing their views on public questions "either orally or through the press."

The same spirit of reform was applied to all branches of the government, notably to the Indian Bureau which had been a scandalous pie for politicians and alert rascals. Hayes did not claim credit for the reforms. He modestly and wisely referred to the pledges of improved civil service contained in the platforms of each major party. He acted avowedly upon the recommendation of specific investigating commissions. Unquestionably he was responding to a clear mandate from the people.

It would be naive, of course, to assume that Hayes forever put an end to patronage, favoritism, and recurrences of graft, that party leaders henceforth had no more influence than "equally respectable citizens." Aided by the public wrath, he accomplished a notable housecleaning for the time being, and he restored the integrity of the White House to a level from which it has seldom receded. Whatever the subsequent lapses from honesty and efficiency, they no longer had "the sanction of usage."

Scandalous conditions continued to recur from time to time in state and city administrations; but the federal government became an ideal of proper behavior. The public does not tolerate moral failures in the federal service with complacency, and serious corruption in the federal administration since Hayes' time has been rare. For setting this tone, for frankly facing the fact of corruption in government, for cleaning it up, for enunciating principles of conduct, the good Hayes deserves his special place in the roster of the presidents. His influence for clean government has endured.

3

In the realm of public finance, the trend of liberal thought has oscillated with the times. It is unsafe to pigeonhole a past president as liberal or conservative according to his fiscal measures. Jefferson and Coolidge were budget-balancers. A real dose of the original Jackson would have startled many modern New Dealers. In fact, Hayes like Jackson was opposed to sizable expenditures for public improvements, and he was a "hard money" man. In these respects, Hayes, like Jackson, collided with the perennial wishful-thinkers who believe that prosperity may be poured out inexhaustibly from the public till. Why not print enough money for everyone? Hayes fought a hard persistent battle against that doctrine.

During Hayes's regime, the Greenback-Labor Party was at its peak and elected fourteen members to Congress. Its main demand was for the continued issuance of irredeemable paper money. During the Civil War the government had issued bills of credit printed in green on one side of the paper. These became known as "greenbacks" and were in circulation as currency, though they were essentially undated notes of the government, worth only as much as the market estimate of the government's good faith. By 1865, greenbacks had sunk to less than half their par value in terms of gold. The fiat money advocates believed that relief for the financial burdens caused by the Civil War lay in currency inflation. Pay off the creditors in depreciated dollars, in which many of the debts had been contracted.

Hayes held to the opposite course, that the only sound bottom for public and national credit was a record of meeting all obligations at their face value. In his Inaugural he urged "an early resumption of specie payments," namely, the redemption of outstanding greenbacks in gold coin. A law, passed during Grant's administration with his approval, already provided for the resumption effective January 1, 1879. Mints were working overtime in preparation for the event. The fiat money feeling was so strong in both parties, however, that a bill for repeal passed the House, though failing in the Senate. The immediate prospect of redemption in gold brought the "greenbacks" close to par by 1878.

The inflationists had yet another measure to their purpose, namely the plea for a bimetallic currency. This proposal had a strong appeal. Silver was hard money. Silver was one of America's great resources. Plentiful mining of silver brought prosperity to certain areas of the country. Bimetallism had the support of some leading British financial authorities. The idea was destined to persist until 1896, and in 1878 took the form of the Bland-Allison Act, which was passed over Hayes's veto. The Act provided for the coinage of silver at a stated volume per month, and at an artificially pegged value per dollar. It fell short of the "unlimited free coinage of silver" goal of the extremists, but made a steady drain on the nation's gold reserves. The law stayed in effect until 1890, when it was replaced by the Sherman silver-purchase law; which was repealed in 1893.

The attempt to give the silver dollar a fixed value in excess of its actual value, and to make it legal payment for debts which had been contracted for at full dollar value was, in Hayes's opinion, a fraud.

"The standard of value should not be changed without the consent of both parties to the contract," Hayes said in his veto message of February 28, 1878. "National promises should be kept with unflinching fidelity. There is no power to compel a nation to pay its just debts. Its credit depends upon its honor . . . The obligation of the public faith transcends all questions of profit or public advantage. Its unquestionable maintenance is the dictate as well of the highest expediency as of the most necessary duty . . . A currency worth less than it purports to be worth will in the end defraud not only creditors, but all who are engaged in legitimate business, and none more surely than those who are dependent on their daily labor for bread."

Earlier in the Hayes administration proposals had been made to pay off United States bonds in fiat money. Hayes, here as elsewhere, opposed any effort to destroy the public credit. The result of his continuous stand for honesty in all things was to strengthen the financial stability of the government. In January, 1879, the Treasury was able to sell government bonds in America and Europe to the amount of $140,000,000. It could be argued, however, that at this stage inflation was needed, and the Hayes policy may have been unwittingly unjust to the debtor classes.

4

The restoration of the South, however, as has been suggested at the beginning of this chapter, was Hayes's monumental achievement. Conceivably no one else could have accomplished so much in so short a time. Had Tilden, the Democrat, been declared elected, and had he attempted to free the South from military rule, the issue would have been regarded as a party measure and might have been kept alive for years. But Hayes, leader of the oppressor Republicans, made the initial moves. The Northern Democrats, dependent for future majorities on Southern support, could not object. Though Hayes's removal of carpet-bag government at the outset was a political deal, he adhered to his principles long after there could be any personal consideration.

The status of the South under Reconstruction nullified the principles of the Gettysburg address. There was no government by the people as long as a large section of the country remained under military rule. The cleavage between North and South was now more acute than that caused by slavery before the Civil War. Lincoln and Johnson had foreseen the evils that would flow from impoverishment of the South and from attempted reformation by force. Hayes, himself a veteran of the war, and a Northerner, held no bitterness. He had seen the evils grow and spread. In words reminiscent of Johnson, but with calmer temperament and in quieter times, he sought to restore the Republic. He had declared in his Inaugural:

Let me assure my countrymen of the Southern States that it is my earnest desire to regard and promote their truest interests—the interests of the white and of the colored people both and equally—and to put forth my best efforts in behalf of a civil policy which will forever wipe out in our political affairs the color line and the distinction between North and South, to the end that we may have not merely a united North or a united South, but a united country.

Shades of Thaddeus Stevens and Charles Sumner! These were not mere words. Hayes ordered the removal of federal troops from South Carolina on April 3, 1877, and on April 20 from Louisiana. The old die-hards were in a frenzy. Ben Wade, William Lloyd Garrison, James G. Blaine, Wendell Phillips, Ben Butler poured out their oratory against Hayes. Only a few notables, such as Schurz, stayed by him; but Hayes did not need to be concerned. He asked no favors for the future.

Moreover, with political despotism removed, the South staged an extraordinary educational and economic revival. Ideals, capital, energies, which had lain dormant under impractical and intolerable restrictions sprang into life. The fields were rich with harvest. The nation was one again.

Yet the situation was far from being idyllic. The Negro problem remained unsolved. It had been augmented by the attempts at enforced reformation. Fear had been instilled in the Southern whites to the extent that now the accent on the future of the colored race was first on self-preservation for the whites. The resentment against the Northern carpetbaggers was even more acute. The word "damyankee" was added to the Elizabethan diction of the Southerners. Even the statistical improvement in the South was relative, a change from destitution to better days. The war had stripped the Confederacy of basic resources, dollars, horses, clothing, homes, the paraphernalia of existence, so that full recovery was many years hence. All this was true, the halting imperfections of re-union; yet Hayes must be credited with laying the foundations for a spiritually united country.

The significance of Hayes as a moral reformer can hardly be overemphasized. The American dream of the free life has included the implication of the good life, freedom for goodness, for self-realization in a noble worthy sense.

No other nation has the motto on its coin "In God We Trust." The test of high personal character has been required for the presidential office; and it was the special task of Hayes to affirm that honesty of purpose and conduct is the first requisite in government.

Big country, big country, everything was getting big.

Biggest rise in population; biggest cities in the world; New York bigger than London, well almost.

Biggest immigration anywhere; most railroad miles; most kerosene lamps; most illuminating gas. Largest wheat crops, corn, hogs, packing houses.

Biggest fortunes ever. Chicago department store daughter marries a duke. Carnegie worth $300,000,000, at least. Boston bulges with copper and wool money. Money in trusts and combines. Railroad princes build personal residences bigger than their terminals.

Riches sprouting from the ground, or there for the digging. Oil, silver, lead, iron, coal unequaled elsewhere. New states come into the Union, making forty-five. The South stays poor mostly. The peddlers, ferrymen, coalbreakers, benchmen, who don't catch the boat may fare meagerly. For the farmer in the North and West, a secure life is assured with almost no risk. Fertile lands are available, millions of new urban mouths must be fed. But, city or rural, everyone has a ticket in the national sweepstakes.

The panic of 1893. Hold everything! There's been much discontent. The Greenback Party, the Populists, Knights of Labor, Pullman Car strike, railway strike. LaFollette, Debs, disturbing notes. Bryan almost won.

The Klondike, biggest gold-find ever. Spanish-American War. Spain, supposed major power, capitulates.

Stand back, please. No criticism, please: The United States of America— the biggest show on earth!

9
Dawn of the Modern World

*Men are qualified for civil liberty in exact proportion
to their disposition to put moral chains upon their own
appetites.*

EDMUND BURKE

I

In the era following the retirement of Hayes to the close of the century,
America came of age.

The life of most of her people had remained rural. Her contests had been
political and racial, for the most part. The presidency had not been im-
pelled to concern itself extensively either with international affairs or with
modern industrialism.

The United States, however, was rapidly becoming a modern state. As such,
it was due to re-examine its domestic police policies over industry and to
become increasingly committed to new phases in its foreign relationships.
Grover Cleveland in 1895 chose to re-interpret the Monroe Doctrine in a
manner destined to lead to the end of American isolationism.

Monroe, encouraged by John Quincy Adams, Jefferson, Madison, and
Calhoun, had declared that any extension of the European system in the
Western Hemisphere would be regarded as an "unfriendly disposition" to
the United States.

On various subsequent occasions, the Doctrine had been invoked by Tyler,
Polk, Buchanan, and Grant. The United States had stopped short of proclaiming the principle as part of international law, or of threatening to establish it by force.

In Cleveland's second term, however, Venezuela had become involved in
a dispute with Great Britain over the boundary between Venezuela and
British Guiana. She was unable to get attention for her claims, and appealed
to the United States. Cleveland entered into diplomatic negotiations with
Great Britain which were unavailing, and finally appointed an American
arbitration commission.

This decision to invoke arbitration in a controversy in which no territorial claims of the United States were involved was communicated to the
American and British publics by Cleveland's message to Congress on December 2, 1895, and created such a stir that the British ministry was shaken
out of its previous attitude of studied indifference. The ministry found that
Parliament was sympathetic to arbitration, but in its reply objected to Cleveland's implication that the Monroe principle was an accepted part of international law.

Cleveland responded in a special message to Congress of December 17, in language bold and definite. He assumed that this was not a fact-finding issue *per se,* but an attempt by Britain to enlarge her frontier and hence her territory in the Western Hemisphere. He affirmed that the Doctrine was "essential to the integrity of our free institutions and the tranquil maintenance of our distinctive form of government. It was intended to apply to every stage of our national life and cannot become obsolete while our Republic endures." In effect, the Western Hemisphere was the United States' sphere of influence, and any issue therein, related to European intrusion was her concern.

Cleveland reiterated his demand for arbitration; but threatened that the United States could not submit "supinely" to a continuance of the present situation. The war clouds seemed close at hand, but Britain agreed to a Joint Commission and the affair was settled peaceably.

Theodore Roosevelt amplified the Doctrine in expounding the policy of the United States, following the dispute with Colombia over the Panama Canal Zone. The Latin American republics had regarded the assumed protectorate of the United States with mixed feelings. The fact that the Republic of Panama had been encouraged by American interests to revolt against Columbia was regarded in many quarters as territorial aggression threatening the future independence of the Latin nations.

Roosevelt responded to this in various official papers. In his annual message of December 5, 1905, he pledged that the United States would in no way use the Doctrine for aggrandizement or territorial aggression. He held that it was a source of strength which any Western Hemisphere nation might call upon, that all were guarantors of the principle and were meeting "on a basis of entire equality."

If the Roosevelt position lacked something in realism, it nevertheless had significance as a statement of principle. In his first annual message he had said "it is simply a step . . . toward assuring the universal peace of the world by securing the possibility of a permanent peace on this hemisphere." Combined with the theory of equality among nations, the concept forecasted the various league ideas which were to develop.

Roosevelt by temperament and conviction, however, was an ardent nationalist. He advocated arbitration and world peace conferences, as shall be seen; but with reservations on points involving "national honor." It remained for President Taft to take the position that all issues might be subject to arbitration. The admission of that point was a prerequisite to the idea of a Union of Nations under whatever name.

The presidency in the closing years of the nineteenth century, as at most times, stood in a moderate position. The White House view did not reflect the extremists, while mass opinion tended to be uninformed and sluggish. Probably few citizens comprehended the steps by which the presidency was leading the country into long-range international commitments. Once the

Monroe Doctrine had become an official active principle, however, the country could not retreat from its participation in the world scene. Meanwhile it was far more absorbed in its domestic struggles.

2

Theodore Roosevelt, twenty-sixth president of the United States, was the first severe shock to the business circles of the modern world. In America the conduct of finance and business, with few exceptions, had been uncontrolled.

There had been Populists and Greenbackers. The brilliant black-haired William Jennings Bryan, that Western troubadour, had scared the wits out of the settled classes in 1896. All these efforts, however, had been defeated. No elected president had hitherto challenged the powers of big business, yet Theodore Roosevelt did so from the beginning.

Andrew Jackson, to be sure, had fought the financiers controlling the United States Bank, but large widespread corporate enterprise had not emerged in Jackson's era. The trust, namely a company or group of companies controlling a sizable proportion of the output in an industry, had developed since the Civil War. It was made possible by modern machinery requiring large capital investment, by railroad transportation opening up interstate markets, and by the economies of volume production which gave the trust a socially useful stature, whatever its social liabilities might be.

The trust initially won more praise than criticism from the public. It was big; America was big, getting ever bigger, and proud of it. Here were the greatest freedom, the greatest resources, the greatest opportunities, the greatest fortunes. America, like most young countries, was a boasting country, and could point to its unequaled development under a system which knew virtually no limits to individual activity.

Between Hayes's retirement in 1880 and the presidency of Roosevelt beginning in 1901, American industry had developed as a robust phenomenon on a national scale. Hitherto each area had been served by its own group of factories and artisans. Now shoe machinery was displacing the hand cobblers, glass-blowing machinery took the place of skilled artisans. Standard Oil encompassed a host of local refineries. United States Steel, established in 1901, included eight large concerns, each of which was a combination of its predecessors. A new type of industrial power thus had arisen, destined to be the chief issue in the republic for generations to come. Should industrial concentrations be broken into small units? Taken over by the government? Controlled? Or wholly let alone? Theodore Roosevelt was keenly aware of the problems posed.

Industrial power was not separate from financial power, obviously the two were closely intertwined. But financial influence hitherto had been visualized as concerned with credits and securities. Finance had even appeared as hostile to industry in times of contracting credits. Industry was in the foreground: It visibly affected employment, prices, the rise or fall of communities. It was more tangible than finance, in many aspects beneficial, and generally hailed as an evidence of a growing and independent America. As industry grew, its alliance with finance became indispensable.

The federal government since the Civil War had, as a rule, favored industry. The Republicans in particular advocated protective tariffs to bolster American manufacture and to maintain higher American wage scales against foreign competition. It was to be expected that a Republican president would favor the industrial system as it stood without interference. But Theodore Roosevelt had read some handwriting on the wall.

The railroads were the first corporations in the country to grow to enormous size. They had, moreover, a clear and tangible effect on the whole life of the people. The location of their routes controlled trade. By their rate-making powers they could foster or wither industries and industrial centers. Changes in rates, for example, could and did move the furniture-making center of the North from Indianapolis to Grand Rapids. The railroads in many instances were aided by public land grants and other public favors. Not surprisingly, they were the first objects of public control.

Hayes had been succeeded by Garfield, then by Arthur, Cleveland, Harrison, Cleveland again, and McKinley. All through the period there had been a growing demand for government regulation railroad practices, with a sidelong glance toward the regulation of major corporations. The Interstate Commerce Commission was established in 1887 with limited controls over railroad operations and rates, and the Sherman Anti-Trust Law was passed in 1890. In neither case did the then current president take conspicuous leadership in the reform. Benjamin Harrison in his First Annual Message stated that in the year ending June 30, 1888, over two thousand railroad employees were killed in service and more than twenty thousand injured, and called upon Congress to require improvements in the construction of cars and in safety appliances; but he did not address his attention to the fundamental economics of rail transportation.

Cleveland skated close to the subject in his Inaugural Address of March 4, 1893, when he referred to the "immense aggregation of kindred enterprises and combination of business interests." He observed that "to the extent that they can be reached and restrained by Federal power, the General Government should relieve our citizens from their interference and exactions"; yet Cleveland was no zealous reformer.

The right of the federal government to regulate business, while virtually unexercised in fact, was not new in principle. While the Constitution was being framed, James Madison wrote in issue No. 10 of *The Federalist*, "A landed interest, a manufacturing interest, a mercantile interest, a moneyed interest, with many lesser interests, grow up of necessity in civilized nations and divide them into different classes, actuated by different sentiments and views. The regulation of these various and interfering interests forms the principal task of modern legislation, and involves the spirit of party and faction in the necessary and ordinary operations of the government."

Since the interests referred to by Madison, landed, manufacturing, etc., had been largely local in scope during the first hundred years of the republic, they had not provoked attempts at federal control; hence the earlier stages of public regulation are to be found in state laws. By the 1890's, however, there were widespread popular clamors for economic reform. Robert M. LaFollette was fighting a strenuous battle against the monopolists in the Northwest, and his fiery career in Congress had already made him a national figure. Bryan had devoted his chief attention to the cause of free silver, but his 1896 platform also had said that "the absorption of wealth by the few, the consolidation of our leading railroad systems, and the formation of trusts and pools require a stricter control by the Federal government of those arteries of commerce."

Theodore Roosevelt was one of the most conspicuous cases of a political accident, coming to the leadership of the people via the wheel of fortune. The channeling of liberalism through that individual mind presumably accelerated the theories of government controls by some years, for the public had twice rejected Bryanism, in 1896 and in 1900. The facts underlying his rise exemplify the unpredictable possibilities in a democratic state.

3

Roosevelt was born October 27, 1858. He was graduated from Harvard in 1880 and undertook to study law. The law soon bored him. He then engaged in the writing of history, in ranching in the Dakota territory and in New York politics. As a native son of New York City, coming from a well-to-do and respected family, and not seeking any financial gain from politics, Roosevelt was a useful asset to the Republican organization. At the age of twenty-six he was a delegate-at-large to the national convention. In 1889 he was appointed a Civil Service Commissioner under Harrison, and for six years Roosevelt and his wife studied the politics of official Washington.

In 1895 he became police commissioner of New York, and in 1897 assistant secretary of the navy. From the latter post he resigned to organize a volunteer cavalry regiment in the Spanish-American war.

The performance of Roosevelt and his Rough Riders in that successful conflict made Theodore Roosevelt a national hero. He became popularly known as "Teddy" and "T.R."

The Spanish affair has been dwarfed by the World Wars of later times, but in 1898 and '99 it seemed a glorious enterprise. The United States for the first time since 1812 had challenged a supposedly major power, and on this occasion had won an extraordinarily easy victory. The United States, also, in taking possession of the Philippine Islands had become for the first time an imperial nation. There were many who viewed the new era with misgivings, but they were in the minority.

"T.R." was perhaps the most conspicuous figure of the new day, and at the close of the war he was elected governor of New York. He won by only a modest majority, however, as the machine of each party regarded him with a dubious eye.

Upon the renomination of President McKinley in 1900, Roosevelt was put on the ticket as the running mate. This was against his wishes. Four years in the vice-presidency might well condemn him to obscurity, which was just what the politicians had in mind; but the assassination of McKinley at Buffalo made Roosevelt president, and he took the oath of office on September 14, 1901.

Like many liberal leaders Roosevelt was something of an enigma, inconsistent, impatient of the checks and balances of the Constitution, egotistic, yet wise enough not to yield to the temptations of dictatorship.

"T.R." was a showman, and the trappings of his act have become so dated as to obscure him, somewhat as the stately diction, the powdered wig, and colonial garb alienate us from George Washington.

Roosevelt had been handicapped in childhood by asthma and defective eyesight. He had determined to overcome or to compensate for these weaknesses. He taught himself to ride, shoot and box. He became by choice an athlete and an outdoors man, consciously vigorous and aggressive. He championed "the strenuous life."

He spoke with a high clear bark. His blue eyes were alert behind the gleaming eye-glasses, and his wide smile bared his strong white teeth. He was fond of such shouted expressions as "Bully!" and "Dee-lighted." An observer has said of him, "he hissed his sibilants and boomed out his vowels. When, after the presidency, he would come to the Scribner offices the glass of the partitions vibrated with his voice; his words filled every corner." [1] This was a new tone for the White House.

One of Roosevelt's noted phrases, however, was "speak softly and carry a big stick." In his initial message to Congress December 3, 1901, he spoke of industry in deceptively mollifying terms:

The growth of cities has gone on beyond comparison faster than the growth of the country, and the upbuilding of the great industrial centers has meant a startling increase, not merely in the aggregate of wealth, but in the number of very large individual, and especially of very large corporate, fortunes. . . .

The process has aroused much antagonism, a great part of which is wholly without warrant. It is not true that as the rich have grown richer the poor have grown poorer . . . There have been abuses connected with the accumulation of wealth; yet it remains true that a fortune accumulated by the person specially

---

[1] Roger Burlingame, *Of Making Many Books.*

benefited only on condition of conferring immense incidental benefits upon others.

The slightest study of business conditions will satisfy anyone capable of forming a judgment that the personal equation is the most important factor in a business operation; that the business ability of the man at the head of any business concern, big or little, is usually the factor which fixes the gulf between striking success and hopeless failure.

He denounced the agitator: "Many of those who have made it their vocation to denounce the great industrial combinations which are popularly, although with technical inaccuracy, known as 'trusts,' appeal especially to hatred and fear."

Nevertheless, he went on to say: "There is a widespread conviction in the minds of the American people that the great corporations known as trusts are in certain of their features and tendencies hurtful to the general welfare . . . It is based upon sincere conviction that combination and concentration should be, not prohibited, but supervised and within reasonable limits controlled; and in my judgment this conviction is right."

The big stick was now apparent. In the name of "a square deal" for the public he began on a career of government control and "trust busting" which was a new departure in the role of the presidency; and he established firmly in popular opinion the idea of the public accountability of individual enterprises.

Repeatedly in messages and speeches the President returned to the same theme song—large business enterprises were good for the country, great fortunes could be generally beneficent, but measures of appraisal and control were necessary. He denounced "malefactors of great wealth," but aimed to distinguish between "good trusts" and "bad trusts." To accomplish his purpose he succeeded in the creation of a new Cabinet Department, namely that of Commerce and Labor. Publicity he regarded as the initial remedy, affirming that the government "should have the right to inspect and examine the workings of the great corporations engaged in inter-state business" and also should "assume power of supervision and regulation over all corporations doing an interstate business."

The Department of Commerce and Labor was designed to accomplish that object. In it the Bureau of Corporations was supposed to gather data and publicize the workings of corporations, presumably determining which were or were not in the public interest.[2]

In 1903 Roosevelt obtained a strengthening of the Sherman Antitrust Law in terms which also made the Interstate Commerce Act more effective. The force of these measures was affirmed by the decision of the U. S. Supreme Court, March 14, 1904, in the Northern Securities Case which prevented the combination of the Great Northern and the Northern Pacific Railroads. On

[2] The Bureau of Corporations was succeeded by the Federal Trade Commission.

July 1, 1905, five corporations and seventeen individuals in the meat-packing industry were indicted for violation of the Sherman Antitrust Law, later pleaded guilty, and were fined.

The radicals complained that fines were an inadequate deterrent. The breaking-up of certain trusts did not wholly do away with friendly under-standings which continued the effects of monopoly; but, compared with an atmosphere of earlier times which had been free from official criticism or re-straint of business, the change was vast. The fact that two such huge corpora-tions as the Great Northern and Northern Pacific could be stopped against their will from carrying out a proposed commercial agreement was a land-mark in social policy.

"T.R." of course was denounced as a traitor to his class. The charge was inaccurate. He was far from being a democratic liberal in the equalitarian sense. He even had the effrontery to characterize critics of corporations, other than himself, as "muckrakers." His personal life at the White House was elegant compared to his predecessors. The White House coachmen in his regime wore livery and cockades, reminiscent of the formal days of the Federalists.

"T.R.'s" interests were catholic. He entertained prize fighters, royalty, editors, writers, historians, economists, with a zealous enthusiasm not evi-dent in the White House since the days of Jackson or equaled subsequently until the days of the second Roosevelt; but he did not seek the society of commoners for commonalty's sake. He was too extreme an individualist to have authentically the common touch.

4

As in the case of Jefferson and the Louisiana Purchase, one of the most notable and lasting of "T.R.'s" contributions to the nation was the building of the Panama Canal. Like Jefferson he stretched his powers uncomfort-ably far in order to achieve a quick result.

The idea of a canal connecting the Atlantic and Pacific oceans had been projected for many years. Since 1846 the United States had officially claimed that its interest required the right to maintain and to police traffic across the Isthmus of Panama. The government had entered into a treaty to that effect with New Granada, the name of the country which then occupied the isthmus. The United States had repeatedly reaffirmed its position with successive governments in that area and from time to time had landed troops to maintain order.

The first canal route had been surveyed by H. de la Soma in 1527, who ex-plored the area for Charles V of Spain. Spanish and English interests had considered the project and a French company actually undertook the work in 1881, but went bankrupt. For some years the United States had been negotiating with Great Britain on the subject and Roosevelt's secretary of state had concluded the Hay-Herran treaty which gave the United States a free hand. Congress then passed a bill which enabled the president to make a treaty with Colombia, or if that failed to undertake a canal through Nicaragua. Colombia was at that time the sovereign state of the Panama territory.

The Colombian delegates signed an agreement which gave their country $25,000,000 in cash and other favorable terms. To the surprise of Roosevelt and the United States, the Colombian Congress rejected the treaty. Roosevelt and many others in the United States and Latin America suspected that the Colombian government, aiming to improve its bargain, made no serious effort to obtain ratification.

Either a long indeterminate period of argument with Colombia, or a transfer to the Nicaraguan route, seemed indicated. Another possibility was that the citizens of Panama, who were frequently in revolution, might revolt again, throw off the rule of Colombia and make a treaty with the United States. This potentiality was enhanced by the fact that the Colombian soldiers on the isthmus had not received any pay from their government for some months.

Roosevelt was infuriated at what he regarded as the duplicity of the Colombian negotiators, and at seeing a great accomplishment apparently snatched from his grasp. Officially, he was powerless to move to set up a revolutionary government. The new Panama Canal Company, however, which was the corporate agent responsible for building the canal, was able to foment the idea, and Roosevelt dispatched Navy ships to the isthmus ostensibly to preserve order. Panama seceded November 31, 1903, without a shot being fired. The United States promptly recognized the new government, and Roosevelt officially advised Colombia of the fact.

A storm of comment ensued. By what right did the President treat with Panama even if the revolution were *bona fide*? In his Third Annual Message to Congress which followed shortly, on December 7, 1903 the President defended his action in these words:

When the Congress directed that we should take the Panama route under treaty with Colombia, the essence of the condition, of course, referred not to the Government which controlled that route, but to the route itself; to the territory across which the route lay, not to the name which for the moment the territory bore on the map. The purpose of the law was to authorize the President to make a treaty with the power in actual control of the Isthmus of Panama. This purpose has been fulfilled.

The logic may seem a little specious; yet, as a new government was in control on the Isthmus, the canal could now go forward. Congress, if it denied Roosevelt's interpretation of its language, would be faced with repudiating the agreement with Panama, possibly returning Panama to the role of Colombia and with opening negotiations with Nicaragua. The building of the canal was permitted to continue.

Politicians, some historians, and certain of the opposition press have aimed to present this event as a robbery of Colombia by "T.R.," and as undertaken under secret circumstances of which the Congress had no knowledge. The latter point certainly cannot be supported.

The records in the case were immediately demanded by Congress, were received, and were accompanied by a special message of the President giving complete details. Elaborate research by the opposition, at the time and subsequently, has produced nothing to impugn the truth of the President's report. In Harding's administration the Senate ratified a treaty with Colombia which had been initiated by Wilson, whereby $25,000,000 indemnity was paid Colombia, though without the apology which Wilson had favored. The act may have been politically advisable as a matter of relations with Latin America; but the history of the canal area and its record of revolutions give plausible support to the President's position; yet "I took the Canal zone and let Congress debate," Roosevelt is quoted as saying in a *New York Times* report, March 24, 1911. Almost the identical words were used in the report of the address as carried in the University of California *Chronicle*. Apparently Roosevelt wanted to have it both ways: bold and daring, yet legal and proper.

It was difficult at times to determine what were Roosevelt's real views. The President had a politically convenient code of ethics. He did not hesitate to speak on any and all subjects, and if he made a blunder he was quick to call the person quoting him a liar. Soon many notables were members of his "Ananias Club." He chose to regard his statements as trial balloons, and even took the position that nothing said by him should be regarded as an accurate quotation unless subsequently authorized by him.

He inevitably made many mistakes of which possibly the most serious was being constantly misled by Japan, encouraging her invasion of Korea and Manchuria and fostering her ambitions to become a major power in the Russo-Japanese War.

5

Roosevelt's qualified views on internationalism have already been noted, yet he looked toward The Hague as the hope for an enduring world peace. A meeting of delegates from all major nations, to encourage arbitration as a substitute for war had been called at The Hague in the Netherlands, in 1899 by the Tsar of Russia. This occasion, known as the First Hague Conference, was the first effort in modern times to establish a unity among nations.

This initial meeting did establish a so-called "Permanent Court of Arbitration." The initial court and its successors became familiarly known as The

Hague Tribunal. The Hague Tribunal, in its time, was the outstanding symbol of international peace and co-operation. The First Conference went only as far as to name a panel of possible arbitrators from which contending states might select judges for the purposes of arbitration if they so chose. Literally, the panel was neither a court nor permanent, but it was a practical beginning since twenty-one arbitrations were held under it.

Roosevelt used his influence repeatedly to strengthen the Tribunal. In 1904, he addressed a circular note to the powers reminding them that a Second Conference had been agreed to on the first occasion. As a result, the Second Hague Conference was held in 1907 where the American delegation sought for the establishment of a World Court, with paid judges who would devote their entire time to the rendering of decisions in international law. They were to be paid by an international fund and sit in regularly scheduled terms. Though the proposal was not adopted, the influence of The Hague Tribunal was enhanced by the continuing discussions, and Roosevelt gave it still further prestige by persuading a number of the powers who had certain grievances against Venezuela to accept the judgment of a court chosen from The Hague panel.

The successful outcome of the Venezuela case, which was accepted by all parties thereto, accelerated arbitration treaties between states and gave further impetus to the idea of unity among nations.

6

One of "T.R.'s" most lasting accomplishments which has become less emphasized with the passage of time was the enlargement of the public forestry, park, and other preserves. Under his administration millions of square miles were added to the public lands, an inestimable benefit to the future. He established a Public Lands Commission in 1903, appointed civilian experts, turned the spotlight on the theme of natural resources, and named a Conservation Commission.

Theodore Roosevelt's years following his presidency need not concern us here where his impress on the office is the matter in hand. More than most presidents he had captured the popular imagination and had made the presidency an instrument of positive policy. To the extent that a liberal tradition implies change, "T.R." was a shining example. Whatever he touched changed. The Monroe Doctrine, peace organizations, controls over industry, forest preserves, were changed and enlarged. While there were passive presidents among his successors, his example established a new modern pattern, giving impetus to continued reform.

Wilson was the first president to head a nation of forty-eight states. Oklahoma had come in in 1907. New Mexico and Arizona in 1912. All of the far western area had been included in the Union by 1896.

There was a feeling of completeness and maturity. Not quite the "era of good feeling" of Monroe's time, yet a sense of confident progress untinged by desperate necessity, or harsh conflict.

Socialists were politely received. One of them was a vice-president of the New York Life Insurance Company. Another became mayor of Berkeley, California. A third, inheritor of copper wealth, married a Jewish settlement worker.

The social settlement movement flourished. Hull House in Chicago, South End House, Denison House, et al in Boston; Greenwich House, the University Settlement, Cristadora House, Hudson Guild, the Henry Street Settlement, the Neighborhood House, in New York; all were working to give opportunity to the lowest economic levels, in recreation, job training, slum clearance, health.

Columbia had its Beard, Kirchwey, Woodberry, Seligman, J. H. Robinson; Harvard its William James, Muensterberg, Santayana; Wisconsin its Ely, Commons (later at Columbia), and E. A. Ross; no omissions are intentional. Many universities and colleges testified to a new intellectual ferment.

In literature, Dreiser, Frank Norris, Kathleen Norris, Upton Sinclair, Willa Cather, Edith Wharton and Ellen Glasgow, to name but a few, developed the novel as a reflection of contemporary realistic life. A new generation of journalists, Ida Tarbell, Ray Stannard Baker, Charles Edward Russell, David Graham Phillips, cried havoc.

Wilson was by no means the sole political apostle of enlightenment, but he was the one who was elected to the chief office; and his role seemed relatively easy. No more war. The wicked and greedy were being exposed, and the remedies were recognized and ready to be applied. The mood was almost millennial, as if there were at hand what Don Marquis called "the almost perfect State."

10

The New Freedom

Freedom today is something more than being let alone.
WOODROW WILSON, *The New Freedom*

I

The rise of Woodrow Wilson and the pattern of his liberalism are significant examples of the interaction of events and personality in their influence on the presidency.

Wilson, in his own eyes and in those of his times, was an ardent liberal, but he was poles apart from the Socialists, and from statism, and he had little of the vocal emotionalism of Theodore Roosevelt.

He was the spiritual heir of citizen Thomas Jefferson as a philosopher of the rights of man; yet he was less flexible than Jefferson, and far more the instinctive administrator.

Born of Scotch Irish stock on December 28, 1856, in Staunton, Virginia, the son of a Presbyterian minister, Wilson had in him more of the stubborn Scot than of the ease of the Old Dominion.

He early had ambitions for political life and to this end studied for the law at the University of Virginia. Failing to obtain sufficient clients or to find his way into politics, he turned to teaching, in which he was an extraordinary success.

By the age of thirty-four he had become president of Princeton University and had written a number of historical works primarily on constitutional government. The schooolmaster role was natural to him, as by temperament he was scholarly and didactic, and he was the only full-time university professor to occupy the White House. Lantern-jawed, confident of his superior intellectual powers, and having a gift for what he called "public utterance," he was accustomed to bend others to his will. His determination was increased by a conscience at peace with itself, and the conviction that what he advocated was for the good of those affected.

That Wilson was one of the greatest men in American history is unquestionable, even though his inflexibility proved to be his personal tragedy and robbed him of a still larger place in history.

His accession to the presidency, as in the case of Jefferson, seems the work of Providence, as each man arrived in office by unexpected routes.

At Princeton Wilson had attempted to democratize the undergraduate life by limiting the social groups and advocating the quadrangle system of dormitories in which the students were compelled to reside. The uproar which this caused brought him to the attention of New Jersey politicians at a time when the Democrats needed a well-known and respectable candidate for the governorship. Wilson was elected, and forthwith embarked upon a number of reforms restraining the privileges of corporations. That in turn made him available as a possible nominee as the Democratic candidate for the presidency.

Champ Clark of Missouri came to the convention with the greatest number of pledged votes; but William Jennings Bryan, still the most influential member of the party, insisted on a candidate who would specifically reject the support of the Tammany Hall Democratic organization in New York. Wilson's advisers urged him not to take that risk; but in this instance his uncompromising temperament was justified and Wilson unequivocally declined the Tammany endorsement. Bryan swung his support to the Jersey governor and he was nominated.

That was the next to final step in a chain of circumstances which brought Woodrow Wilson to the White House. The other vital factor was the split in the Republican ranks. Theodore Roosevelt had become embittered against his successor Taft. Taft, although easy-going and conservative by temperament, had in fact continued most of the Roosevelt policies. Taft had had a liberal record as a judge. He had championed international arbitration, and the League to Enforce Peace. He had effectuated a treaty with Canada, which virtually provided for free trade between the two countries. The Parcels Post Act and the Postal Savings Bank Act were passed with his support; but temperamentally he was not attuned to the liberal element, and still less did he like being regarded as Roosevelt's rubber stamp. "T.R." had spent some time hunting in Africa following his retirement, and upon his return he reached an open break with his successor. At the Republican convention, both Taft and Roosevelt were candidates. When the latter was defeated he formed the Progressive Party.

Had a World War not followed the campaign of 1912 within a few years, the election might have had relatively little significance. Some degree of social reform was inevitable, but the public was not zealous for national controls. The nation was living in an age of innocence. There had been no major war since the Franco-Prussian conflict of 1870. Norman Angell of England had written *The Great Illusion* which seemed to prove that another war was impossible because both the financial interests and common-sense of an enlightened world would not permit it. Any war of major proportions would be far more costly than any benefits which could be achieved by it. Americans further were convinced that they lived in a Promised Land which nothing could disturb.

The wave of reform, which had begun in 1896 had been lulled during the McKinley years and had been resumed during the T. Roosevelt era, was essentially a clamor for honesty in business and in public affairs. The muckrakers, beginning in the early 1900's, had kept up their drumfire of at-

tack on big business and corrupt politicians. Ray Stannard Baker, Ida Tarbell and others who had written their sensational articles in the old *McClure's
Magazine* had formed the new *American Magazine* in 1906 and were continuing their exposes.

The country, however, was intrinsically prosperous. It did not seek change,
but rather the curtailment of the exploiters and the preservation of individual
opportunity. A small minority, primarily Socialists, championed old age
pensions and other forms of security, but in the main, especially outside of
the large cities, the average citizen could be assured of making a living and
being taken care of through his own efforts and savings from the cradle to the
grave.

The Wilson campaign, therefore, was not a contest between a liberal government and "the interests." True, the more conservative groups rallied
around Taft, but Roosevelt's following was as liberal as Wilson's and in many
instances more radical. When the votes were counted it was found that Wilson
was the leading candidate, yet with a minority of the total vote. He had
something over 6,000,000 votes, to around 4,500,000 for Roosevelt, 3,400,000
for Taft and 900,000 for Eugene V. Debs, the Socialist candidate. The total
vote of "T.R.," Debs and Wilson (which however included the solid South)
represented a substantial liberal victory.

Wilson immediately revealed the nature of his mind as a national leader.
First of all, for the first time since Jefferson's initial and sole attempt, the
President personally addressed both Houses of Congress in his inaugural
speech. By this action, he aimed to emphasize the need for a closer tie between the legislative and executive branches, with the intent to enhance the
prestige of the latter. He carried trust-busting a step further than "T.R." by
advocating various government controls of industry, a reduction of the tariff
and a reform of the banking laws. The address was hardly a surprise, since
it reaffirmed the principles he had advocated in "The New Freedom," as
his collated campaign addresses were called. The message indicated the
consistency of his intentions, and that he had no thought of compromising
upon coming to office. Its forthrightness rallied about him liberal support
from all parties.

While Wilson's immediate program differed little from those of T. Roosevelt and Taft, "The New Freedom" proclaimed that there had been a basic
change in American society. "We are in the presence of a new organization
of society . . . The life of America is not the life that it was twenty years
ago . . . We have changed our economic conditions absolutely from top to
bottom . . . We are facing the necessity of fitting a new social organization
. . . to the happiness and prosperity of the great body of citizens." [1]

Again, where T. Roosevelt had seen merit in large scale business if ethically
conducted, Wilson inveighed against the intrinsic power of size. "Don't de-

[1] Woodrow Wilson, *The New Freedom,* edited by William Bayard Hale, pp. 3, 4.

ceive yourselves for a moment as to the power of the great interests which now dominate our development. They are so great that it is almost an open question whether the Government of the United States can dominate them or not." [2]

As an historian, he knew better than most presidents the *laissez-faire* elements of the liberal movement, and he specifically rejected that approach, saying, "Freedom today is something more than being let alone. The program of a government of freedom must in these days be positive, not negative merely." [3]

His avowed program of lower tariff, workmen's compensation, the right of labor to organize, shorter hours, and the like, was similar to that of earlier reformers. His major domestic ideal, however, was to break up large business units into small enterprises. He recalled, as stated in "The New Freedom," small manufacturing towns in Indiana and elsewhere where production was carried on by relatively small units, worker, owner, and manager being neighbors and often overlapping in their functions.

Later sociologists have demonstrated that the small factory was seldom ideal from the average worker's standpoint, except that the benchman of exceptional ability had greater opportunity to rise. The employer of small industry offered no other special advantages to the hands. Hours and security benefits were often inferior to those in larger enterprises. The history of working conditions in American small factories was, in fact, deplorable. The chance to quit, rise, and compete, was the chief redeeming note.

To the small business men, both owners and managers, Wilson's advocacy of smallness had strong appeal. The multiplicity of small enterprises spelled a multiplicity of executive posts, more opportunities to be "the boss," a wider range of independence for thousands on the managerial tier. The championing of small enterprise was an appropriate position for the leader of the Democratic party whose economic strength was derived from such sources.

There is no evidence that Wilson took this position as a matter of political astuteness. He did not make the time, the times made him. Because he was a philosopher of the moderate-income classes, neither Tory nor Laborite, he was the leader of that day. An English critic of the day referred to the United States as a nation of villagers and shopkeepers, a description which many Americans welcomed with nostalgia. Wilson hoped that the country would be restored to that ideal. Wilson's dream of small industry has persisted; but neither he nor any of his successors have reversed the trend toward consolidation. Wilson tackled easier, special problems first and before he could move on to his supposedly major objective of decentralization, a world war had raised new issues of pressing importance.

[2] *Ibid.*, p. 285.
[3] *Ibid.*, p. 284.

2

During Wilson's first two years in office he met with almost no opposition. A tariff-for-revenue-only had long been a slogan of the Democratic Party. High protective tariffs had encouraged the development of infant industries in the United States; but the now dominant agricultural South and West desired lower prices for industrial products and a freer foreign trade for their markets.

Cattle growers sought protection against Argentine beef; but in the main the rural interests favored a low tariff on manufactures. Within hardly more than six months after Wilson's inaugural, the Underwood tariff was passed in October 1913, not as drastic as the free-traders would have liked, but carrying substantial reductions.

The federal income tax was enacted, a proposal which had been the subject of agitation for many years. The income tax became a means for reaching at last the pockets of large personal fortunes and achieved in part Wilson's desire to limit wealth and power.

In December 1913, Wilson accomplished the passing of the Federal Reserve Act. This was a long overdue improvement on Van Buren's project of an independent Treasury. The central United States Treasury served the business of the federal government, but it left the chief financing of the national economy in private hands. The new system served to co-ordinate the financial needs and policies of the government with the private banking facilities of the nation, under the general direction of the Federal Reserve Board.

Under the Federal Reserve System, the country was divided into twelve districts, each with its Federal Reserve Bank, each supposed to take care of the financial needs of its area. This step in its time was regarded virtually as the economic millennium. It was believed that elasticity in the Federal Reserve System would prevent future panics and depressions, a dream from which the public did not awaken until a generation later.

One further curb on special privilege which Wilson established was the creation of the Federal Trade Commission which was empowered to investigate and denounce a wide range of unfair practices including monopoly, unfair advertising, misrepresentation of products, and the like. It was the successor to Theodore Roosevelt's Bureau of Corporations, but had more teeth. This and other measures, however, were not contemplated to effect any change in the nation's general social structure, but to protect the small business man and the individual against exploiters.

At the outset Wilson had been faced with a critical labor situation. In April, 1913, there had been a strike at the Colorado Fuel and Iron Company. The two sides had been unable to reach a settlement and a state of civil war had followed. Wilson dispatched two thousand troops to keep order, the strike had been broken and a substantial part of the labor element had become critical of the President. In other respects, however, labor leaders received a notable boon from the Administration in the passage of the Clayton Act, which specifically exempted labor unions from prosecution under the anti-trust legislation which prohibited other types of combinations.

By the time Wilson had achieved these two years of legislation, which were not due to him alone but were the culmination of a long period of reform, his popularity began to wane. For the many evils that had been so strenuously expounded before the public, there were now a multitude of corrective laws. The cup of progress was filling up. Moreover, the public was beginning to tire of the same old story. It was significant that the liberal *American Magazine* began to fall into a decline, until the business manager in 1914 said: "Let me edit the magazine. I know what the people want and you fellows don't." He turned it into a "success magazine," glorifying accomplishment rather than criticism, and its circulation increased enormously. Moreover, the change in the tariff schedules had affected numerous industries adversely by early 1914. Business and employment declined, and the prestige of Wilsonism was momentarily dimmed.

3

One of the phases of the age of innocence was a confidence in the complete efficacy of moral suasion regardless of physical force. Pacifists said glibly that economic blockades would suffice to curb recalcitrant nations. (They failed to turn back to Jefferson's unhappy experience on that score.) Bryan, appointed secretary of state, had drawn up a host of treaties between nations which were accepted as additional guarantees of peace. To prevent hasty or surprise attacks, "cooling-off periods" were agreed to in the Bryan treaties. All of these steps were commendable and idealistic efforts to find peaceful solutions for international differences; and no one seemed to conceive the possibility that some nations might choose not to abide by the rules. Teddy Roosevelt had said: "Speak softly, but carry a big stick," but the new method was to speak loudly and carry a little stick.

The United States traditionally had had a small standing Army, and wanted no other policy. On the other hand, tradition had favored a sizable Navy to protect our vast stretches of coast line. Now, however, both the administration and the public desired a reduction in naval establishments.

As long as national policy, as it had been until the Spanish War in '98, was to keep out of affairs beyond the Western Hemisphere, a nonmilitary procedure was logical. A nonimperialistic policy was in keeping with the American temperament, with the American devotion to individual freedom, with the American dislike of regimentation by the military or otherwise.

Therefore, when Wilson began to extend his zeal for reform beyond our own shores, he was armed only with the sword of "public utterance" and the breastplate of moral suasion. The country was entirely unprepared in materials, trained man-power, or intention to back up any presidential ukases.

Wilson may have suffered delusions of grandeur from the ease with which he had steered the ship of state into more liberal seas, for there he was running with the tide. He did a skillful job of piloting. He avoided rocks and eddies that might have ruined a duller captain, and he went forward; but he was in fact integrating and effectuating the popular will rather than forming it. Wilson's contribution to statecraft on the domestic front was not in rousing or liberating the people, but in translating their desires into practical instruments of government. The times needed his intellect, his working knowledge of history and political procedures, his determined clarity; and he did the job. Most of the new measures of government adopted under his regime, such as the Federal Reserve System, remain substantially unaltered to this day.

But the ease of the success led him to an almost naive self-confidence in foreign affairs. When Huerta captured the presidency of Mexico by murder of his predecessor in 1913, Wilson refused to recognize the new regime even though most other foreign powers had done so. Moreover, he read that country a lecture stating that the United States would never recognize a government which came to power by unconstitutional means. In Mexico a forcible accession to power had been virtually standard practice. Wilson's decision to pass upon the constitutionality of foreign regimes was a new and difficult policy.

The President's attempt to prevail by moral suasion proved ineffective. Some American sailors were arrested by the Mexican authorities at Tampico. Wilson demanded an apology from the Huerta government, which was refused. Another incident occurred at Vera Cruz, and Wilson dispatched some gunboats to that harbor, but only as a gesture. Mexico was not intimidated and the United States stood appalled at the President's procedure in getting the country involved. The President said, "I do not see what other course was open to us or how we could have avoided taking such steps as we have taken. The next move is for Huerta. It depends upon him how far this thing shall go. I sincerely pray God it may not have to go to the length of definite war." [4] Fortunately for him, Argentina and Brazil and Chile on April 25, 1914, offered to mediate the affair and Wilson was able momentarily to save face.

Mexico, having discovered that Wilson didn't wish to fight and that the country was not prepared to do so, continued to goad him, being encouraged in this course by Germany, as the facts later developed.

Wilson, jeered at by political opponents at home as well as by Huerta and the bandit leader Villa, had to take the stand that there was such a thing as being "too proud to fight." At length, in the spring of 1916 when Villa made a raid across the Texas border, Wilson dispatched the army on a "puni-

[4] R. S. Baker, *Life,* vol. IV, p. 332.

tive expedition" into Mexico, and called the National Guard into service. In foreign affairs, Wilson's policy of moral suasion had thus far proved a complete failure.

Meanwhile a far more serious crisis had shaken the world. In August 1914, Germany had marched into Belgium, disregarding its guarantee of the neutrality of that country as a "military necessity" and calling its treaty a "scrap of paper." To most of the United States west of the eastern seaboard, the war in Europe seemed none of its affair. For weeks at a time after the initial outbreak, the war news was not even on the front pages of the inland newspapers. Even when Germany began its submarine warfare and the British liner, *Lusitania,* was sunk on May 7, 1915, with many Americans on board, the chief clamor came from the states on the North Atlantic coast. Wars had come and gone in Europe, balances of power had shifted often in the century and a half of the existence of the United States. The nation had remained aloof, holding to its traditional policy of non-involvement in European affairs.

This time there was the important emotional difference that the security of England was threatened. While twisting the lion's tail always had been a favorite American sport, the ties between the two nations had been close, because of similarity in language, the preponderance of English descendants in the United States, and the mutual economics and defense interests of the two countries. Also there was similarity of laws and customs. As long as England remained strong, as long as the British Navy was mistress of the seas with a non-aggressive policy toward us, America had nothing to fear from Europe.

The cause of the Allies was further helped in the United States by the fact that France had helped America during her Revolution. Those sentimental and friendly ties had continued. Nevertheless, during the first year or more of war on the Continent, only a minority of sentiment in the United States favored the nation being drawn into the war.

11

A War for Democracy

*An evident principle runs through the whole program
I have outlined. It is the principle of justice to all peoples and nationalities, and their right to live on equal
terms of liberty and safety with one another, whether
they be strong or weak.*

WOODROW WILSON, *Address to
Congress on the Fourteen Points*

I

When Germany began sinking without warning any vessel found in
Allied waters, or on sea lanes supplying the Allies, Wilson rebuked her in a
series of firm messages. He outlined principles of international law as he
conceived them, and stated how far Germany could or could not go. Anything
beyond the limit would be considered an "unfriendly act."

While there was in these messages until the very end of the series, no
threat of war, they were sharp and corrective in their tone. It was historically
useful for Wilson to have tried to discipline Germany by moral force before
actually going to war. Had the method worked it might have been a cornerstone of international peace. Indeed, the notes were heeded for a time.

The chance of Germany being influenced by Wilson's persuasions at this
point were small. Her case was too desperate. Adherence to the international
code would have rendered the submarine useless, but seemingly it was Germany's best chance for a victorious issue.

The danger of Wilson's procedure was that on his own initiative he was
departing from the traditional isolation policy of the country and if he failed
his very contribution brought the United States nearer to the conflict. Had
his messages to Germany been stalling for time to educate the opinion of the
United States and get prepared for war, his procedure might be regarded as
a masterful piece of strategy.

Wilson's diary and letters indicate, however, that he thought he could make
Germany recede, and that he could exert the moral force of the United
States without any physical involvement.

Right in the midst of this issue, in 1916, came the national presidential
elections. The Progressive Party of "T.R." had faded from the political scene.
The Republicans ran Charles Evans Hughes, who retired from the chief
justiceship of the Supreme bench to enter the race.

Hughes was a man of vigor and probity, formerly governor of New York,
and famous for his prosecution and reform of major insurance companies.
He had several weaknesses as a candidate, however. He had been on the

bench and out of politics for so long that he had lost his touch. Furthermore, he had a full beard in a smooth-faced era. Grant, Garfield, Hayes and Benjamin Harrison had been possessors of handsome facial hair without suffering any political liability thereby; but by 1916 the public beard was obsolete, limited chiefly to kings of England and elderly farmers. Hughes also had been associating too long with "the best people." His special campaign train which toured the Far West included a committee of ladies from New York's upper social strata, a bad political *faux pas* which cost many votes.

With all the advantages of office and of a bungling opposition, Wilson nevertheless had a close call. The Democrats' campaign slogan was: "He kept us out of war," and for that he had the passionate support of wide areas of the country, though his strength in the East had sharply dwindled. A sizable public opinion along the Atlantic seaboard held that the United States should be in the war, or could not avoid being in it, and that the country should be led by a man who believed in that policy. Conversely, many of those who wished America to stay out of the conflict believed that Wilson's procedure was bringing the country rapidly nearer the brink and that a prudent statesman like Hughes had the best chance to extricate the country from its situation. When the votes were counted the Eastern seaboard was so heavily for Hughes that for twenty-four hours he was thought to be elected, but the South and West supported Wilson solidly and California's vote assured him of re-election by a small margin.

Wilson had barely been inaugurated for the second time when Germany began a new series of overt acts which led Wilson in 1917 to ask the Congress for a declaration of war, which was promptly voted. From that time on until the beginnings of peace, Wilson's administration added nothing to the liberal tradition of the White House. In the name of national security, critics of the administration were jailed, including Eugene V. Debs, the mild and naive leader of the Socialist Party. Hundreds of citizens were prosecuted for real and alleged subversive acts.

The Selective Service Law was passed (realistically known as the Draft Act), and an American expeditionary force landed on European soil. America had entered an entirely new era in her history. Cleveland, Theodore Roosevelt and Taft had comprehended the need for international law, but the United States now had become a party to international action.

As the war years continued, Wilson's megalomania increased, or at the least, he evidenced less self-control. As commander-in-chief, with civil restraints removed, his normal impatience toward opposition or even advice was no longer thwarted.

The public interest, in fact, had been channeled into the one thought of winning the war. Liberalism had been less repudiated than forgotten. In the fall of 1918, Wilson tolled the bell by requesting that everyone as a patriotic duty should vote for Democratic candidates.

The country, already bewildered by the change which had shaken its hitherto comfortable and near utopian world, was deeply shocked and resentful. It rejected the advice of the President and Wilson found himself for the first time lacking a majority in the Congress.

His attitude now revealed his tragic nature. It is to no purpose to wish that he had been otherwise, for he was not otherwise. Imbued with his sense of destiny and rightness, he learned nothing from his repudiation at the polls. In his own eyes, whatever he did was the only course to take, and he desired as colleagues only those who would agree.

Before the ultimate victory of the Allies became apparent, though not before the toll of war was becoming intolerable to both sides, the President issued his Fourteen Points which he offered as the terms on which Germany could make an honorable surrender. They were general in their terms and intrinsically were never repudiated. The German Foreign Office wished to ask for more specific definition, but the German headquarters' staff soon advised its government that the Points should be accepted, for the internal economy of Germany and hence her military power were approaching exhaustion. The points as presented by Wilson to Congress on January 8, 1918, were:

I. *Open covenants of peace, openly arrived at,*[1] after which there shall be no private international understandings of any kind but diplomacy shall proceed always frankly and in the public view.

II. *Absolute freedom of navigation upon the seas,* outside territorial waters, alike in peace and in war, except as the seas may be closed in whole or in part by international action for the enforcement of international covenants.

III. *The removal, so far as possible, of all economic barriers and the establishment of an equality of trade conditions* among all the nations consenting to the peace and associating themselves for its maintenance.

IV. *Adequate guarantees given and taken that national armaments will be reduced* to the lowest point consistent with domestic safety.

V. *A free, open-minded, and absolutely impartial adjustment of all colonial claims,* based upon a strict observance of the principle that in determining all such questions of sovereignty the interests of the populations concerned must have equal weight with the equitable claims of the government whose title is to be determined.

VI. *The evacuation of all Russian territory and such a settlement of all questions affecting Russia* as will secure the best and freest cooperation of the other nations of the world in obtaining for her an unhampered and unembarrassed opportunity for the independent determination of her own political development and national policy and assure her of a sincere welcome into the society of free nations under institutions of her own choosing; and, more than a welcome, assistance also of every kind that she may need and may herself desire. The treatment accorded Russia by her sister nations in the months to come will be the acid test

---

[1] Italics by the author, to highlight the principles stated; but note that on several points there are scuttling qualifications.

of their good will, of their comprehension of her needs as distinguished from their own interests, and of their intelligent and unselfish sympathy.

VII. *Belgium,* the whole world will agree, *must be evacuated and restored,* without any attempt to limit the sovereignty which she enjoys in common with all other free nations. No other single act will serve as this will serve to restore confidence among the nations in the laws which they have themselves set and determined for the government of their relations with one another. Without this healing act the whole structure and validity of international law is forever impaired.

VIII. *All French territory should be freed* and the invaded portions restored, and the wrong done to France by Prussia in 1871 in the matter of Alsace-Lorraine, which has unsettled the peace of the world for nearly fifty years, should be righted, in order that peace may once more be made secure in the interest of all.

IX. *A readjustment of the frontiers of Italy* should be effected along clearly recognizable lines of nationality.

X. *The peoples of Austria-Hungary,* whose place among the nations we wish to see safeguarded and assured, *should be accorded* the freest opportunity *of autonomous development.*

XI. *Rumania, Serbia, and Montenegro should be evacuated;* occupied territories restored; Serbia accorded free and secure access to the sea; *and the relations of the several Balkan states to one another determined* by friendly counsel *along historically established lines* of allegiance and nationality; and international guarantees of the political and economic independence and territorial integrity of the several Balkan states should be entered into.

XII. *The Turkish portions of the present Ottoman Empire* should be assured a secure sovereignty, but the other nationalities which are now under Turkish rule should be assured an undoubted security of life and an absolutely unmolested opportunity of autonomous development, and the Dardanelles should be permanently opened as a free passage to the ships and commerce of all nations under international guarantees.

XIII. *An independent Polish state should be erected* which should include the territories inhabited by indisputably Polish populations, which should be assured a free and secure access to the sea, and whose political and economic independence and territorial integrity should be guaranteed by international covenant.

XIV. *A general association of nations must be formed* under specific covenants for the purpose of affording mutual guarantees of political independence and territorial integrity to great and small states alike.

The President after stating, and making certain comments on, the Points, then said:

We have no jealousy of German greatness, and there is nothing in this program that impairs it. We grudge her no achievement or distinction of learning or of pacific enterprise such as have made her record very bright and very enviable. We do not wish to injure her or to block in any way her legitimate influence or power. We do not wish to fight her either with arms or with hostile arrangements of trade if she is willing to associate herself with us and the other peace-loving nations of the world in covenants of justice and law and fair dealing. We wish her only to accept a place of equality among the peoples of the world,—the new world in which we now live—instead of a place of mastery.

It will be recalled that in the spring of 1918, the Allies faced dark days, but the tide turned rapidly in the summer. The Allies accepted the Fourteen Points on November 5, 1918. Meanwhile, the Germans overthrew the Hohenzollern dynasty and, as stated, had accepted Wilson's proposals as the basis for peace.

Among Wilson's Fourteen Points, his chief one and his great contribution was the last—the League of Nations. The idea was not original with him, to be sure; it was centuries old. Greece, Rome, the Holy Alliance, the formation of many of the modern nations including the United States and the British Empire had been coalitions of hitherto rival states. Now the League offered hope to a world in which national rivalries had proved to be well-nigh suicidal.

2

Wilson determined to effectuate the idea and to do it in person. He decided to attend the peace conference. That move was the first of a series of glaring errors. Wilson at home still enjoyed a vast personal popularity. Abroad, he was regarded as a Messiah. The Allies realized that the troops and the finances of America were the margin that had made victory possible. The vanquished saw some measure of hope in the Fourteen Points. At the least here was a victor who brought the semblance of an olive branch, rather than breathing vengeance. Had Wilson not tried to play the politician with such adepts as Clemenceau and Lloyd George, the French and British leaders, he might have remained at home as an Olympian critic stating what would or would not be acceptable to him.

More deplorable, his policy refused American leadership in the cause to anyone other than Woodrow Wilson. The Foreign Affairs Committee of the Senate ultimately would have the responsibility of passing upon the terms of the peace treaty. Constitutionally, two-thirds of the Senate had the power to accept or reject the treaty. Wilson appointed none of the committee and no senator on the American peace mission which accompanied him. He had experts and technicians of great ability who commanded public respect, but no Democrat or Republican who was important in the political sense.

The peace negotiations began in January, 1919, at Paris, and by the end of April, a committee of fifteen headed by Wilson, presented to the Peace Conference the Covenant of the League of Nations, which was adopted. To secure its adoption he had been obliged to accept definitions of his Fourteen Points which had seriously crippled their intent. But he had his League.

The Covenant provided for a council holding the primary power and for an assembly which was largely advisory. The council was to consist of the United States, Great Britain, France, Italy, Japan and four additional powers to be chosen by the assembly. Thirty-two nations soon joined the League, and fifty-five ultimately were members. The seat chosen for the new world government was Geneva, Switzerland.

Whatever faults the League might have had in detail, it was by far the greatest step toward international harmony in the history of the world. It was assumed by Wilson and by most people abroad and at home that the United States would be one of the first and most influential members of the League. The problems which would confront the League would be numerous and would come promptly, beginning with the redrawing of the map of Europe and the setting up of new nationalities which had been provided for in the peace treaty. Wilson was no longer convinced of the sufficiency of public utterance and moral suasion, and dear to his heart was Article Ten of the Covenant which provided for an international police force composed of soldiery from the leading powers, to enforce, if necessary, the League's determinations.

The President presented the treaty, including the League Covenant, to the United States Senate in July, 1919, saying in effect: "This is it."

To his apparent surprise, there was immediately a vocal minority opposition. The President had offended and had done nothing to conciliate the critical elements. He seemed to have forgotten that America for 150 years had lived under a policy of international isolation,[2] which the public believed had been established by President Washington as a fundamental principle for the nation's welfare. The public had endured two years of intensive regimentation. It had submitted to the draft act, and had seen more than two million of its sons shipped to foreign soil. Wilson, further, had delayed recognizing the Kerensky liberal government in Russia and thus contributed to Kerensky's fall and the advent of the Communists; and he had shipped American troops to Archangel, Russia, for purposes which were not explained. There was more than a little fear that Wilson was becoming a naive, if innocent, tool of Europe's power politics.

These conditions made fertile soil for critics of the League. Henry Cabot Lodge, senior senator from Massachusetts, seized upon Article Ten as an obnoxious feature. Keep some of our boys indefinitely in Europe? No! Other clauses were attacked. It was inevitable that the Foreign Affairs Committee of the Senate, acting within its prerogatives, and hitherto almost insultingly ignored, should wish to introduce some face-saving qualifications; but Wilson would have none of it. He was a tired man, and ill. He had suffered an attack of influenza in Paris from which he had not fully recovered. Opposition, never welcome to him, was now well-nigh unbearable. Instead of trying to conciliate the Senate, he determined to stump the country in a campaign of speeches in different cities to appeal to the mass of the people;

[2] Except for the Monroe Doctrine and a sortie against the Barbary pirates, and the war with Spain.

but in an address, at Pueblo, Colorado, on September 25, 1919, he suffered a nervous breakdown and was brought back to Washington.

There, stricken with paralysis, he refused to relinquish the reins of office. Robert Lansing, Secretary of State, because of the prior death of the vice-president, was the constitutional heir-apparent, and desired to carry on the government. Wilson resented Lansing's intervention and dismissed him. The President became inaccessible not only to party leaders, but even to Colonel E. M. House who had been his unofficial adviser for many years. Wilson remained alive until February 3, 1924, but after his collapse in September, 1919, he took no active part in public life.

The Senate, after nine months' wrangle, failed to adopt the League in a vote in November, 1919. A second vote was held in January, 1920, when a majority was mustered, but not the necessary two-thirds. Thus Wilson's great dream came to a pitiful end, not to be revived until a quarter-century later.

The mass of the population in cities were no longer hewers of wood and drawers of water, as long as they had the wherewithal.

They turned the faucet and the water flowed. Central heating in their apartments or houses kept them warm. Fuel was brought to the door in trucks. They pressed a button or pulled a switch, and there was electric light; as long as they could pay the bill.

The post-Wilson decade brought the greatest material advance for the common man that America had seen to date, in both labor- and mind-saving devices. The 1920–1930 era marked the great rise of the motor car, the automatic refrigerator, the washing machine, modern lighting, and home tenantry. Freedom from muscular labor and financial responsibility had reached a new apogee.

In the mental field motion pictures and phonographs provided mass entertainment at lower cost than had been available through stage, lyceum, or piano. Radios came on the market in the 1920s. Self-created amusement such as folk dancing was relegated to remote regions and to faddists. "How ya gonna keep 'em down on the farm, after they've seen Paree?" How indeed? That was the dominant social question which brought them swarming to the already congested cities.

This was the era of the high standard of living in mechanical terms. Psychologically the new standards were as persuasive as the influence of the Crusades in the Middle Ages, though in a different manner. The orientation of America toward the possibilities and the content of life had changed.

The beneficial aspects were obvious. The rural dwellers who could afford the new machinery saved hours of toil, had more physical and mental mobility; and the city populations enjoyed unprecedented gains in easy comforts.

To be sure, if a man lacked the cash he became suddenly less than the hewer of wood and the drawer of water. In the city he was far from the woodlot, and it was conspicuous and humiliating to haul water by the pail from a public tap. And if without a job his case became as desperate as a serf exiled from a feudal barony. But for most, in this decade of the '20's, the cash flowed in a seemingly inexhaustible stream.

The era also was characterized by a literary renaissance. Seemingly even iconoclastic art paradoxically flourishes best in times of prosperity. Maxwell Anderson, Eugene O'Neill, Ernest Hemingway, Paul Green, John Dos Passos, Sinclair Lewis, James T. Farrell, Thomas Wolfe, T. S. Eliot—to name but a few—gave America a rebirth in letters. As in the times just preceding World War I, there was a bright confidence in the sure march of progress.

12

Interlude

The times are wild.

II Henry IV

I

Wilson had been America's most liberal president of modern times in the line of social planning. On the home front he had opposed economic power. He had offered the United States as a leader in world peace. Judged by Thomas Jefferson's "absolute acquiescence in the will of the majority," Wilson and his liberalism were, for the time being, repudiated. Warren Gamaliel Harding was elected in 1920 by a huge vote on the platform "back to normalcy."

Harding was a large, handsome man with big soft hands who looked like a statesman and had good intentions. His nomination had been engineered in part, however, by a rascally group who were soon appointed to office and began to fill their pockets from the public till. In the midst of a storm of financial scandals which did not touch Harding personally, but involved various of his officials, the new President died on August 2, 1923. He had been kind, humanitarian, good-tempered, but inadequate.

Calvin Coolidge, the vice-president, succeeded. He had been governor of Massachusetts and was a native of Vermont. He was one of the few plain unmoneyed men ever to occupy the White House. While the majority of presidents were farm-born, they were or became men of considerable financial substance before reaching the presidency. Sandy-haired, sparse of figure, and taciturn, Coolidge looked like a village postmaster. Harold Laski has said that "Coolidge adored rich men," but this is nonsense. Coolidge admired and was staunchly befriended by several men of wealth, including Andrew Mellon, his secretary of the treasury, Dwight Morrow, a college classmate, who later became a partner in J. P. Morgan & Company, Frank Stearns, another classmate who inherited a Boston department store, and W. Murray Crane, a Massachusetts paper manufacturer, who had helped Coolidge at the start of his political career; but the faculty for adoration was not a Coolidge characteristic. He winced when Middlewesterners greeted him with boisterous enthusiasm. He had a dry wit, the gift of silence and the manner of a persimmon.

Coolidge, while far from exuberant, was not a puritan. He liked his tumbler of whiskey and he believed in live and let live. The country found him restful.

His political principles came out of the little red schoolhouse; thrift, honesty and diligence. As a believer in home rule, he was perhaps closer to Jefferson than to any other predecessor and in a town meeting he might have seemed to be the perfect liberal, although he probably would have been shocked by such a designation.

The practical effects of the Coolidge *laissez-faire* policy in the complicated economic structure of the decade following the first World War were to give free rein to speculation, inflation and business activity on a large scale.

On the favorable side, a broad commercial prosperity was achieved. The production of motor vehicles and household conveniences rose to new heights. Farm values and farm prices recovered substantially from their 1921 deflation. The four million soldiers returning from Europe and the American training camps found ample employment. There were many "soft spots" in both farming and industrial areas, but in the main there had been no peacetime period in recent decades when there was less poverty or material distress.

Coolidge himself realized, however, that there were abuses and overexpansion. After one elected term following his succession to office because of Harding's death, he did "not choose to run" again in 1928. He had no comprehension of an elaborate social state; and in an article written after his retirement he avowed that he had never understood the subject of tariffs.

By the time Coolidge was ready to retire, the many abuses in the midst of prosperity, the numerous failures of businesses (some dishonestly or incompetently administered), the millions of persons on fixed incomes who enjoyed no benefit from the prosperity of high prices, had begun to build up considerable liberal sentiment, critical of things as they were.

Herbert Hoover seemed like an answer to the country's need. In view of the end of his career and the "typing" of him as a Bourbon by the Democrats, his liberal reputation at the time of his nomination has been almost forgotten.

He was the great engineer, the poor Iowa boy who had made a sizable fortune and had spent much of it in good works. He was the great humanitarian, the Wilson appointee who had fed the starving Belgians. When hundreds of Americans had been stranded in Europe at the opening of the war in 1914, it was Hoover who had organized a committee to get them home and had financed many of them out of his own pocket. He had stayed out of politics except for a competent term as secretary of commerce under Coolidge, in which he had avoided controversial issues. Hoover, in spite of the host of enemies that he made later, was singularly worshiped by the people who worked directly for him, either for pay or as volunteers, and it was largely these zealots who obtained the Republican nomination for him.

Hoover was in the unfortunate position of having been mislabeled and misadvertised to the electorate as a liberal. Though probably as devoted to the nation and the public as any man who has occupied the White House, he was lacking in exterior warmth of personality. Nor did he have Wilson's facility for projecting his ideas in glowing terms. Colonel Starling, secret service man at the White House through five administrations, has described the Hoover personality succinctly: [1]

President Hoover himself was a man of tremendous ability, and surely he was as earnest and as honest as any man who ever held the office. He was handicapped, I felt, by certain habits he had acquired during his career as an engineer, and by the fact that he thought of humanity as an abstract quality instead of a collection of highly differentiated personalities. Thus he believed that all tasks could be accomplished by adequate planning and sufficiently expert supervision, and the American people could be served and aided without reducing them to individualized portions of creative expression.

In the first year and a half of his administration, Hoover's influence on public affairs was inconspicuous. The Wall Street bull market was at its peak and general prosperity was undeflated. Few important governmental measures were undertaken, except for certain attempts toward the standardization of products and efforts to simplify the structure of the government. These matters, however, had no outstanding public appeal.

Hoover soon alienated himself from the press through a shyness and reserve which gave the impression of arrogance. He was testy under questioning and was unable or unwilling to clothe his views in popular terms. He canceled press conferences without apparent reason, claimed he was misquoted, and often went for days without being accessible to the press at all. Yet while disregarding the press, his chief potential channel of information to the people, his mind was conceiving of the state as a force which could be engineered in the public interest.

Any good intentions which he had, however, were beclouded by the stock market crash of October, 1929, and the series of disasters which ensued for several years following.

Hoover promptly went to work to stem the tide, and some of his measures, such as the Federal Farm Board, and the Reconstruction Finance Corporation, were accepted, amplified, or reconstituted by his successor; so, likewise, was his policy of large expenditures for public works to cushion unemployment. His successful appeals to industry to maintain wage rates was hailed by the liberals; and it was the first time in the country's history that wage rates had been maintained in the face of general deflation.

In many respects, Hoover's policy was clearly to the left of center and it was not until later years that anyone thought to describe him as a reactionary; but he made a series of mistakes that accentuated even the unfortunate conditions which inescapably had to be faced. To placate the farmers he supported the Hawley-Smoot tariff for increases on farm products primarily, although other items were included. This precipitated retaliations by other countries, dimmed our fading foreign trade and damaged the economy

[1] Col. E. W. Starling and Thomas Sugrue, *Starling of the White House* (Simon & Schuster, 1946).

of European nations which had already been in a depression for some time. He had a mania for "fact finding," appointing numerous committees to report on special problems, holding that if the public had the facts the solutions would be forthcoming. This in practice was a form of delay and avoidance which was peculiarly distressing.

Hoover's fundamental error, moreover, was in believing that the depression would be short lived. Restoration of public confidence was his prime remedy. He might have been right, but it can never be proved because public confidence was not restored, and did not yield even to heroic measures. John D. Rockefeller, Sr., immediately after the big crash stated on October 30, 1929, that "there is nothing in the business situation to warrant the destruction of values that has taken place"; [2] the selling panic persisted and the market continued to sag. Nevertheless, as late as the autumn elections of 1932, the administration and its Cabinet officers barnstormed the country preaching that all signs were favorable, and that the storm would be over as soon as the public had confidence.

This optimism in the face of widespread financial distress throughout the land made a worse impression than a candid realization of the facts would have. The mere wiping out of speculators would not have been disastrous. The real blow to conservative opinion in the country was in the ruination of thousands who had followed the Coolidge doctrine of thrift and saving. In the year 1932, scores of savings banks had closed their doors. Two major concerns who specialized in guaranteed mortgages, supposedly a prudent investment for widows and trust funds, went to the wall, even though they had had a record of many years without a single default in payments. One of Boston's most conservative banking houses and a trustee for numerous family accounts, failed. It was not merely the speculators, or the men who had made sudden fortunes, who lost, but the millions of sober diligent citizens who saved for a rainy day, never expected riches, and had not benefited noticeably during the lush years of the twenties.

The Hoover administration was not idle in the face of disaster. The Reconstruction Finance Corporation, for example, was founded to strengthen the credit of the banking structure and to arrest the deflationary process generally. It began operations on February 12, 1932, with a fund of $500,000,000 with which some heroic work was done; yet it was severely attacked by the very liberal organs that were crying out for an adequate relief policy. The R.F.C. was hotly criticized for rescuing banks which allegedly did not deserve to be saved, and in turn for allowing other banks to close.

The total loss to depositors during the depression years will never be known. The figures of losses to depositors in closed banks, however, indicate the

[2] *New York American,* October 31, 1929. This, and statements that William Rockefeller and his son were "buying heavily" appeared widely in the press and had only momentary effect.

trend. In 1929 the losses to depositors amounted to $77,000,000, in 1930 to $237,000,000, in 1931 to $391,000,000.[3]

By 1932 the losses to depositors in closed banks dropped to $168,000,000 for the year. This fact and other circumstances give support to President Hoover's contention that things were already on the mend when he stood for re-election. Whether because of Roosevelt policies or not, the losses in 1933 rose to an all-time high of $540,000,000.[4]

Three-quarters of the reported losses in bank failures were on balances not exceeding $5,000. The losses on the larger accounts often contributed to the ruination of businesses, and accelerated the downward spiraling of unemployment. Figures for depositors' losses reported do not include mutual saving institutions which operate in seventeen states, but are the totals of commercial banks including trust companies, stock savings banks, in short the bulk of deposits. The losses of stockholders in the closed banks were even larger than those of the depositors, and the surviving banks absorbed millions of dollars of losses, by writing down the book value of their impaired assets.

Most of the closed banks ultimately reopened either under the same management or under reorganization. The average per cent of loss to the depositors was small, though there were thousands of instances where even ultimately the loss to individuals was complete. Moreover, whenever a bank closed, the shocked depositors had no way of knowing whether they were completely wiped out, or if not wiped out what would be the extent of their recovery. Many months, and sometimes years, ensued before they knew the answer. Statistically, most of the loss from the financial crash was salvaged, but for millions of Americans their former sense of security, stability and opportunity was irretrievably lost. The feeling of insecurity in turn shook the hitherto rigid conservatism of the middle classes and made the public at large receptive to change.

[3] From Annual Report of the Federal Deposit Insurance Corporation for the year ended December 31, 1940.
[4] *Ibid.*

Christmas Eve, 1932, Eighth Street, Greenwich Village, New York. An attractive young married couple are playing violin and saxophone, standing on the sidewalk near their flat. A small wicker basket near by invites contributions. They have enterprise, they have buried their pride, and on this particular eve, they have a good "take." But they are among the new unemployed.

They were graduates of a notable Western university, where he continued for his law degree. They had married when he got a job in a New York firm. In the general financial collapse, the job expired. He and she believed that native talent and a willingness to work would assure at least a modest living for anyone. But now all the intellectual trades had shrunk. Opportunities, for the time being—and they had to live in the time being—did not exist. They were willing under necessity to do any manual work, but they found competition there even more acute.

This new crisis had little to do with the merit of the individual worker.

In 1932, a man who lived elsewhere owned a house in Massillon, Ohio. He couldn't pay his mortgage interest or taxes, as his funds were in a closed trust company. The Massillon bank which held the mortgage refused to foreclose, though the owner was willing, for there were no potential buyers. The public authority would not take the property for taxes, for the same reason. The tenant, privileged to have rent free until better times, left because he had no money to buy coal. The house, a good one, stood empty, a useless equity, victim of a collapsed financial machinery.

13

"Happy Days"

*. . the liberal deviseth liberal things; and by liberal
things shall he stand.*

Isaiah XXXII, 8

I

The ease with which Roosevelt was elected,[1] and the catastrophic national conditions attending his early months in the White House, have tended to blur the record of just how he came into being as the leading statesman of his time. "Happy Days Are Here Again," his campaign song, symbolized the public's wish to escape from the immediate past.

When the period 1912–1945 becomes foreshortened by future years, the Wilson-Roosevelt regimes may come to be regarded as a single unit, though broken in the middle. Wilson made the more thorough-going studious presentation against the size and power of large private enterprises. He established certain governmental counterbalances through legislation, and he concluded by turning from a national reform program to emphasis on international unity. In a broad sense F. D. Roosevelt followed the same pattern, had similar goals.

In temperament and procedures the two men were different. Though Wilson was by no means the pioneer in clearing the forest, he had tilled the soil which Roosevelt fertilized and cultivated. Wilson, moreover, was preeminently the philosopher. He usually told the public specifically where he was trying to go at any moment and what was his long range direction. Wilson was a liberal through informed scholarly conviction, whereas Franklin Roosevelt—the term is not used invidiously—was an opportunist, who at times tried to go in several directions at once. Wilson was authoritarian and could easily have been a fundamentalist in all respects if his mind had found that answer in his books, while Roosevelt was not at home in any fixed scheme of things. Once when Roosevelt was asked about his philosophy, he replied: "Philosophy? I am a Christian, and a Democrat—that's all." [2] The answer rings true. He had a devout Christian faith which was religious rather than theological, and his political zeal was integral with his concept of the Democratic Party.

Franklin D. Roosevelt was a liberal by nature. He was a prime example of the fact that the liberal is known by his intent and public acceptance, rather than by his belief in specific measures. In measures alone he was inconsistent

---

[1] His popular vote was 57 per cent (57.32) of the total.
[2] Frances Perkins, *The Roosevelt I Knew.*

and changing, but he was consistent in his desire to try new things and in being fascinated by change.

He was an enigma to many persons in his first candidacy, when he came to the White House, and indeed throughout his presidency. As Frances Perkins, his devoted secretary of labor, said of him in *The Roosevelt I Knew*: "Franklin Roosevelt was not a simple man. That quality of simplicity which we delight to think marks the great and noble was not his. He was the most complicated human being I ever knew and out of this complicated nature there sprang much of the drive which brought achievement." [3]

Born of an old New York Dutch family, educated at the selective Groton School and at Harvard University, he was regarded by many of his social colleagues as "a traitor to his class." It might be said equally that they were traitors to him, because in his first presidential campaign, when his platform was moderate almost to conservatism, most of his "class" supported not him but the outlander, Herbert Hoover.

It is interesting to speculate on the possible modifying effect on Roosevelt policy had his school and university friends, and their community of wealthy men, flocked to Roosevelt as one of their own, even as most of the Virginia aristocracy embraced Jefferson.

Roosevelt wore no man's collar, but he was susceptible to ideas, and in his early days in the presidency entertained a procession of diverse advisers, being receptive at least to hearing their views. At times, indeed, he seemed like an Aeolian harp, moved by the latest winds of advice, and not until his later years in the presidency did his cumulative record of social reform make his course more or less predictable.

Mr. Roosevelt was, of course, committed to the Democratic Party, having been assistant secretary of the navy under Wilson, and a candidate for the Vice-Presidency in 1920. Such was the range of party opinion, however, that the label itself implied little that was specific, for throughout the 1920's Wilsonism had not been fashionable in Democratic circles.

In two terms as governor of New York, Roosevelt's interest had been markedly along humanitarian lines. He had espoused better housing, old-age assistance, and relief to agriculture, all reasonably moderate measures, though his efforts at public control of water power and electrification, together with the incurring of a huge state debt, had alarmed the conservatives. Perhaps, too, some of the conservatives were aware of his Sunday evening gatherings at Hyde Park, antedating his nomination by many months, where assembled economists, professors, persons of many points of view, met to discuss what ailed the nation and what should be done about it.

It was in a radio address from Albany on April 17, 1932, that he first summarized his basic intent in a way that captured the public's imagination. He called for "faith once more in the forgotten man at the bottom of the economic

[3] *Ibid.*, p. 3.

pyramid." Yet this same address deplored drastic measures of public spending, pointing out that millions of dollars for public works could employ only seven or eight million persons at most, and referring to such expenditure as "a stop gap."

More than specific measures, it was Roosevelt's personality and characteristics which had a wide public appeal that his opponents continued to underestimate. He had remarkable diction, putting things in simple terms that everyone could understand, rather than in closely reasoned economic treatises. He had a warm, easy speaking voice, well adapted for radio, which was just in the early stages of its vast popularity. He was approachable, genial, almost devil-may-care in manner, probably the most informal man to seek the presidency since Lincoln, and certainly a contrast to his immediate predecessors.

Along with this cheerfulness was the fact that he had fought his way back from infantile paralysis, and was still partially paralyzed. Such an example of fortitude, of handicaps daily endured, won general admiration and respect.

The White House, with all its responsibilities, is America's greatest show. It symbolizes and dramatizes the Republic as both king and premier represent Great Britain. For this role Mr. Roosevelt had a natural flair. When VanLear Black, aviator and part owner of the Baltimore *Sun,* offered to fly Mr. Roosevelt to Chicago to accept the nomination, he promptly consented. Cooler heads protested the risk, but fearlessness to personal danger was another quality which made Roosevelt a natural popular leader.

Accepting the nomination in person on the convention floor was another innovation, where he pledged himself to follow the principles of "the unquenchable progressive soul of our commander-in-chief, Woodrow Wilson"; and he referred to the Democratic Party as the "bearer of liberalism and progress and, at the same time, of safety to our institutions."

The reference to Wilson may have been significant, or perhaps it was just a glowing tribute to the last Democratic president to occupy the White House. There was no note calling for our entry in the League of Nations, and the same address affirmed that government cost too much and that unnecessary functions of government must be eliminated.

Here it was that he first referred to a new deal, but a lower-case new deal not a definite set of measures, when he said, "I pledge you, I pledge myself, to a new deal for the American people."

Thus far, the liberal program of Roosevelt went no further than might be expected from any presidential candidate, and indeed receded from the social planning of Hoover. In Roosevelt's radio address of July 30, 1932, he expounded and quoted from the Democratic platform, saying, "Let us have the courage to stop borrowing to meet continuing deficits. Stop the deficits . . . insist on a sound currency." He also opposed the cancellation of debts owed the United States by foreign nations, condemned the "excessive use of money in political activities," and pledged himself to repair the national economy, all in familiar terms.

Indeed, Miss Perkins, herself a life-long liberal, has discovered no fundamentally radical framework, no framework at all, in the President's thinking. "Roosevelt took the status quo in our economic life as much for granted as his family," she says. "He had, I am sure, no thought or desire to impose any overall economic or political change on the United States . . . It was his way to be concerned about the concrete situations." [4]

There was, as noted in the preceding chapter, a series of accelerated financial calamities, these served to stiffen the attitude of the President-elect. He had little support from the financial community with whom he was familiar. Hence influence in thought from that quarter was negligible. He realized after the election that his initial responsibility was not to devise either a liberal or a conservative program, in whatever terms that either might mean, but to rescue the nation from its complete economic paralysis.

A complete shutdown of the banks was on his doorstep at the time of his First Inaugural Address, all the more appalling because the supposedly adequate Federal Reserve System had been unable to avert the crisis. The President said in his Inaugural that "the only thing we have to fear is fear itself"; but his most drastically significant statement was in these words: "If we are to go forward, we must move as a trained and loyal army willing to sacrifice for the good of common discipline . . . We are, I know, ready and willing to submit our lives and property to such discipline, because it makes possible a leadership which aims at larger good."

There was hardly a dissenting voice from any quarter at such bold assumption of responsibility. The speech, indeed, was greeted with general acclaim. It was a milestone, leading whither no one knew. Never in peacetime had a president made such demands for virtually unlimited powers. Congress passed the necessary emergency legislation, and the country waited to see what would be built on the new foundations.

There is reassurance in the traditions of democracy in the months that followed, partial parallels from other countries notwithstanding. The principle, as Roosevelt stated it, would cover the activities of Hitler in the Third Reich, of Mussolini in his rule of Italian economy, and of the Russian statist government. It was accepted without fear by the American public, however, conscious that Roosevelt had no intent of dictatorship, and that they voluntarily would go along with whatever measures seemed to work until the nation pulled out of the crisis.

2

The program adopted in the ensuing months was a strange phantasmagoria of miscellaneous ideas suggested by many and diverse advisers of the President. To the expectable acts of social and economic reform were added a mass of avowedly experimental legislation. When the schemes failed to work perfectly, the advocates of a planned society attributed the failure to the fact

[4] *Ibid.*, pp. 328, 332.

that the plan was lopsided. Not enough legislation had been passed, in their opinion, and the Supreme Court later threw out certain parts of it. The criticism was well founded, if one accepts the desirability of a fully planned society. The aim to establish a balanced control of all phases of American economic life never was achieved. The program which was passed did, for a time, go a long way toward statism, and had manifold provisions for policing various segments of the public.

3

The President's personality went far toward persuading the public of the merits of the New Deal. Having a chameleonlike nature, a love of popularity, and a native taste for politics, the President tended to promise all things to all men, and then to do as he chose. In time this habit created enemies; but he moved blithely and swiftly from point to point and his critics were never quite sure where their target would be found next.

In the first hundred days of Congress, beginning March 9, 1933, however, the President advocated an extensive and detailed program of "recovery and reform."

In Roosevelt's Inaugural he announced an era of drastic change. In Jacksonian language he said that the "rulers of mankind's goods have failed through their own stubbornness and their own incompetence, have admitted their failure, and have abdicated . . . True they have tried, but their efforts have been cast in the pattern of an outworn tradition." The New Deal, a special new deal with initial caps, was at hand.

There is no need here to recapitulate all the multitudinous Acts, Proclamations, and Directives which introduced a new method of government in the United States; but a classification of the main measures adopted in the hundred days of Congress beginning March 9 may be useful. These measures may be divided into those for immediate relief, those in the pattern of expectable reform, and those marking a clear break with the past. The relief measures comprised:

The Wagner-Costigan-LaFollette Act, granting $500,000,000 to the states for unemployment relief.

An act creating the Civilian Conservation Corps, providing work relief for 250,000 young men in the national parks and forests.

An act establishing the Home Owners' Loan Corporation, with $200,-000,000 capital supplied by the government and with authority to issue $2,000,000,000 worth of bonds guaranteed by the government, all for the purpose of protecting the mortgages of small homes.

A new Agricultural Credit Act, providing for $2,000,000,000 worth of bonds guaranteed by the government, to be issued by the Federal Land Bank System to save farm mortgages from foreclosure. It also provided that

$100,000,000 be loaned to the Joint Stock Land Bank System so that it would not need foreclose the mortgages on its books. The act further provided for the appointment of a Farm Loan Commissioner empowered to lend $200,000,000 worth of government money to farmers for any necessary purpose.

These measures had wide approval throughout the nation. The public economy had been paralyzed by a persisting panic psychology. All institutions, banks, life insurance companies, mortgage concerns, were trying to collect the obligations due them, all at the same time, which was an obvious impossibility. Unemployment was so widespread that masses of people did not have the means for subsistence, let alone paying taxes, rent, or the principals of obligations. The huge loans and credits might relieve many individual crises.

In the second group of bills were obvious and expectable bills of reform:

The Securities Act provided for elaborate reports by corporations whose securities were on sale to the general public. The intent here was similar to Theodore Roosevelt's Bureau of Corporations, and Woodrow Wilson's Federal Trade Commission, but was more forceful and comprehensive in its supervision. Though cumbersome in some of its aspects, it was a necessary protection to the buying public. While it could not remove the risks inherent in any investment, it went far toward driving "blue sky" promoters out of business. It was also a protection to legitimate business which no longer needed to compete with shady enterprises for the available capital supplied by the public.

The Banking Act extended the federal authority over banking, endeavoring to accomplish what the Federal Reserve System had been expected to do in protection of the security of banks. Under this Act, the United States Treasury contributed the first $150,000,000 of capital to a federal corporation for the purposes of insurance, and the banks provided up to one-half of one per cent of their deposits, after which the corporation was empowered to issue bonds to an undetermined figure, estimated not to exceed $2,000,000,000.

The Railroad Act created a federal Railroad Coordinator who was supposed to improve and correlate the railroad systems of the country. Neither the need for, nor the accomplishments of, this measure have been very clear.

The Economy Act empowered the President to cut $1,000,000,000, if possible, out of the government's ordinary annual expenditures. This was responsive to the campaign pledge for economy, but had little practical effect.

There were four further measures, so drastic in their concept, so penetrating to everyone's pocketbook and way of life, that they constituted a bloodless revolution:

The Tennessee Valley Authority Act had some shadow of precedent in the municipal ownership of public utilities in many cities and in the federal creation of dams for general water supply and irrigation. The intent of the act, however, as a yardstick for public utility costs and as a program to revise the whole economy of the one section of the country was new.

The Agricultural Adjustment Act had an innocent title, as did its sub-section "The Emergency Farm Mortgage Act." No one would guess from these titles that the measure provided for enormous funds to peg the prices of farm products, or, secondly, for an elaborate scheme for the devaluation of the dollar. Of this, more later.

The Joint Resolution of the Congress abrogated the gold clause in all public and private contracts.

The National Industrial Recovery Act, more often referred to as the National Recovery Act, provided for national cartels of industry. Of this, also more later. The Public Works Act was likewise included as a sub-title in this measure.

The direct and potential expenditures under all of these measures amounted to almost $11,000,000,000, which may be summarized as follows: [5]

DIRECT APPROPRIATIONS AND AUTHORIZATIONS

Grants to states for unemployment relief	$500,000,000
To expedite certain public works	148,000,000
Loans to the Joint Stock Land Banks	100,000,000
To the Farm Loan Commissioner for direct loans to farmers	200,000,000
For farm relief rentals and benefits	100,000,000
For Federal Land Banks on account of depleted funds and loss of interest	65,000,000
To the Farm Credit Administration to make loans for crop production and marketing	40,000,000
For capital in the Home Owners' Loan Corporation	200,000,000
To buy preferred stock in federal loan & savings associations	100,000,000
For capital in the Federal Bank Deposit Insurance Corporation	150,000,000
For public works, under the National Recovery Act	3,300,000,000
	$4,903,000,000

CONTINGENT LIABILITIES

On account of bonds to be issued by the Federal Land Banks, guaranteed by the government	$2,000,000,000
On account of bonds to be issued by the Tennessee Valley Authority	50,000,000
On account of bonds to be issued by the Home Owners' Loan Corporation, guaranteed by the government	2,000,000,000

On account of bonds to be issued by the Federal Deposit Guar-

[5] Tabulation from Garet Garrett, "The Hundred Days," *The Saturday Evening Post,* August 12, 1933.

antee Corporation	2,000,000,000
Total contingent liabilities	$6,050,000,000
Add direct appropriations and authorizations as above	4,903,000,000
Grand total emergency dispositions of public credit	$10,953,000,000

The size of these appropriations, though often highly publicized, was not their significant feature. Not all these dollars were to be called for at once, and a sizable share of them constituted capital which was intended to be self-liquidating.

The 1933 expenditures of the government were about $4,300,000,000, less than the approximately $5,000,000,000 expended by Hoover in 1932. The high point of peacetime New Deal spending was around $9,000,000,000 in 1936.

The real significance of the New Deal financing was that for the first time the government had addressed its capital resources to meet a peacetime national emergency, on a scale which hitherto had been thought feasible only in the prosecution of wars.

Possibly the most radical of all the steps undertaken by the New Deal was that of the Emergency Farm Mortgage Act, referred to above. It authorized the government to print $3,000,000,000 of paper money and exchange it for outstanding interest-bearing obligations of the government. It permitted the administration to fix the ratio of gold and silver, and to devalue the dollar at any point short of 50 per cent of its value at the time the government went off the gold standard.

The President himself never seemed too eager to refer to this phase of his program, and the very fact that it was attached to an agricultural bill suggested a desire to screen it from public attention.[6] Senator Elmer Thomas of Oklahoma, who introduced the measure in Congress, on behalf of the Executive, stated its purpose boldly: "Two hundred billion dollars of wealth and buying power now rests in the hands of those who own the bank deposits and fixed investments, bonds and mortgages . . . If the amendment carries and the powers are exercised in a reasonable degree, it must transfer that $200,000,000,000 in the hands of persons who now have it, who did not buy it, who did not earn it, who do not deserve it, who must not retain it, back to the other side—the debtor class of the Republic, the people who owe the mass debts of the nation."

The real justification for the gold and dollar legislation was the difficult position of the United States in world finance, politics and trade, as the only nation on the gold standard. Furthermore, the devaluation of the dollar caused an immediate inflation of prices, including those of the deflated stocks and bonds. Within a few months after this measure had been passed the securities on the New York Stock Exchange had appreciated in value by

[6] For full text on the general finance parts of the act, see *Public—No. 10—73rd Congress* (H.R. 3835), Title II, Part 5, Sec. 38; Title III, Secs. 44-46.

twenty billions of dollars. They were different dollars, but the effect was salutary.

As suggested above, the President seemed to have some qualms on the subject. The diary of Henry Morgenthau, Secretary of the Treasury, as reported in *The New York Times* of December 31, 1946, refers to the President's attitude on the subject. Says the *Times* report:

> Beginning on Oct. 25, each morning the President conferred with Mr. Morgenthau and Jesse Jones to set the price of the gold for the day. While the President breakfasted, usually on scrambled eggs, the trio discussed the gold reports from abroad. On the first day, gold was $31.02 in London and $31.09 in Paris. Mr. Morgenthau suggested $31.36 for the first day's price . . . "All right," said the President, "we will make it $31.36."
>
> "The actual price on any given day made little difference and was determined arbitrarily," the diary says. One day, for example, the bedside conference decided on a rise of 21 cents.
>
> "It's a lucky number," the President remarked, "because it's three times seven."
>
> In his diary, Mr. Morgenthau commented: "If anybody ever knew how we really set the gold price through a combination of lucky numbers, etc., I think they would really be frightened."

The apologists for President Roosevelt on this matter have suggested that he had a sense of humor and that Mr. Morgenthau did not. On the other hand, the instance suggests that Mr. Roosevelt was a realist, that he knew there was no statistically right figure at which to set devaluation, that any learned formula on the subject would be just so much mumbo-jumbo, and that the amount of devaluation would necessarily be a matter of trial and error. Hence it may be surmised that he was indulging in the luxury of being shockingly honest in the bosom of his official family.

4

The National Recovery Act was a strange device to come from a liberal source. The N.R.A., in many respects, established the structure of a corporate state. Under it, every industry was called upon to set up a code of agreement, and six hundred industries did so.

These codes provided for a fixing of prices and regulation of production, with severe penalties for violations. While each code was administered by a special Code Authority having a governmental official in charge, the personnel of the Authority was usually identical with trade association leaders of the particular industry, and it was customarily the trade body who drew up the details of the code.

Plans for the N.R.A. were drawn up for transportation and farming. Roosevelt characterized these arrangements as "a partnership between government and farming and industry and transportation, not a partnership in profits, for the profits still go to the citizens, but rather a partnership in planning, and a partnership to see that the plans are carried out."

In contrast to the "hold the line" price policy of later years, the goal now was to push prices up. Production was to be kept within limits everywhere. In industry, production and prices could be controlled by agreement. In agriculture, under collateral legislation, bonuses were paid to the farmers for plowing crops under, or for not raising as much as in previous years.

Some manufacturers who believed in their superior ability to compete and preferred free markets, were opposed to N.R.A. But broadly speaking, there was considerable zeal for trying out the system. Never before had there been such government protection of prices, such elimination of the cut-throat competitor. If the public could and would buy under these conditions, it looked like a field-day for industry.

One clause in the act, however, made an important exception to the pattern. That was the famous 7(a), which said:

Every code of fair competition, agreement, and license approved, prescribed, or issued under this title shall contain the following conditions: (1) that employees shall have the right to organize and bargain collectively through representatives of their own choosing, and shall be free from the interference, restraint, or coercion of employers of labor, or their agents, in the designation of such representatives or in self-organization or in other concerted activities for the purpose of collective bargaining or other mutual aid or protection; (2) that no employee and no one seeking employment shall be required as a condition of employment to join any company union or to refrain from joining, organizing, or assisting a labor organization of his own choosing; and (3) that employers shall comply with the maximum hours of labor, minimum rates of pay, and other conditions of employment approved or prescribed by the President.

In short, the price which industry was obliged to pay for its special protections was the advantage which 7(a) gave to organized labor. Actually, several years elapsed before unions fully grasped their opportunities, but 7(a) was the foundation stone of Roosevelt's labor policies.

For the next two years there was general improvement in employment and profits. Most of the banks reopened. The N.R.A. system operated with little apparent pain. The emergency was presumably over.

There had always been, however, considerable doubt as to the constitutionality of the National Industrial Recovery Act, and in test cases the United States Supreme Court, by two decisions, declared the act unconstitutional. The President seemed to take this as a personal affront. His brain child had been strangled.

From this time on he regarded the Supreme Court as his enemy and an enemy to progress. It is probable, however, that the ending of N.R.A. was beneficial to the President. As a measure taken *in extremis,* it helped to restore public confidence, but whether so restricted a system would have served an expanding economy is at least debatable. Certainly, its extinction had no extensive effect on recovery.

Roosevelt, nevertheless, regarded the slaughter of the N.R.A. as the work of industrialists and capitalists; and in his campaign of 1936, he moved into his second phase of active and avowed opposition to the financial community as such. In his acceptance speech at Philadelphia, June 27, 1936, he said:

Out of this modern civilization economic royalists carved new dynasties. New kingdoms were built upon concentration of control over material things. Through new uses of corporations, banks and securities, new machinery of industry and agriculture, of labor and capital—all undreamed of by the fathers—the whole structure of modern life was impressed into this royal service.

There was no place among this royalty for our many thousands of small business men and merchants who sought to make a worthy use of the American system of initiative and profit . . .

His words were reminiscent of Theodore Roosevelt, but even more so of Andrew Jackson. He continued:

It was natural and perhaps human that the privileged princes of these new economic dynasties, thirsting for power, reached out for control over Government itself. They created a new despotism and wrapped it in the robes of legal sanction. In its service new mercenaries sought to regiment the people, their labor, and their property. . . .

The hours men and women worked, the wages they received, the conditions of their labor—these had passed beyond the control of the people, and were imposed by this new industrial dictatorship. The savings of the average family, the capital of the small business man, the investments set aside for old age—other people's money—these were tools which the new economic royalty used to dig itself in.

The royalists of the economic order have conceded that political freedom was the business of the Government, but they have maintained that economic slavery was nobody's business. They granted that the Government could protect the citizen in his right to vote, but they denied that the Government could do anything to protect the citizen in his right to work and his right to live.

Today we stand committed to the proposition that freedom is no half-and-half affair. If the average citizen is guaranteed equal opportunity in the polling place, he must have equal opportunity in the market place.

These economic royalists complain that we seek to overthrow the institutions of America. What they really complain of is that we seek to take away their power.

The whole campaign was in the tone of what G. B. Shaw has referred to as, "the crude Marxist melodrama of 'The Class War: or the Virtuous Worker and the Brutal Capitalist.'" It was an echo of "T.R.'s" denunciation of "the malefactors of great wealth," and it was reminiscent of Oliver Cromwell's literal "off with their heads" practice toward his enemies. Such an attitude naturally stirred up violent countercriticism in many quarters.

Roosevelt's general popularity, however, was at its peak. The times were vastly better than when he had come into office. Many admitted wrongs had been corrected, and if some new wrongs had been committed and mistakes made, which the President conceded, the public decided that the result was strongly in his favor. In his second election, the President carried slightly over 60 per cent of the popular vote, the highest majority of any president since the Civil War, with the exception of the sweep of President Harding.

Even as Cromwell abolished the Commonwealth in favor of the Protectorate, Roosevelt, armed with this vote of public confidence, became increasingly impatient of opposition. He was now determined to curb the power of the Supreme Court which had declared several major measures of the New Deal to be unconstitutional. On February 5, 1937, the President addressed the Congress denouncing the Supreme bench as "nine old men" and presenting a bill for reorganization of the judiciary which in effect would enable the president to control the complexion of the Court. This court-packing proposal has been generally regarded as the President's greatest mistake, even by many of his most liberal followers. The refusal of Congress to adopt this proposal, despite administrative pressure, is an indication that the liberal sentiment of the country will curb even a markedly liberal president when he tries to go too far beyond the checks and balances which are characteristic of the American system of government.

Roosevelt later claimed that he was by no means defeated on this issue because after his attack, the Court reversed itself on several important points (though not on N.R.A.). This thesis is set forth persuasively by Roosevelt in the Introduction to the Sixth Volume of his Public Papers and Addresses. Fate also helped Mr. Roosevelt, for the retirement or death of several of the justices soon gave him an opportunity to name the majority of the court. Nevertheless, the attempt to establish the principle of subservience of the court to the Executive had failed. In that defeat as in the loss of N.R.A., the President could be considered fortunate for it relieved him of a responsibility too heavy for any single human being to assume.

14

The Four Freedoms

*Is the world as it was, man? Which is the way? Is it
sad, and few words? or how? The trick of it?*
                                        Measure for Measure

I

Sumner Welles has said that since the autumn of 1936, Roosevelt "had
become ever more engrossed with foreign policy." [1]

Rexford Guy Tugwell, one of the earliest and most utopian of the President's Brain Trust, says of him, "He was a progressive of the Nineteenth
Century in economic matters and it was in economics that our troubles lay.
For their solution his progressivism, his New Deal, was pathetically in-
sufficient, which was why in 1944 he wanted it to be forgot." [2]

Tugwell's statement is obviously extreme, but there is ground for thinking
that the President was becoming progressively bored with his New Deal
program once his second election was assured. Both the novelty and the
honeymoon atmosphere were over. The Supreme Court had rejected the
N.R.A. as well as several other New Deal measures. The President had been
criticized in many quarters for his "court-packing" bill which had failed to
pass the Congress, in which his party had a large majority. While his popularity as a person continued high, the policies of himself and his advisers
were no longer accepted even by the Democrats as the inspired word.

An outstanding source of controversy, particularly in Roosevelt's second
term, was his labor program. Conservatives have sometimes referred to
Roosevelt's administrations as "a labor government," but this is only a half-
truth. The National Labor Relations Act, known as the Wagner Act was
passed in 1935, two years after the start of the New Deal. Roosevelt sought
the political support of organized labor, used the influences of the government to foster and maintain labor organizations, but never allowed himself
to be drawn into a position of subservience to the labor powers. The top
union leaders had ready access to the President, but they were not his personal intimates.

Perhaps his most liberal advance in the field of labor was the first wide
curtailment of child labor in the United States and this was a personal achievement of the President. His first step was to insist on prohibition of child
labor in the cotton code under the N.R.A., and he later obtained legislation
forbidding child labor in all enterprises engaged in interstate commerce.

The organization of labor in thousands of enterprises throughout the na-

[1] Sumner Welles, *Where Are We Heading?* p. 3.
[2] R. G. Tugwell, *The Stricken Land*, p. 681.

tion was accomplished largely through the activities of the National Labor Relations Board and other Labor boards which operated in a spirit of experimentalism that was typically Rooseveltian. F. V. Morley, a war labor board panel chairman who said, "I knew nothing whatever about government or labor relations and did not want to learn" has described the situation: [3]

All that a chairman of a National War Labor Board panel had to do in those early days was very simple—succeed or perish. That much was easy to understand. The rest was a little more difficult. What one was really called upon to exercise, without anybody knowing upon what authority, was judicial capacity, in a realm where there wasn't any law. I don't know how the other chairmen felt, for we were much too busy ever to see each other, but in many, many cases that I handled I was scared stiff. It might be a powder company, it might be surgical instruments; it might be the aircraft industry, or glass, or textiles, or furniture makers. It might be Insurance, it might be Laundries, it might be the Migratory Oil Drillers. It wasn't like any ordinary judicial career, because these were new problems, and there was no precedent whatever.

The organizations brought before these jurisdictions naturally did not regard them lightly, in fact were outraged and appalled at being the guinea pigs; yet this very casualness about serious matters was a characteristic which enabled the President to muddle through problems that would have been overpowering if undertaken in a heavy spirit. Better wages, shorter hours, minimum wage scales, organized bargaining, these were his goals, and to him the method was secondary if they were accomplished.

One further basic change in the national structure brought about by Mr. Roosevelt was the introduction of the government into the field of social security. Tugwell might be entitled to characterize this as nineteenth century liberalism on the basis that the idea was prevalent in the nineteenth century. Bismarck had established old-age pensions and similar provisions in Germany under the Kaiser as a sop to the growing unrest in that country. Similar measures had been advocated by the Socialist Party in America for many years. The Social Security Act which was passed in 1935 provided for unemployment compensation, old-age pensions and other social benefits.

It is difficult to know just when the President's interest began to veer away from the domestic scene, because the administration's army of publicists kept shouting the virtues of the program in a continuous roar.

Never before had government been so assiduously interpreted to the public. Every government department, board, and agency had its public relations specialists. At one time there were ninety men on the government's payroll specifically assigned to publicity for different branches and agencies, and there were a host of others who swelled the chorus.

Judge Samuel I. Rosenman, for example, compiled and edited the public papers and addresses of the President together with introductions and foot-

[3] F. V. Morley, *My One Contribution to Chess*, pp. 63, 68.

notes in a form which would provide an excellent campaign document. Throughout his various administrations the President reiterated justifications of his past activities. His introductions to the Rosenman volumes covering the years 1937, 1938, 1939 and 1940 were all signed between June 3 and July 17, 1941. They were an *ex post facto* formulation of the merits of the President's domestic policy but did not necessarily reflect his major current concerns as late as 1941.

Whether the President did or did not have a continuing preoccupation with the domestic reforms which he had established is pertinent only because of the transfer of his attention to the international scene and the change which that brought in the national policy of the United States.

2

Mrs. Roosevelt on looking back on the transition from the domestic to the world scene has said:[4]

While my husband was in Albany and for some years after coming to Washington, his chief interest was in seeing that the average human being was given a fairer chance for "life, liberty, and the pursuit of happiness." That was what made him always interested in the problems of minority groups and of any group which was at a disadvantage.

As the war clouds gathered and the inevitable involvement of this country became more evident, his objective was always to deal with the problems of the war, political and military, so that eventually an organization might be built to prevent future wars.

America in the twenty years following World War I, had become increasingly isolationist. A second world war had seemed impossible. One of the most popular songs had been "I Didn't Raise My Boy To Be A Soldier." Pacifism was actively taught in many classrooms. Only a minority regretted that the United States had declined to participate in the League of Nations. That minority was composed of individuals from various political parties. Franklin D. Roosevelt himself, addressing the Woodrow Wilson Foundation, said regarding the League, "We are not members and do not contemplate membership." Isolationists later were scorned as pro-German and anti-humanitarians, but for a long time isolation was the official policy of the government. In the early stages of the European war, American ships were not permitted to be armed for self-defense or to transport munitions. The Communist Party and varying degrees of leftist organizations sympathetic to it were isolationist until the Russian break with Germany.

Roosevelt and his administration had for a number of years been pacifistic isolationists. He advocated the joint resolution on neutrality which prohibited the export of arms to belligerent nations and also restricted the travel by American citizens on the ships of nations at war. In approving this measure

[4] Eleanor Roosevelt, "My Day," April 17, 1945.

in August 31, 1935, he said that it was "the fixed desire of the government and the people of the United States to avoid any action which might involve us in war . . . the policy of the government is definitely committed to the maintenance of peace and the avoidance of any entanglements which would lead us into conflict. At the same time it is the policy of the government by every peaceful means and without entanglement to cooperate with other similar minded governments to promote peace."

Commenting on this neutrality legislation the President said in an address at Chautauqua, N.Y., on August 14, 1936, "We can keep out of war if those who watch and decide have a sufficiently detailed understanding of international affairs to make certain that the small decisions of each day do not lead toward war and if, at the same time, they possess the courage to say 'no' to those who selfishly or unwisely would let us go to war."

The failure of the United States to participate in the League of Nations, the government's policy of neglecting national defense and its appeasement attitude toward Japan and Germany during the period 1933–1939 were again bringing about conditions similar to those which involved this country in World War I.[5] Like Wilson, Mr. Roosevelt addressed reproachful words to the belligerent nations, to which, of course, they did not give heed. At length, on July 14, 1939 the president sent a special message to Congress asking repeal of the arms embargo provision. The arms embargo was one of the few instances in which the President ever admitted error. "Although I approved this legislation when it was passed originally," he said, "and when it was extended from time to time, I have regretted my action." [6]

During the summer of 1940 the German army had swept across western Europe, and England was fighting desperately for survival. The President had obtained authorization for a two-ocean navy. His mind was directed to the possibility or probability of the United States' being drawn into the war. For weeks before the party convention he had refused to commit himself in respect to a third term, and also declined to suggest anyone as a possible successor. When he was renominated by acclamation his opponents were certain that he had arranged for events to turn out that way. Roosevelt himself in his acceptance speech affirmed that he was a tired man, that he had discharged his responsibilities to public office, and that only the complex and delicate condition of the country in respect to the war moved him to accept the demand to run again. He was re-elected by 55 per cent (54.68) of the popular vote.

The President still had the hope or at least pretended to hope that the country could keep out of war and yet determine the issues of the conflict by the use of economic power. The United States was to be the arsenal

[5] The President, however, urged the fortification of Guam and the building of a two-ocean Navy before many isolationists had changed their minds.
[6] *Public Papers*, vol. 8, p. xxxii.

of democracy. In his "Four Freedoms Address" to Congress on June 7, 1941 he affirmed that the national safety was "overwhelmingly involved in foreign events." He said that "our actions and our policy should be devoted primarily—almost exclusively to meeting the foreign peril." He affirmed that in the 1940 election "there was no substantial difference between the two great parties in respect to our refusal to acquiesce in a peace dictated by aggressors" and he went on to say "they do not need manpower."

He then put forth a picture of America as the producer and supplier for the democracies of the world and stated what he considered to be the "Four Essential Human Freedoms":

The first is freedom of speech and expression—everywhere in the world.

The second is freedom of every person to worship God in his own way—everywhere in the world.

The third is freedom from want—which, translated into world terms, means economic understandings which will secure to every nation a healthy peacetime life for its inhabitants—everywhere in the world.

The fourth is freedom from fear—which, translated into world terms, means a world-wide reduction of armaments to such a point and in such a thorough fashion that no nation will be in a position to commit an act of physical aggression against any neighbor—anywhere in the world.

That is no vision of a distant millennium. It is a definite basis for a kind of world attainable in our own time and generation. That kind of world is the very antithesis of the so-called new order of tyranny which the dictators seek to create with the crash of a bomb.

The policy of the Four Freedoms was further expounded in the so-called Atlantic Charter issued jointly by President Roosevelt and Prime Minister Winston Churchill on August 14, 1941 as "Common principles in the national policies of their respective countries." The Atlantic Charter may be regarded as the parent of the United Nations. Sumner Welles has said that it "represented the first major reversal of isolationist policy which the American people had been pursuing since the close of the First World War." In other words it was a return to Wilsonism. The essence of the Charter had been contained in the Fourteen Points. Whatever the future may hold, the United States at last had committed itself to the program which Wilson advocated. In this, Roosevelt's influence, of course, was paramount. The points of the Charter aimed high:

First, their countries seek no aggrandizement, territorial or other;

Second, they desire to see no territorial changes that do not accord with the freely expressed wishes of the peoples concerned;

Third, they respect the right of all peoples to choose the form of government under which they will live; and they wish to see sovereign rights and self-government restored to those who have been forcibly deprived of them;

Fourth, they will endeavor, with due respect for their existing obligations, to further the enjoyment by all States, great or small, victor or vanquished, of access, on equal terms, to the trade and to the raw materials of the world which are needed for their economic prosperity;

Fifth, they desire to bring about the fullest collaboration between all nations in the economic field with the object of securing, for all, improved labor standards, economic advancement and social security;

Sixth, after the final destruction of the Nazi tyranny, they hope to see established a peace which will afford to all nations the means of dwelling in safety within their own boundaries, and which will afford assurance that all the men in all the lands may live out their lives in freedom from fear and want;

Seventh, such a peace should enable all men to traverse the high seas and oceans without hindrance;

Eighth, they believe that all of the nations of the world, for realistic as well as spiritual reasons must come to the abandonment of the use of force. Since no future peace can be maintained if land, sea or air armaments continue to be employed by nations which threaten, or may threaten, aggression outside of their frontiers, they believe, pending the establishment of a wider and permanent system of general security, that the disarmament of such nations is essential. They will likewise aid and encourage all other practicable measures which will lighten for peace-loving peoples the crushing burden of armaments.

Viewed in the light of present events the world evidently has a long distance to go before it establishes all the principles of the Charter.

When Japan attacked Pearl Harbor on December 7, 1941, all doubt concerning the nation's active participation in the war was removed. Roosevelt, as Commander-in-chief, avoided many of Wilson's mistakes, and carried on with a tolerance to all shades of opinion that has rarely been seen in public office in time of war. Conscientious objectors were permitted to engage in useful tasks, in camps especially assigned to them, without the stigma of public disgrace. There was no shackling of political opponents. By appointing two eminent Republicans to the critical Cabinet posts of war and navy, the President gave national rather than party direction to the conflict. By naming two immigrants, William S. Knudsen and Sidney Hillman, to the War Production Board, he dramatized to first-generation Americans that the war was as much their affair as that of the native born. His recognition of Russia in 1933 had placed the United States in equal relationship with all the leading powers. His inclusion of the House and Senate Committees on Military and Naval Affairs in major conferences and commissions relating to the war both nationally and internationally, assured the participation of the legislative branches in the war- and peace-making councils.

In the early autumn of 1944, at the behest of President Roosevelt the United States, Great Britain, Russia, and later China, met at Dumbarton Oaks, Virginia, to formulate proposals for the United Nations organization. As Welles has pointed out, the United States made an error in not consulting the Latin American countries in advance, and recent revelations regarding the conferences of the great powers at Teheran and Yalta suggest that Roosevelt, Churchill and Stalin always expected to dominate any world-wide structure, while preserving the appearance of an internationally democratic body. This is not to suggest that the United Nations was or is a sham; but events have already demonstrated the difficulty of developing an effective and democratic international sovereignty. The more that fact is comprehended the greater may be the likelihood of a successful solution.

It seemed inevitable that Roosevelt would be renominated in 1944. If the public could take the hurdle of an unprecedented third term, a fourth term appeared a smaller obstacle. Moreover, he was so thoroughly involved in what were evidently the closing phases of the war, that a change seemed unlikely. Dewey, the Republican opponent, hammered on the slogan, "It's time for a change," but the public seemed to feel "Not quite yet."

The nature of the campaign displayed for the fourth time, in their quintessence, Roosevelt's gifts for popular leadership. He entertained Frank Sinatra and other stars of the radio, stage and screen. He cultivated popular writers. He complained bitterly that the bulk of the newspaper editors were against him, though a large share of the correspondents and columnists were close to the White House. They, and the headline writers, were with him. These were the minnesingers and troubadours of the people, and no other president had approached Roosevelt's wisdom in making sure of their support.

In spite of all this, Roosevelt did not have complete assurance of victory. The public customarily is resentful of the accompaniments of war, such as wage controls, shortages of fuel, food, housing and a host of other limitations. Moreover, the well-founded report was being circulated everywhere that the President was in bad health, and that to elect him might simply be to elect his vice-president. In reply to this, Mr. Roosevelt made perhaps the most gallant gesture of his career. To prove his physical capacity, he planned a tour of Greater New York. When the time came, there was a furious, driving rainstorm; but undaunted, the President made the entire trip in an open touring car. From that time on, there was little doubt of his victory, and he was re-elected for the fourth term by 53 per cent (53.31) of the popular vote.

A few months afterward on April 12, 1945, he died in office, deprived of the opportunity to demonstrate fully what he might or might not have accomplished toward world peace and reconstruction.

If the United Nations grows in prestige and power, and consistently directs itself to the achievements of the Four Freedoms, that will be President Roosevelt's chief monument. In that event, changes which he effected in national policy in time will be dimmed, for the new order will gradually become international in scope, and nationalism will become obsolete.

On national matters Roosevelt, and Wilson, specifically thought of the presidential office in terms of a particular style of liberalism, a liberalism of governmental control which Roosevelt summed up in these words—"As new conditions and problems arise beyond the power of men and women to meet as individuals, it becomes the duty of the Government itself to find new remedies with which to meet them. The liberal party insists that the Government has the definite duty to use all its power and resources to meet new social problems with new social controls."

The former things had passed away.

World War II had seared the mind of man until memory had the hardness and paralysis of a scar.

Even in prosperous America, financial opportunity was halved. A safe 6 per cent on savings had dropped to 3 per cent. Rainy-day bank accounts once adequate for comfortable old age could now provide a mere subsistence. The chance for rapid independent rise of the individual diminished as high taxation curtailed profits and savings.

In the Western Hemisphere few wept over the decline of possible fortune, for the average well-being, the average comfort, remained high. Yet over all was the cloud of the future and insecurity. In most countries undernourishment and disorganization prevailed.

Survival rather than comfort was the cardinal issue, for Cassandra carried jet rockets and an atomic bomb.

Yet the earth could support its people. The resources and the technology to do it were extant. Only peace and good will among men were needed for the fruition.

The American presidency more than any other office in the world's history had found the path of peace in crisis after crisis. It had made steady advances toward the union of nations.

Its influence may guide the world's future.

15

Trends Toward Tomorrow
(The End of the Presidency)

To the efficacy and permanency of your union a government for the whole is indispensable . . . an indissoluble community of one nation.

GEORGE WASHINGTON

The governments of the United Kingdom and the French Republic make this declaration of indissoluble union.

ANNOUNCEMENT BY BRITISH GOVERNMENT, June 16, 1940

Modern man is obsolete.

NORMAN COUSINS

I

The liberal tradition today is reputed in some quarters to be bankrupt. The very nature of reform causes it to go through cycles of apparent extinction. Where liberal measures of the moment succeed, the mission loses its newness, or where they fail it is discredited.

The confusion and change inherent in liberal politics, "tending in the direction of freedom or democracy," as Oxford defines it, are, however, signs of vitality. The liberal tradition in the presidency has been inconsistent, but its changeability has been realistic and hence resilient.

The form of the liberal tradition in the past has, we re-emphasize, been molded by the lives and temperaments of those occupying the White House, as fully as by the conditions of their times.

The nation might never have made a firm beginning under any other person than Washington. At the outset it could have been easily split by the stubbornness of an Adams, or could have fallen apart through the localism of a Jefferson.

Jefferson and Jackson are examples of how much personal experience and environment may affect the course of presidential policy. Each was a sizable planter in slaveholding parts of the country. Neither made strenuous efforts to free the black man. Jefferson was well-nigh hopeless in the face of the problem; and Jackson's liberal advisers were resentful of the Abolition movement, as distracting attention from other issues which they regarded as more important.

Conceivably, a strong Northern president at that period might have been able to start a program of liberation, as was under way in other countries. It is doubtful if any man likely to be elected during that time would have pursued a liberal policy toward the red man, as the white settlers were determined to clear the Indians away from the extending frontiers.

166

The value of pointing out how past leaders have been inconsistent with pure unalloyed liberalism lies not in the dimming of reputations, but in strengthening the belief that progress persists in spite of the inconsistencies of human nature. G. B. Shaw has even gone so far as to say that modern man tends to set his ideals impossibly high, thereby involves himself in hypocrisy, and because of the fog thus created, hampers his own progress. The point, of course, is debatable, for if the ideals were not projected all sense of direction might be lost.

To continue briefly with the might-have-beens: A weaker president than Lincoln could have allowed the Confederate states to depart in peace, thus committing the United States to a future like that of the Balkans. On the other hand, Thaddeus Stevens as president might have prosecuted the Civil War more quickly and more relentlessly, and destroyed the possibility of real national unity for many generations.

If President McKinley had not been assassinated, the trend of economic balances and public controls might have been diverted or delayed. The vigorous, ambitious personality of Theodore Roosevelt blasted away large segments of conservative opinion, and laid the groundwork for the extensive economic changes under Wilson and F. D. Roosevelt.

Substitute Champ Clark or Oscar Underwood for Woodrow Wilson, and Newton D. Baker for Franklin Roosevelt, and the whole world picture might be far different. Conceivably, the United States might have been in neither world war. All Europe, including Britain, might have been a German state.

Some may hold that events are inexorable, that whatever men have occupied the White House were predestined to be there. Even if this be true, at least we have reflected on whatever our destiny may have been, and we have noted the course along which the presidency has led the nation.

2

The trends for tomorrow are marked by certain clear signs. They point to future national policies on the one hand, and again to America's place in world affairs.

The United States for more than one hundred years' has continued, in the words of Washington, to offer "the fairest prospects for happiness and prosperity." Freedom and the democratic life were accepted as the guiding principles from the beginning. Compared with most of the rest of the world the people of America have the best living standards and best opportunities. In considering the liberal trend of the future therefore, we are thinking in terms of degree, starting ahead of the experience of most of mankind beyond America's borders.

There may be a more widely democratic status in Switzerland and the Scandinavian countries, more peace of mind in the philosophic people of Guatemala (or other non-industrial areas); but this does not solve the problems of so diversified and complicated a country as the United States.

The battleground on the economic front for the next generation, unless interrupted by war, will be between divergent concepts of liberalism. The outlook for probable solutions, fair to the interests of society as a whole, is more encouraging than in past eras, since in the past quarter century the fallacies of various sides have been brought out through vigorous debate. Trials of strength have proved that no single school of thought, no particular body of citizens, can dominate over the whole.

The nineteenth century liberals, following Adam Smith, spoke for the free market and free enterprise and opposed government controls or interference. The function of government, under that theory, was merely to be a police power restraining citizens from injuring one another and protecting against injury from outside sources. This phase of liberal doctrine released great energies, developed the material wealth of the country and created mass opportunities.

The rise of nationalism, however, and the development of huge concentrations of machinery, capital and control made the theory unrealistic. Where there are tariff walls, the free market no longer exists on a world-wide basis. Where there is rate-setting by large privately controlled units, the public retains some element of the free market through the avenue of refusing to buy. Where there is rate-setting by state or federal control, as in the case of railroad rates and public utility charges, the free-market virtually has vanished.

In the field of enterprise, when large concentrations of power developed through the control of capital and machinery, it was logical for the government to attempt to counter-balance the situation by government controls and by encouraging concentrations of power in industrial and trade unions. The Socialist theory, which never won wide acceptance in the United States, held that the solution was for the government to own and operate all the means of production.

Experience has demonstrated that the clash between the powerful opposing groups creates danger to each and causes wide public suffering. The liberal purpose of the future will be to protect as far as possible the rights of all groups to operate freely without the conferring of special privileges upon any. All must have equal rights before the law. That, of course, is easier said than done. The presidency for nearly a half century has accepted the role of economic mediator, and often has sought it. The government, in short, has become an advisory consultant on management, often with power to act.

There is a growing disposition on the part of most groups to recognize the indispensability of government as a common meeting ground for the solution of national economic affairs, and, whether welcome or not, that will probably be the future course. The necessity for reaching solutions tends steadily to diminish angers and frictions within the national framework and to give promise of a gradually improving society.

3

The opportunity for a gradually improving nation, however, assumes that it is progressing in the midst of a calm and comfortable world. That was the broad, general assumption in the United States in 1912, just before World War I. Today, the American public recognizes that it cannot be independent of world conditions. Because of the atom bomb, "modern man is obsolete," as Norman Cousins has put it. The liberal tradition, if followed, leads logically to international sovereignty and the end of the presidency.

That is the logical course, but not necessarily the inevitable course of destiny. Nor is the alternative inescapably the destruction of the world. Long ago, the Western nations grasped the warfare potentials of the discovery of gunpowder. Coupling this with the gift for organization, they soon subjugated the rest of the world to their purposes.

For America, however, to embark on a course of imperial domination would be to turn back on its tradition.

While the United States does have the record of having wrested its frontiers from the red man, while only lately in its history has it concerned itself with economic justice to all races within its borders, its over-all commitment to freedom would hardly permit the country rapidly to embark on a program of world conquest. And such a plan would need to be effected rapidly, if it were to be successful.

On the contrary, in spite of a so-called isolation policy through most of its history, the presidency has consistently led the country toward the conclusion of a world state, in which each nation ultimately would surrender its sovereignty to an international government.

Washington, of all the presidents, talked the most about the dangers of foreign alliances, a different matter from international government. He also presented the broadest testament for a sovereign government embracing the span of a continent. His arguments for an indissoluble union would serve in many respects as a program for the United Nations when the time comes to draw up its permanent constitution.

Here was a new country, made up of thirteen colonies, free of all tariff walls, united for mutual security and mutual growth, united by a common body of law, including a Bill of Rights. There were jealousies and economic conflicts, but Washington pointed out how union strengthened rather than superseded local interests. The situation in many particulars was not parallel to the present, but the principles have had a continuing vitality.

Though Jefferson repeatedly championed state sovereignty and thereby weakened the national prestige, when in the presidency he delivered one of the most forceful arguments for the general government. "I believe this . . . the strongest government on earth," he said in his first Inaugural. "I believe it the only one where every man, in the cause of the law, would fly to the standard of the law, and would meet invasions of the public order as his own personal concern."

As we have seen, it remained for Jackson and Lincoln to reaffirm and re-establish the validity and endurance of the national constitution beyond further dispute.

The United States, however, by no means stayed within its continental boundaries, despite its supposed isolationism. The Monroe Doctrine has been referred to in previous chapters. From the day that Monroe proclaimed that the extension of European power in the western hemisphere would be re-garded as an unfriendly attitude toward the United States, the country was headed toward a united nations' policy embracing half the globe. As we have seen, other presidents invoked the principle in the discussion of specific events. Cleveland claimed the right to interfere as a mediator between Venezuela and England, and affirmed the Doctrine as a part of international law. Theodore Roosevelt interpreted the Doctrine as a mutual principle which the Latin republics might appeal to on their own initiative. He pledged that the United States would not use the Doctrine for territorial aggrandizement. Thereby the United States distinguished between imperial policy and its desire to act as part of a western family of nations.

Wilson strengthened this attitude by accepting mediation of three Latin American republics in one of his disputes with Mexico. The good faith of the United States in its western hemisphere attitude was further demon-strated in World War I. German government documents, ultimately seized and made public, revealed that Germany had counted on the United States' grasping the obvious opportunity to take possession of Canada and Mexico. The United States, of course, was so far from imperial intent that such a project was never even in the public consciousness. A large section of the American public was always critical of the United States' position in the Philippines, and their return to self-government is another evidence of Ameri-can nonimperialism.

The extension of the Monroe Doctrine, however, on the basis of hemisphere security was a logical precursor to the League of Nations, and more. Wash-ington's indissoluble union was a preparation for the idea of indissoluble hemisphere security. That in turn helped to make acceptable an indissoluble world union, of which the League of Nations might have been the feeble beginning.

As Emery Reves and many others have pointed out, the intrinsic fault of the League of Nations, or of any similar group, lies in its being a collection of sovereign states. Alliances and treaties fall apart when national interests interfere. The idea of a league, *per se,* has fallen apart repeatedly through the retention of national sovereignty. The Holy Alliance of 1815 was composed of powers presumably strong enough to enforce the peace of the world, but it was soon dissolved.

The failure of the League of Nations perhaps was inevitable, even if the United States had been a participant. Nevertheless, there was a disposition at that time at least to modify national sovereignty in the interest of world security. William Howard Taft had been prepared to submit even questions of national honor to arbitration, and Wilson was disposed to go a long distance toward international government and international law, but lacked the necessary persuasiveness. Possibly no one of his time could have done otherwise, for the war intensified the emotion of nationalism, even while it pointed to the need for international unity.

The international ideal obviously did not die. The Atlantic Charter and the United Nations to date continue to have the weakness, from the international government standpoint, of retaining national sovereignty.[1]

A beginning, however, must be made somewhere. There can be obviously no loyalty to a vacuum. The Continental Congress and the Articles of Confederation were weak beginnings, but were necessary demonstrations to the American people that a strong central government with a common body of law was essential to survival.

Such departures from accepted habits of thought come only under strong pressures, but the departures and the pressures have been accumulating. At the peak of the German advance in World War II, Britain offered an indissoluble union with France, not simply an alliance; but it was too late, too late to serve at that particular time.

The obstacles to the establishing of a world government obviously are huge, but less so than at any prior time in history. It is not the function of this book to argue that case on either side, but to observe the course of liberal tradition in the presidency, a course which seems to be leading to the end of the presidency as we presently conceive it. Hamilton Holt has said, "The one way for a man to rise above the presidency of the United States is to ascend into the international realm and there work for peace through justice." That is the trend.

•The trend of a nonimperial, democratic state must be toward a world democracy under a common body of law, under which each country is willing to sacrifice its national sovereignty. Under the permanent constitution of the United Nations, or under some world sovereignty not many years distant, the United States may become a participating power in the common enterprise, having limited reserved rights, but subordinate to a general world government. The prospect need not be too fearful, for the loyalties are not necessarily mutually exclusive. No American citizen need have a lesser pride in his home town or in his state because of his primary loyalty to his country, or less love for his country if it becomes part of an international state.

When and if the transition comes, the presidency will cease to be the high-

---

[1] The case for world government is exhaustively and brilliantly stated in Emery Reves, *The Anatomy of Peace.*

est office in the American consciousness. It will be secondary to some international head, comparable to a governorship.

4

The body of law of any world state obviously must be based upon the moral law for all people and reflect their desires to have such law and to observe it. No exterior charter for the world or for the village can save man against himself. As Reves has observed, the effectiveness of the Bill of Rights implies the acceptance of the Ten Commandments.

The fact that there is a hope for an ever improving form of government for the world assumes a belief that the state was made for man, not man for the state. It regards individual man, in the words of the Psalmist, as a little lower than the angels and crowned with glory and honor.

Whether the presidency and the people accept or reject the logic of the liberal tradition as presented here, they can not escape far-reaching change in this our time. The words of Abraham Lincoln come back hauntingly—"The dogmas of the quiet past are inadequate to the stormy present . . . we must disenthrall ourselves, and then we shall save our country."

And the world.

Appendix

Herewith are presented documents bearing on particular points in the preceding chapters. Some of these documents, such as the *Notes on the State of Virginia* excerpts and the *Specie Circular*, are available in only a few libraries. No documents are quoted for presidents after Theodore Roosevelt because of the greater availability of public records since that time.

The selections on the following pages include:

1. *George Washington,* from First Annual Address: comment on defense; manufactures and public education in relation to freedom.
2. *George Washington,* from Farewell Address: his relation to the public; thorough exposition of union; national sovereignty compared to state sovereignty; implications of consent of the governed; policy toward other nations; government by law.
3. *Kentucky Resolutions of 1799,* inspired by Jefferson and Madison, affirming state sovereignty.
4. *Thomas Jefferson,* from First Inaugural: in a mood of national unity; government based on law; its limits of jurisdiction; essential principles of the Republic.
5. *Thomas Jefferson,* from *Notes on the State of Virginia,* Query XIV: views on slavery and the colored people; colonization; speculations on their inferiority; on their capacities; difficulty of assimilation.
6. *Thomas Jefferson,* from *Notes on the State of Virginia,* Query XIX: on industry and on city labor; against manufactures; values of a rural economy; degeneracy of city workmen.
7. *James Monroe,* on the Monroe Doctrine, from Seventh Annual Message to Congress.
8. *Andrew Jackson,* on Bank of the United States, from First Annual Message to Congress: hazards of monopoly; president may make his own interpretation of Constitution; attack on the financial interests.
9. *Andrew Jackson,* on the Indians, from various messages to Congress: progressive stages in proposing the extinction of the red man.
10. *Andrew Jackson,* on national sovereignty, from message of January 16, 1833, and proclamation of December 10, 1832: thoroughly reasoned treatise on the liberal necessity of national authority, paralleling the arguments of Washington.
11. *Specie Circular,* often noted and seldom quoted, a document issued by the Treasury Department, July 11, 1836, at the instance of Jackson and effectuated under Van Buren. Calls for payment for public lands in hard cash.
12. *Martin Van Buren,* on noninterference by government, from Special Session Message, September 4, 1837: a manifesto of nineteenth century liberalism, proclaiming that government should neither interfere in private businesses, nor provide relief for them in distress.

13. *Abraham Lincoln,* on proposal to purchase slaves. Note: His Second Annual Message to Congress, December 1, 1862, was his last appeal before the enforced Emancipation Proclamation went into effect.

14. *Andrew Johnson,* on restoration of the Union, from First Annual Message to Congress: "with malice toward none" the national policy.

15. *Andrew Johnson,* on Reconstruction, from various veto messages: the hazards of military rule and "reform" exposed.

16. *Grover Cleveland,* on the Monroe Doctrine, from Special Messages to Congress: invokes it as international law.

17. *Theodore Roosevelt,* on Monroe Doctrine, from Fifth Annual Message, December 5, 1905: all American republics may invoke it; the United States pledges "no territorial aggressions."

18. *Theodore Roosevelt,* on International Peace, from Fifth Annual Message, December 5, 1905: participation in Hague Conferences; limited agreement to arbitrate.

1. Washington on Defense, Manufactures, and Public Education

From First Annual Message to Congress, January 8, 1790

To be prepared for war is one of the most effectual means of preserving peace.

A free people ought not only to be armed, but disciplined; to which end a uniform and well-digested plan is requisite; and their safety and interest require that they should promote such manufactories as tend to render them independent of others for essential, particularly military, supplies. . . .

Knowledge is in every country the surest basis of public happiness. In one in which the measures of government receive their impressions so immediately from the sense of the community as in ours it is proportionably essential. To the security of a free constitution it contributes in various ways—by convincing those who are intrusted with the public administration that every valuable end of government is best answered by the enlightened confidence of the people, and by teaching the people themselves to know and to value their own rights; to discern and provide against invasions of them; to distinguish between oppression and the necessary exercise of lawful authority; between burthens proceeding from a disregard to their convenience and those resulting from the inevitable exigencies of society; to discriminate the spirit of liberty from that of licentiousness—cherishing the first, avoiding the last—and uniting a speedy but temperate vigilance against encroachments, with an inviolable respect to the laws.

2. George Washington's Farewell Address
September 17, 1796

It appears to me proper, especially as it may conduce to a more *distinct expression of the public voice,* that I should now apprise you of the resolution I have formed to decline being considered among the number of those out of whom a choice is to be made. . . .

In the discharge of this trust I will only say that I have, with good intentions, contributed toward the organization and administration of the Government the best exertions of *which a very fallible judgment was capable.* Not unconscious in the outset of the inferiority of my qualifications, experience in my own eyes, perhaps still more in the eyes of others, has strengthened the motives to diffidence of myself; and every day the increasing weight of years admonishes me more and more that the shade of retirement is as necessary to me as it will be welcome. Satisfied that if any circumstances have given peculiar value to my services they were temporary, I have the consolation to believe that, while choice and prudence invite me to quit the political scene, patriotism does not forbid it. . . .

UNION ESSENTIAL TO INDEPENDENCE [1]

The *unity of government* which constitutes you one people is also now dear to you. It is justly so, for it is a *main pillar in the edifice of your real independence,* the support of your tranquillity at home, your peace abroad, of your safety, of your prosperity, of that very liberty which you so highly prize. But as it is easy to foresee that from different causes and from different quarters much pains will be taken, many artifices employed, to weaken in your minds the conviction of this truth, as this is the point in your political fortress against which the batteries of internal and external enemies will be most constantly and actively (though often covertly and insidiously) directed, it is of infinite moment that you should properly estimate the immense value of your national union to your collective and individual happiness. . . .

MUTUAL INTERESTS OF DIFFERENT SECTIONS

The North, in an unrestrained intercourse with the South, protected by the equal laws of a common government, finds in the productions of the latter great additional resources of maritime and commercial enterprise and precious materials of manufacturing industry.

The South, in the same intercourse, benefiting by the same agency of the North, sees its agriculture grow and its commerce expand. Turning partly into its own channels the seamen of the North, it finds its particular navigation invigorated; and while it contributes in different ways to nourish and increase the general mass of the national navigation, it looks forward to the protection of a maritime strength to which itself is unequally adapted.

The East, in a like intercourse with the West, already finds, and in the progressive improvement of interior communications by land and water will more and more find, a valuable vent for the commodities which it brings from abroad or manufactures at home.

The West derives from the East supplies requisite to its growth and comfort, and what is perhaps of still greater consequence, it must of necessity owe the secure enjoyment of indispensable outlets for its own productions to the weight, influence, and the future maritime strength of the Atlantic side of the Union, directed by an indissoluble community of interests as one nation. Any other tenure by which the West can hold this essential advantage, whether derived from its

[1] Subheadings added by the author.

own separate strength or from an apostate and unnatural connection with any foreign power, must be intrinsically precarious. . . .

MILITARY DANGERS

Hence, likewise, they will avoid the necessity of those overgrown military establishments which, under any form of government, are inauspicious to liberty, and which are to be regarded as particularly hostile to republican liberty. In this sense it is that your union ought to be considered as a main prop of your liberty, and that the love of the one ought to endear to you the preservation of the other. . . .

In contemplating the causes which may disturb our union it occurs as matter of serious concern that any ground should have been furnished for characterizing parties by geographical discriminations—Northern and Southern, Atlantic and Western—whence designing men may endeavor to excite a belief that there is a real difference of local interests and views. One of the expedients of party to acquire influence within particular districts is to misrepresent the opinions and aims of other districts. You can not shield yourselves too much against the jealousies and heartburnings which spring from these misrepresentations. . . .

CENTRAL GOVERNMENT INDISPENSABLE

To the efficacy and permanency of your *union a government for the whole is indispensable.* . . . Respect for its authority, compliance with its laws, acquiescence in its measures, are duties enjoined by the fundamental maxims of true liberty. The basis of our political systems is the right of the people to make and to alter their constitutions of government. But the constitution which at any time exists till changed by an explicit and authentic act of the whole people is sacredly obligatory upon all. The very idea of the power and the right of the people to establish government presupposes the duty of every individual to obey the established government. . . .

VALUE OF ESTABLISHING A TRADITION

Toward the preservation of your Government and the permanency of your present happy state, it is requisite not only that you steadily discountenance irregular oppositions to its acknowledged authority, but also that you resist *with care the spirit of innovation upon its principles, however specious the pretexts.* One method of assault may be to effect in the forms of the Constitution alterations which will impair the energy of the system, and thus to undermine what can not be directly overthrown. In all the changes to which you may be invited remember that time and habit are at least as necessary to fix the true character of governments as of other human institutions. . . .

PERILS OF DICTATORSHIP

The alternate domination of one faction over another, sharpened by the spirit of revenge natural to party dissension, which in different ages and countries has perpetrated the most horrid enormities, is itself a frightful despotism. But this leads at length to a more formal and permanent despotism. The disorders and miseries which result gradually incline the minds of men to seek security and repose in the absolute power of an individual, and sooner or later the chief of some prevailing faction, more able or more fortunate than his competitors, turns this disposition to the purposes of his own elevation on the ruins of public liberty. . . .

RELIGION AS A PILLAR OF LIBERTY

Of all the dispositions and habits which lead to political prosperity, religion and morality are indispensable supports. In vain would that man claim the tribute of patriotism who should labor to subvert these great pillars of human happiness —these firmest props of the duties of men and citizens. The mere politician, equally with the pious man, ought to respect and to cherish them. A volume could not trace all their connections with private and public felicity. Let it simply be asked, Where is the security for property, for reputation, for life, if the sense of religious obligation desert the oaths which are the instruments of investigation in courts of justice? And let us with caution indulge the supposition that morality can be maintained without religion. Whatever may be conceded to the influence of refined education on minds of peculiar structure, reason and experience both forbid us to expect that national morality can prevail in exclusion of religious principle. . . .

PRINCIPLES IN FOREIGN RELATIONS [2]

The great rule of conduct for us in regard to foreign nations is, in extending our commercial relations to have with them as little political connection as possible. So far as we have already formed engagements let them be fulfilled with perfect good faith. Here let us stop.

Europe has a set of primary interests which to us have none or a very remote relation. Hence she must be engaged in frequent controversies, the causes of which are essentially foreign to our concerns. Hence, therefore, it must be unwise in us to implicate ourselves by artificial ties in the ordinary vicissitudes of her politics or the ordinary combinations and collisions of her friendships or enmities.

Our detached and distant situation invites and enables us to pursue a different course. If we remain one people, under an efficient government, the period is not far off when we may defy material injury from external annoyance; when we may take such an attitude as will cause the neutrality we may at any time resolve upon to be scrupulously respected; when belligerent nations, under the impossibility of making acquisitions upon us, will not lightly hazard the giving us provocation; when we may choose peace or war, as our interest, guided by justice, shall counsel.

Why forego the advantages of so peculiar a situation? Why quit our own to stand upon foreign ground? Why, by interweaving our destiny with that of any part of Europe, entangle our peace and prosperity in the toils of European ambition, rivalship, interest, humor, or caprice?

Is it our true policy to steer clear of permanent alliances with any portion of the foreign world, so far, I mean, as we are now at liberty to do it; for let me not be understood as capable of patronizing infidelity to existing engagements. I hold the maxim no less applicable to public than to private affairs that honesty is always

[2] See chapters 1 and 2 for author's comment on Washington's world policies.

the best policy. I repeat, therefore, let those engagements be observed in their genuine sense. But in my opinion it is unnecessary and would be unwise to extend them.

Taking care always to keep ourselves by suitable establishments on a respectable defensive posture, we may safely trust to temporary alliances for extraordinary emergencies.

BEWARE FAVORED NATIONS CLAUSES

Harmony, liberal intercourse with all nations are recommended by policy, humanity, and interest. But even our commercial policy should hold an equal and impartial hand, neither seeking nor granting exclusive favors or preferences; consulting the natural course of things; diffusing and diversifying by gentle means the streams of commerce, but forcing nothing; establishing with powers so disposed, in order to give trade a stable course, to define the rights of our merchants, and to enable the Government to support them, conventional rules of intercourse, the best that present circumstances and mutual opinion will permit, but temporary and liable to be from time to time abandoned or varied as experience and circumstances shall dictate; constantly keeping in view that it is folly in one nation to look for disinterested favors from another; that it must pay with a portion of its independence for whatever it may accept under that character; that by such acceptance it may place itself in the condition of having given equivalents for nominal favors, and yet of being reproached with ingratitude for not giving more. There can be no greater error than to expect or calculate upon real favors from nation to nation. It is an illusion which experience must cure, which a just pride ought to discard. . . .

BENEFIT OF GOOD LAWS

I anticipate with pleasing expectation that retreat in which I promise myself to realize without alloy the sweet enjoyment of partaking in the midst of my fellow-citizens the benign influence of good laws under a free government—the ever-favorite object of my heart, and the happy reward, as I trust, of our mutual cares, labors, and dangers.

3. The Kentucky Resolutions of 1799

Following a preamble the Kentucky Legislature resolved, February 22, 1799, on the broad subject of state sovereignty:

Resolved, That this commonwealth considers the federal Union, upon the terms and for the purposes specified in the late compact, conducive to the liberty and happiness of the several states:

That it does now unequivocally declare its attachment to the Union, and to that compact, agreeably to its obvious and real intention, and will be among the last to seek its dissolution:

That if those who administer the general government be permitted to transgress the limits fixed by that compact, by a total disregard to the special delegations of power therein contained, an annihilation of the state governments, and the creation upon their ruins of a general consolidated government, will be the inevitable consequence:

That the principle and construction contended for by sundry of the state legislatures, that the general government is the exclusive judge of the extent of the powers delegated to it, stop not short of despotism—since the discretion of those who administer the government, and not the Constitution, would be the measure of their powers:

That the several states who formed that instrument being sovereign and independent, have the unquestionable right to judge of the infraction; and, That a nullification of those sovereignties, of all unauthorized acts done under color of that instrument is the rightful remedy:

That this commonwealth does, under the most deliberate reconsideration, declare, that the said Alien and Sedition Laws are, in their opinion, palpable violations of the said Constitution; and, however cheerfully it may be disposed to surrender its opinion to a majority of its sister states, in matters of ordinary or doubtful policy, yet, in momentous regulations like the present, which so vitally wound the best rights of the citizen, it would consider a silent acquiescence as highly criminal:

That although this commonwealth, as a party to the federal compact, will bow to the laws of the Union, yet, it does, at the same time declare, that it will not now, or ever hereafter, cease to oppose in a constitutional manner, every attempt at what quarter soever offered, to violate that compact.

And, finally, in order that no pretext or arguments may be drawn from a supposed acquiescence, on the part of this commonwealth in the constitutionality of those laws, and be thereby used as precedents for similar future violations of the federal compact—this commonwealth does now enter against them its solemn PROTEST.

4. From Jefferson's First Inaugural Address, March 4, 1801

[In this address Jefferson aimed to conciliate all factions. Throughout his presidency he minimized his fears of the general government and tempered his zeal for states' rights. For detailed analysis of the address, see Henry Adams: *The History of the United States under Thomas Jefferson,* Vol. I.]

NATION NOT DIVIDED ON PRINCIPLES [8]

During the contest of opinion through which we have passed the animation of discussions and of exertions has sometimes worn an aspect which might impose on strangers unused to think freely and to speak and to write what they think; but this being now decided by the voice of the nation, announced according to the rules of the Constitution, all will, of course, arrange themselves under the will of the law, and unite in common efforts for the common good.

All, too, will bear in mind this sacred principle, that though the will of the majority is in all cases to prevail, that will to be rightful must be reasonable; that

[8] Subheadings added by the author.

the minority possess their equal rights, which equal law must protect, and to violate which would be oppression.

Let us, then, fellow-citizens, unite with one heart and one mind. Let us restore to social intercourse that harmony and affection without which liberty and even life itself are but dreary things.

And let us reflect that, having banished from our land that religious intolerance under which mankind so long bled and suffered, we have yet gained little if we countenance a political intolerance as despotic, as wicked, and capable of as bitter and bloody persecutions.

During the throes and convulsions of the ancient world, during the agonizing spasms of infuriated man, seeking through blood and slaughter his long-lost liberty, it was not wonderful that the agitation of the billows should reach even this distant and peaceful shore; that this should be more felt and feared by some and less by others, and should divide opinions as to measures of safety.

But every difference of opinion is not a difference of principle. We have called by different names brethren of the same principle. We are all Republicans, we are all Federalists. . . .

GOVERNMENT STRONGEST, BECAUSE BASED ON LAW

If there be any among us who would wish to dissolve this Union or to change its republican form, let them stand undisturbed as monuments of the safety with which error of opinion may be tolerated where reason is left free to combat it. I know, indeed, that some honest men fear that a republican government can not be strong, that this Government is not strong enough; but would the honest patriot, in the full tide of successful experiment, abandon a government which has so far kept us free and firm on the theoretic and visionary fear that this Government, the world's best hope, may by possibility want energy to preserve itself? I trust not.

I believe this, on the contrary, the strongest Government on earth. I believe it the only one where every man, at the call of the law, would fly to the standard of the law, and would meet invasions of the public order as his own personal concern. . . .

Let us, then, with courage and confidence pursue our own Federal and Republican principles, our attachment to union and representative government.

LIMITATIONS ON GOVERNMENT

Still one thing more, fellow-citizens—a wise and frugal Government, which shall restrain men from injuring one another, shall leave them otherwise free to regulate their own pursuits of industry and improvement, and shall not take from the mouth of labor the bread it has earned. This is the sum of good government, and this is necessary to close the circle of our felicities.

ESSENTIAL PRINCIPLES OF THE REPUBLIC

About to enter, fellow-citizens, on the exercise of duties which comprehend everything dear and valuable to you, it is proper you should understand what I deem the essential principles of our Government, and consequently those which ought to shape its Administration. I will compress them within the narrowest compass they will bear, stating the general principle, but not all its limitations.

Equal and exact justice to all men, of whatever state or persuasion, religious or political;

Peace, commerce, and honest friendship with all nations, entangling alliances with none;

The support of the State governments in all their rights, as the most competent administrations for our domestic concerns and the surest bulwarks against anti-republican tendencies;

The preservation of the General Government in its whole constitutional vigor, as the sheet anchor of our peace at home and safety abroad;

A jealous care of the right of election by the people—a mild and safe corrective of abuses which are lopped by the sword of revolution where peaceable remedies are unprovided;

Absolute acquiescence in the decisions of the majority, the vital principle of republics, from which is no appeal but to force, the vital principle and immediate parent of despotism;

A well-disciplined militia, our best reliance in peace and for the first moments of war, till regulars may relieve them;

The supremacy of the civil over the military authority;

Economy in the public expense, that labor may be lightly burthened;

The honest payment of our debts and sacred preservation of the public faith; encouragement of agriculture, and of commerce as its handmaid;

The diffusion of information and arraignment of all abuses at the bar of the public reason; freedom of religion;

Freedom of the press, and freedom of person under the protection of the habeas corpus, and trial by juries impartially selected.

These principles form the bright constellation which has gone before us and guided our steps through an age of revolution and reformation.

5. Jefferson's *Notes on the State of Virginia*

[Jefferson's *Notes on the State of Virginia,* written in his early days, were by his own admission his only systematic comment on a state of government. These notes were written in reply to a series of queries by an overseas friend. In the observations on Query XIV Jefferson showed himself to be fully immersed in the economy of the slavery system despite a few remote suggestions as to ultimate change.]

Query XIV—On Slavery

The administration of justice and the description of the laws?

If any free person commit an offence against the commonwealth, if it be below the degree of felony, he is bound by a justice to appear before their court, to answer it on indictment or information. If it amount to felony, he is committed to jail; a court of these justices is called; if they on examination think him guilty, they send him to the jail of the general court, before which court he is to be tried first by a grand jury of 24, of whom 13 must concur in opinion; if they find him guilty, he is then tried by a jury of 12 men of the county where the offence was committed, and by their verdict, which must be unanimous, he is acquitted or condemned without appeal. If the criminal be a slave, the trial by a county court is final. In every case, however, except that of high treason, there resides in the governor a power of pardon. . . .

Slaves, as well as lands, were entailable during the monarchy: but, by an act of the first republican assembly, all donees in tail, present and future, were vested with the absolute dominion of the entailed subject. . . .

Many of the laws which were in force during the monarchy being relative merely to that form of government, or inculcating principles inconsistent with republicanism, the first assembly which met after the establishment of the commonwealth appointed a committee to revise the whole code, to reduce it into proper form and volume, and report it to the assembly. . . .

The following are the most remarkable alterations proposed:

To make slaves distributable among the next of kin, as other moveables. . . .

PROPOSAL TO COLONIZE SLAVES [4]

To emancipate all slaves born after passing the act. The bill reported by the revisors does not itself contain this proposition; but an amendment containing it was prepared, to be offered to the legislature whenever the bill should be taken up, and further directing, that they should continue with their parents to a certain age, then be brought up, at the public expence, to tillage, arts or sciences, according to their geniuses, till the females should be eighteen, and the males twenty-one years of age, when they should be colonized to such place as the circumstances of the time should render most proper, sending them out with arms, implements of household and of the handicraft arts, seeds, pairs of the useful domestic animals, &c. to declare them a free and independent people, and extend to them our alliance and protection, till they have acquired strength; and to send vessels at the same time to other parts of the world for an equal number of white inhabitants; to induce whom to migrate hither, proper encouragements were to be proposed.

"DISTINCTIONS WHICH NATURE HAS MADE"

It will probably be asked, why not retain and incorporate the blacks into the state, and thus save the expence of supplying by importation of white settlers, the vacancies they will leave? Deep rooted prejudices entertained by the whites; ten thousand recollections, by the blacks, of the injuries they have sustained; new provocations; the real distinctions which nature has made; and many other circumstances, will divide us into parties, and produce convulsions, which will probably never end but in the extermination of the one or the other race. . . .

To these objections, which are political, may be added others, which are physical and moral. The first difference which strikes us is that of color. Whether the black of the negro resides in the reticular membrane between the skin and scarf-skin, or in the scarf-skin itself; whether it proceeds from the color of the blood, the color of the bile, or from that of some other secretion, the difference is fixed in nature, and is as real as if its seat and cause were better known to us.

And is this difference of no importance? Is it not the foundation of a greater or less share of beauty in the two races? Are not the fine mixtures of red and white, the expressions of every passion by greater or less suffusions of color in

[4] Subheadings added by the author.

the one, preferable to that eternal monotony, which reigns in the countenances, that immoveable veil of black which covers all the emotions of the other race? Add to these, flowing hair, a more elegant symmetre of form, their own judgment in favor of the whites, declared by their preference of them, as uniformly as is the preference of the Oranootan for the black women over those of his own species.

ODOR OF WHITES AND COLORED

The circumstance of superior beauty, is thought worthy attention in the propagation of our horses, dogs, and other domestic animals; why not in that of man? Besides those of color, figure, and hair, there are other physical distinctions proving a difference of race. They have less hair on the face and body. They secrete less by the kidnies, and more by the glands of the skin, which gives them a very strong and disagreeable odour. This greater degree of transpiration renders them more tolerant of heat, and less so of cold than the whites. Perhaps too a difference of structure in the pulmonary apparatus, which a late ingenious [a] experimentalist has discovered to be the principal regulator of animal heat, may have disabled them from extricating, in the act of inspiration, so much of that fluid from the outer air, or obliged them in expiration, to part with more of it.

NEGROES NEED LESS SLEEP

They seem to require less sleep. A black after hard labor through the day, will be induced by the slightest amusements to sit up till midnight, or later, though knowing he must be out with the first dawn of the morning. They are at least as brave, and more adventuresome. But this may perhaps proceed from want of forethought, which prevents their seeing a danger till it be present. When present, they do not go through it with more coolness or steadiness than the whites.

MORE ARDENT

They are more ardent after their female: but love seems with them to be more an eager desire, than a tender, delicate mixture of sentiment and sensation. Their griefs are transient. Those numberless afflictions, which render it doubtful whether heaven has given life to us in mercy or in wrath, are less felt and sooner forgotten with them. In general, their existence appears to participate more of sensation than reflection. To this must be ascribed their disposition to sleep when abstracted from their diversions, and unemployed in labor. An animal whose body is at rest, and who does not reflect, must be disposed to sleep of course.

EQUAL MEMORY, LESS REASON

Comparing them by their faculties of memory, reason and imagination, it appears to me that in memory they are equal to the whites; in reason much inferior, as I think one could scarcely be found capable of tracing and comprehending the investigations of Euclid; and that in imagination they are dull, tasteless, and anomalous.

It would be unfair to follow them to Africa for this investigation. We will consider them here, on the same stage with the whites, and where the facts are

[a] Crawford.

not apocryphal on which a judgment is to be formed. It will be right to make great allowances for the difference of condition, of education, of conversation, of the sphere in which they move.

Many millions of them have been brought to and born in America. Most of them indeed have been confined to tillage, to their own homes, and their own society: yet many have been so situated, that they might have availed themselves of the conversation of their masters; many have been brought up to the handicraft arts, and from that circumstance have always been associated with the whites. Some have been liberally educated, and all have lived in countries where the arts and sciences are cultivated to a considerable degree, and have had before their eyes samples of the best works from abroad. . . .

INDIANS COMPARED WITH NEGROES

The Indians, with no advantages of this kind, will often carve figures on their pipes not destitute of design and merit. They will crayon out an animal, a plant, or a country, so as to prove the existence of a germ in their minds which only wants cultivation. They astonish you with strokes of the most sublime oratory; such as prove their reason and sentiment strong, their imagination glowing and elevated. But never yet could I find that a black had uttered a thought above the level of plain narration; never see even an elementary trait of painting or sculpture.

NEGROES AND MUSIC

In music they are more generally gifted than the whites with accurate ears for tune and time, and they have been found capable of imagining a small catch.[b] Whether they will be equal to the composition of a more extensive run of melody, or of complicated harmony, is yet to be proved.

NO POETRY IN NEGROES

Misery is often the parent of the most affecting touches in poetry. Among the blacks is misery enough, God knows, but no poetry. Love is the peculiar oestrum of the poet. Their love is ardent, but it kindles the senses only, not the imagination. Religion indeed has produced a Phyllis Whately; but it could not produce a poet . . . The compositions published under her name are below the dignity of criticism. The heroes of the Dunciad are to her, as Hercules to the author of that poem.

LITERARY LIMITATIONS

Ignatius Sancho has approached nearer to merit in composition; yet his letters do more honor to the heart than the head. They breath the purest effusions of friendship and general philanthropy, and shew how great a degree of the latter may be compounded with strong religious zeal. He is often happy in the turn of his compliments, and his stile is easy and familiar, except when he affects a Shandean fabrication of words. But his imagination is wild and extravagant, escapes incessantly from every restraint of reason and taste, and, in the course of

[b] The instrument proper to them is the Banjar, which they brought hither from Africa, and which is the original of the guitar; its chords being precisely the four lower chords of the guitar.

its vagaries, leaves a tract of thought as incoherent and eccentric, as is the course of a meteor through the sky. His subjects should often have led him to a process of sober reasoning: yet we find him always substituting sentiment for demonstration. Upon the whole, though we admit him to the first place among those of his own color who have presented themselves to the public judgment, yet when we compare him with the writers of the race among whom he lived and particularly with the epistolary class, in which he has taken his own stand, we are compelled to enroll him at the bottom of the column. This criticism supposes the letters published under his name to be genuine, and to have received amendment from no other hand; points which would not be of easy investigation.

The improvement of the blacks in body and mind, in the first instance of their mixture with the whites, has been observed by every one, and proves that their inferiority is not the effect merely of their condition of life. We know that among the Romans, about the Augustan age especially, the condition of their slaves was much more deplorable than that of the blacks on the continent of America. The two sexes were confined in separate apartments, because to raise a child cost the master more than to buy one. Cato, for a very restricted indulgence to his slaves in this particular,[c] took from them a certain price. But in this country the slaves multiply as fast as the free inhabitants. Their situation and manners place the commerce between the two sexes almost without restraint. . . .

The same Cato, on a principle of economy, always sold his sick and superannuated slaves. He gives it as a standing precept to a master visiting his farm, to sell his old oxen, old waggons, old tools, old and diseased servants, and every thing else become useless. 'Vendat boves vetulos, plaustrum vetus, ferramenta vetera, servum senem, servum morbosum, & si quid aliud supersit vendat.'

BETTER CONDITION OF AMERICAN SLAVES

The American slaves cannot enumerate this among the injuries and insults they receive. It was the common practice to expose in the island Aesculapius, in the Tyber, diseased slaves, whose cure was like to become tedious.[d] The emperor Claudius, by an edict, gave freedom to such of them as should recover, and first declared that if any person chose to kill rather than expose them, it should be deemed homicide.

The exposing them is a crime of which no instance has existed with us; and were it to be followed by death, it would be punished capitally. We are told of a certain Vedius Pollio, who, in the presence of Augustus, would have given a slave as food to his fish, for having broken a glass.

ROMAN SLAVES WERE WHITES

With the Romans, the regular method of taking the evidence of their slaves was under torture. Here it has been thought better never to resort to their evidence. When a master was murdered, all his slaves, in the same house, or within hearing, were condemned to death. Here punishment falls on the guilty only, and as precise proof is required against him as against a freeman. Yet notwithstanding these and other discouraging circumstances among the Romans, their slaves were often their rarest artists. They excelled too in science, insomuch as to be

[c] Tous doulous etaxen orismenou nomesmatos homilein tais therapainsin. Plutarch.
[d] Suet. Claud. 25.

usually employed as tutors to their master's children. Epictetus, Terence, and Phaedrus were slaves. But they were of the race of whites. It is not their condition then, but nature, which has produced the distinction.

Whether further observation will or will not verify the conjecture, that nature has been less bountiful to them in the endowments of the head, I believe that in those of the heart she will be found to have done them justice.

THEFT DUE TO SITUATION

That disposition to theft with which they have been branded, must be ascribed to their situation, and not to any depravity of the moral sense. The man, in whose favor no laws of property exist, probably feels himself less bound to respect those made in favor of others. When arguing for ourselves, we lay it down as a fundamental, that laws, to be just, must give a reciprocation of right; that, without this, they are mere arbitrary rules of conduct, founded in force, and not in conscience: and it is a problem which I give to the master to solve, whether the religious precepts against the violation of property were not framed for him as well as his slave? And whether the slave may not as justifiably take a little from one, who has taken all from him, as he may slay one who would slay him? That a change in the relations in which a man is placed should change his ideas of moral right or wrong, is neither new, nor peculiar to the color of the blacks. Homer tells us it was so 2600 years ago.

> 'Emisu, ger t' aretes apoainutai europa Zeus
> Haneros, eut' an min kata doulion ema elesin.
> Odd. 17. 323.
> Jove fix'd it certain, that whatever day
> Makes man a slave, takes half his worth away.

But the slaves of which Homer speaks were whites. Notwithstanding these considerations which must weaken their respect for the laws of property, we find among them numerous instances of the most rigid integrity, and as many as among their better instructed masters, of benevolence, gratitude, and unshaken fidelity.

JEFFERSON RAISES DOUBTS

The opinion, that they are inferior in the faculties of reason and imagination, must be hazarded with great diffidence. To justify a general conclusion, requires many observations, even where the subject may be submitted to the anatomical knife, to optical classes, to analysis by fire, or by solvents. How much more then where it is a faculty, not a substance, we are examining; where it eludes the research of all the senses; where the conditions of its existence are various and variously combined; where the effects of those which are present or absent bid defiance to calculation; let me add too, as a circumstance of great tenderness, where our conclusion would degrade a whole race of men from the rank in the scale of beings which their Creator may perhaps have given them.

REGRETS LACK OF SCIENTIFIC STUDY

To our reproach it must be said, that though for a century and a half we have had under our eyes the races of black and of red men, they have never yet been viewed by us as subjects of natural history. I advance it therefore as a suspicion only, that the blacks, whether originally a distinct race, or made distinct by time and circumstances, are inferior to the whites in the endowments both of body and mind.

It is not against experience to suppose, that different species of the same genus, or varieties of the same species may possess different qualifications. Will not a lover of natural history then, one who views the gradations in all the races of animals with the eye of philosophy, excuse an effort to keep those in the department of man as distinct as nature has formed them?

This unfortunate difference of colour, and perhaps of faculty, is a powerful obstacle to the emancipation of these people. Many of their advocates, while they wish to vindicate the liberty of human nature are anxious also to preserve its dignity and beauty. Some of these, embarrassed by the question 'What further is to be done with them?' join themselves in opposition with those who are actuated by sordid avarice only. Among the Romans emancipation required but one effort. The slave, when made free, might mix with, without staining the blood of his master. But with us a second is necessary, unknown to history. When freed, he is to be removed beyond the reach of mixture.

The revised code further proposes to proportion crimes and punishments. . . .

Slaves guilty of offences punishable in others by labour, to be transported to Africa, or elsewhere, as the circumstances of the time admit, there to be continued in slavery. A rigorous regimen proposed for those condemned to labour.

6. Jefferson's *Notes on the State of Virginia*

[Jefferson, raised in the rural tradition, was suspicious of other economic enterprises.]

Query XIX—On Manufactures and Commerce

The present state of manufactures, commerce, interior and exterior trade?

We never had an interior trade of any importance. Our exterior commerce has suffered very much from the beginning of the present contest. During this time we have manufactured within our families the most necessary articles of clothing. Those of cotton will bear some comparison with the same kinds of manufacture in Europe; but those of wool, flax, and hemp are very coarse, unsightly, and unpleasant: and such is our attachment to agriculture, and such our preference for foreign manufactures, that be it wise or unwise, our people will certainly return as soon as they can, to the raising raw materials, and exchanging them for finer manufactures than they are able to execute themselves.

The political economists of Europe have established it as a principle that every state should endeavor to manufacture for itself: and this principle, like many others, we transfer to America, without calculating the difference of circumstance which should often produce a difference of result.

In Europe the lands are either cultivated, or locked up against the cultivator. Manufacture must therefore be resorted to of necessity not of choice, to support the surplus of their people. But we have an immensity of land courting the industry of the husbandman.

Is it best then that all our citizens should be employed in its improvement, or that one half should be called off from that to exercise manufactures and handicraft arts for the other? Those who labor in the earth are the chosen people of God, if ever he had a chosen people, whose breasts he has made his peculiar deposit for substantial and genuine virtue. It is the focus in which he keeps alive that sacred fire, which otherwise might escape from the face of the earth.

CORRUPTION CAUSED BY CUSTOMERS [5]

Corruption of morals in the mass of cultivators is a phaenomenon of which no age nor nation has furnished an example. It is the mark set on those, who not looking up to heaven, to their own soil and industry, as does the husbandman, for their subsistence, depend for it on casualties and caprice of customers. Dependence begets subservience and venality, suffocates the germ of virtue, and prepares fit tools for the designs of ambition. This, the natural progress and consequence of the arts, has sometimes perhaps been retarded by accidental circumstances: but, generally speaking, the proportion which the aggregate of the other classes of citizens bears in any state to that of its husbandmen, is the proportion of its unsound to its healthy parts, and is a good enough barometer whereby to measure its degree of corruption.

LEAVE WORKSHOPS IN EUROPE

While we have land to labor then, let us never wish to see our citizens occupied at a work-bench, or twirling a distaff. Carpenters, masons, smiths, are wanting in husbandry: but, for the general operations of manufacture, let work-shops remain in Europe. It is better to carry provisions and materials to workmen there, than bring them to the provisions and materials, and with them their manners and principles. The loss by the transportation of commodities across the Atlantic will be made up in happiness and permanence of government.

EVIL OF MOBS

The mobs of great cities add just so much to the support of pure government, as sores do to the strength of the human body. It is the manners and spirit of a people which preserve a republic in vigor. A degeneracy in these is a canker which soon eats to the heart of its laws and constitution.

7. Monroe on the Monroe Doctrine

[The doctrine was previously affirmed in part by Madison in 1811; also invoked by Tyler, Polk, Buchanan, Grant, T. Roosevelt.]

After the overthrow of Napoleon, France, Russia, Prussia, and Austria formed the so-called Holy Alliance in September, 1815, for the suppression of revolutions within each other's dominions and for perpetuating peace.

The Spanish colonies in America having revolted, it was rumored that

[5] Subheadings added by the author.

this alliance contemplated their subjugation, although the United States had acknowledged their independence. George Canning, English secretary of state, proposed that England and America unite to oppose such intervention. On consultation with Jefferson, Madison, John Quincy Adams, and Calhoun, Monroe, in his annual message to Congress in 1823, embodied the conclusions of these deliberations in what has since been known as the Monroe doctrine. Referring to the threatened intervention of the Holy Alliance, the message declares:

From Seventh Annual Message, December 2, 1823

ANY EXTENSION OF EUROPEAN POWER ON WESTERN HEMISPHERE "UNFRIENDLY" TO U.S.

We owe it, therefore, to candor and to the amicable relations existing between the United States and those powers to declare that we should consider any attempt on their part to extend their system to any portion of this hemisphere as dangerous to our peace and safety. With the existing colonies or dependencies of any European power we have not interfered and shall not interfere. But with the Governments who have declared their independence and maintained it, and whose independence we have, on great consideration and on just principles, acknowledged, we could not view any interposition for the purpose of oppressing them, or controlling in any other manner their destiny, by any European power in any other light than as the manifestation of an unfriendly disposition toward the United States.

The promulgation of this doctrine is accredited to Mr. Monroe, but on January 3, 1811, the principle had been substantially enunciated by Mr. Madison. In a message to Congress of that date, while discussing a threat of Great Britain to take possession of a portion of Florida claimed by Spain, he used these words:

I recommend to the consideration of Congress the seasonableness of a declaration that the United States could not see, without serious inquietude, any part of a neighboring territory in which they have in different respects so deep and so just a concern pass from the hands of Spain into those of any other foreign power.

The practical application of this doctrine went no further than to place the United States in opposition to any possible attempt of any European power to subjugate or take possession in whole or in part of any American country. The principle involved was clearly set forth by Secretary of State Richard Olney in his dispatch of July 20, 1895, on the Venezuelan Boundary dispute. He stated that the Monroe Doctrine "does not establish any general protectorate by the United States over other American States. It does not relieve any American State from its obligations as fixed by international law, nor prevent any European power directly interested from enforcing such obligations or from inflicting merited punishment for the breach of them." This interpretation of the Monroe Doctrine was upheld in the most emphatic manner by President Roosevelt in many of his public speeches and his messages to Congress in which he stated that any well-merited punishment inflicted by a European power upon an American State does not violate the Monroe Doctrine, provided that such punishment does not involve any occupation, either permanent or temporary, of American territory. See commentaries quoted in Appendix from both Cleveland and T. Roosevelt.

8. Jackson on the Bank of the United States

From First Annual Message, December 8, 1829

BANK HAS NOT SERVED WELL [6]

The charter of the Bank of the United States expires in 1836, and its stockholders will most probably apply for a renewal of their privileges. In order to avoid the evils resulting from precipitancy in a measure involving such important principles and such deep pecuniary interests, I feel that I can not, in justice to the parties interested, too soon present it to the deliberate consideration of the Legislature and the people. Both the constitutionality and the expediency of the law creating this bank are well questioned by a large portion of our fellow-citizens, and it must be admitted by all that it has failed in the great end of establishing a uniform and sound currency.

From Veto Message, July 10, 1832

USEFUL IF SAFEGUARDED

A bank of the United States is in many respects convenient for the Government and useful to the people. Entertaining this opinion, and deeply impressed with the belief that some of the powers and privileges possessed by the existing bank are unauthorized by the Constitution, subversive of the rights of the States, and dangerous to the liberties of the people, I felt it my duty at an early period of my Administration to call the attention of Congress to the practicability of organizing an institution combining all its advantages and obviating these objections. I sincerely regret that in the act before me I can perceive none of those modifications of the bank charter which are necessary, in my opinion, to make it compatible with justice, with sound policy, or with the Constitution of our country. . . .

PRESENT FORM A MONOPOLY

It enjoys an exclusive privilege of banking under the authority of the General Government, a monopoly of its favor and support, and, as a necessary consequence, almost a monopoly of the foreign and domestic exchange. The powers, privileges, and favors bestowed upon it in the original charter, by increasing the value of the stock far above its par value, operated as a gratuity of many millions to the stockholders. . . .

[6] Subheadings added by the author.

SHOULD BE OPEN TO COMPETITION

It is not conceivable how the present stockholders can have any claim to the special favor of the Government. The present corporation has enjoyed its monopoly during the period stipulated in the original contract. If we must have such a corporation, why should not the Government sell out the whole stock and thus secure to the people the full market value of the privileges granted?

HAZARDS OF MONOPOLY

Is there no danger to our liberty and independence in a bank that in its nature has so little to bind it to our country? The president of the bank has told us that most of the State banks exist by its forbearance. Should its influence become concentered, as it may under the operation of such an act as this, in the hands of a self-elected directory whose interests are identified with those of the foreign stockholders, will there not be cause to tremble for the purity of our elections in peace and for the independence of our country in war? Their power would be great whenever they might choose to exert it; but if this monopoly were regularly renewed every fifteen or twenty years on terms proposed by themselves, they might seldom in peace put forth their strength to influence elections or control the affairs of the nation. . . .

PRESIDENT MAY ACT ON HIS OWN VIEW OF CONSTITUTIONALITY

If the opinion of the Supreme Court covered the whole ground of this act, it ought not to control the coordinate authorities of this Government. The Congress, the Executive, and the Court must each for itself be guided by its own opinion of the Constitution. Each public officer who takes an oath to support the Constitution swears that he will support it as he understands it, and not as it is understood by others. It is as much the duty of the House of Representatives, of the Senate, and of the President to decide upon the constitutionality of any bill or resolution which may be presented to them for passage or approval as it is of the supreme judges when it may be brought before them for judicial decision. The opinion of the judges has no more authority over Congress than the opinion of Congress has over the judges, and on that point the President is independent of both. The authority of the Supreme Court must not, therefore, be permitted to control the Congress or the Executive when acting in their legislative capacities, but to have only such influence as the force of their reasoning may deserve. . . .

PRESIDENT NOT CONSULTED

The bank is professedly established as an agent of the executive branch of the Government, and its constitutionality is maintained on that ground. Neither upon the propriety of present action nor upon the provisions of this act was the Executive consulted.

INFLUENCE OF RICH AND POWERFUL ON GOVERNMENT

It is to be regretted that the rich and powerful too often bend the acts of government to their selfish purposes. Distinctions in society will always exist under every just government. Equality of talents, of education, or of wealth can not be produced by human institutions. In the full enjoyment of the gifts of Heaven and the fruits of superior industry, economy, and virtue, every man is equally entitled to protection by law; but when the laws undertake to add to these natural and just advantages artificial distinctions, to grant titles, gratuities, and exclusive privileges, to make the rich richer and the potent more powerful, the humble members of society—the farmers, mechanics, and laborers—who have neither the time nor the means of securing like favors to themselves, have a right to complain of the injustice of their Government.

INVADES THE RIGHTS AND POWERS OF THE STATES

Nor is our Government to be maintained or our Union preserved by invasions of the rights and powers of the several States. In thus attempting to make our General Government strong we make it weak. Its true strength consists in leaving individuals and States as much as possible to themselves—in making itself felt, not in its power, but in its beneficence; not in its control, but in its protection; not in binding the States more closely to the center, but leaving each to move unobstructed in its proper orbit. . . .

Many of our rich men have not been content with equal protection and equal benefits, but have besought us to make them richer by act of Congress. By attempting to gratify their desires we have in the results of our legislation arrayed section against section, interest against interest, and man against man, in a fearful commotion which threatens to shake the foundations of our Union. It is time to pause in our career to review our principles, and if possible revive that devoted patriotism and spirit of compromise which distinguished the sages of the Revolution and the fathers of our Union. If we can not at once, in justice to interests vested under improvident legislation, make our Government what it ought to be, we can at least take a stand against all new grants of monopolies and exclusive privileges, against any prostitution of our Government to the advancement of the few at the expense of the many, and in favor of compromise and gradual reform in our code of laws and system of political economy.

From Eighth Annual Message, December 5, 1836

LESSON FOR THE PUBLIC

The lessons taught by the Bank of the United States can not well be lost upon the American people. They will take care never again to place so tremendous a power in irresponsible hands, and it will be fortunate if they seriously consider the consequences which are likely to result on a smaller scale from the facility with which corporate powers are granted by their State governments.

9. Jackson on the Indians

[Jackson, the Indian fighter, was not sympathetic to the original, or at least the prior, inhabitants of America, whom he desired to replace. Jackson in relation to the Indians at best was an unqualified imperialist. When the democratic liberals of his era desired to rationalize the Indian policy with the brotherhood of man, they encountered a losing battle, which was the lost cause of the Indian. The language of Jackson on Indian matters, as contained in his official papers, seems quite unlike his rugged diction, more like Amos Kendall. Jackson's regime enhanced the status of the common white man but marked the doom of the red man in America.]

From Second Annual Message, December 6, 1830

HUMANITY WEEPS FOR THE INDIAN [7]

Humanity has often wept over the fate of the aborigines of this country, and Philanthropy has been long busily employed in devising means to avert it, but its progress has never for a moment been arrested, and one by one have many powerful tribes disappeared from the earth. Philanthropy could not wish to see this continent restored to the condition in which it was found by our forefathers. What good man would prefer a country covered with forests and ranged by a few thousand savages to our extensive Republic, studded with cities, towns, and prosperous farms, embellished with all the improvements which art can devise or industry execute, occupied by more than 12,000,000 happy people, and filled with all the blessing of liberty, civilization, and religion? . . .

PROPOSAL TO ACQUIRE INDIAN LANDS

The present policy of the Government is but a continuation of the same progressive change by a milder process. The tribes which occupied the countries now constituting the Eastern States were annihilated or have melted away to make room for the whites. . . . Does Humanity weep at these painful separations from everything, animate and inanimate, with which the young heart has become entwined? Far from it. . . . How many thousands of our own people would gladly embrace the opportunity of removing to the West on such conditions! If the offers made to the Indians were extended to them, they would be hailed with gratitude and joy.

From Third Annual Message, December 6, 1831

FINEST OHIO LANDS REMOVED FROM THE INDIAN

During the present year the attention of the Government has been particularly directed to those tribes in the powerful and growing State of Ohio, where con-

[7] Subheadings added by the author.

siderable tracts of the finest lands were still occupied by the aboriginal pro-
prietors. . . . It is pleasing to reflect that results so beneficial, not only to the
States immediately concerned, but to the harmony of the Union, will have been
accomplished by measures equally advantageous to the Indians. What the native
savages become when surrounded by a dense population and by mixing with the
whites may be seen in the miserable remnants of a few Eastern tribes, deprived
of political and civil rights, forbidden to make contracts, and subjected to guardians,
dragging out a wretched existence, without excitement, without hope, and almost
without thought. . . .

IMPROVED OPPORTUNITY FOR CHRISTIAN INSTRUCTION

But the removal of the Indians beyond the limits and jurisdiction of the States
does not place them beyond the reach of philanthropic aid and Christian instruction. . . . Now subject to no control but the superintending agency of the
General Government, exercised with the sole view of preserving peace, they may
proceed unmolested in the interesting experiment of gradually advancing a community of American Indians from barbarism to the habits and enjoyments of
civilized life.

From Seventh Annual Message, December 7, 1835

INDIANS CANNOT PROSPER IN CIVILIZED COMMUNITY

The plan of removing the aboriginal people who yet remain within the settled
portions of the United States to the country west of the Mississippi River approaches
its consummation. It was adopted on the most mature consideration of the condition of this race, and ought to be persisted in till the object is accomplished,
and prosecuted with as much vigor as a just regard to their circumstances will
permit, and as fast as their consent can be obtained. *All preceding experiments for
the improvement of the Indians have failed.* It seems now to be an established
fact that they can not live in contact with a civilized community and prosper.

A PROGRAM OF INDIAN RESERVATIONS OUTLINED

Ages of fruitless endeavors have at length brought us to a knowledge of this
principle of intercommunication with them. The past we can not recall, but the
future we can provide for. Independently of the treaty stipulations into which
we have entered with the various tribes for the usufructuary rights they have
ceded to us, no one can doubt the moral duty of the Government of the United
States to protect and if possible to preserve and perpetuate the scattered remnants
of this race which are left within our borders. In the discharge of this duty an
extensive region in the West has been assigned for their permanent residence. It
has been divided into districts and allotted among them. Many have already removed and others are preparing to go, and with the exception of two small bands
living in Ohio and Indiana, not exceeding 1,500 persons, and of the Cherokees,
all the tribes on the east side of the Mississippi, and extending from Lake Michigan
to Florida, have entered into engagements which will lead to their transplanta-
tion. . . .

A POLICY OF PROTECTED SEGREGATION

Such are the arrangements for the physical comfort and for the moral improvement of the Indians. The necessary measures for their political advancement and for their separation from our citizens have not been neglected. The pledge of the United States has been given by Congress that the country destined for the residence of this people shall be forever "secured and guaranteed to them." A country west of Missouri and Arkansas has been assigned to them, into which the white settlements are not to be pushed. . . .

LIQUOR TRAFFIC FORBIDDEN

Summary authority has been given by law to destroy all ardent spirits found in their country, without waiting the doubtful result and slow process of a legal seizure. I consider the absolute and unconditional interdiction of this article among these people as the first and great step in their melioration. . . .

LEFT TO THE "PROGRESS OF EVENTS"

After the further details of this arrangement are completed, with a very general supervision over them, they ought to be left to the progress of events. These, I indulge the hope, will secure their prosperity and improvement, and a large portion of the moral debt we owe them will then be paid.

10. Jackson on National Sovereignty

[Jackson was the connecting link between Washington and Lincoln on the principle of national sovereignty. Those who doubt that either Washington or Jackson were liberal in their insistence on the necessity for a strong central government to preserve the freedom asserted by union may turn to Jackson's exposition. Presumably the Jackson words were written by Amos Kendall and others, but Jackson signed them.]

From Special Message to Congress, January 16, 1833

RIGHT TO SECEDE CANNOT BE ACKNOWLEDGED [8]

The right of the people of a single State to absolve themselves at will and without the consent of the other States from their most solemn obligations, and hazard the liberties and happiness of the millions composing this Union, can not be acknowledged. Such authority is believed to be utterly repugnant both to the principles upon which the General Government is constituted and to the objects which it is expressly formed to attain. . . .

[8] Subheadings added by the author.

UNION INDISSOLUBLE

I have determined to spare no effort to discharge the duty which in this conjuncture is devolved upon me. That a similar spirit will actuate the representatives of the American people is not to be questioned; and I fervently pray that the Great Ruler of Nations may so guide your deliberations and our joint measures as that they may prove salutary examples not only to the present but to future times, and solemnly proclaim that the Constitution and the laws are supreme and the Union indissoluble.

From Proclamation, December 10, 1832

RIGHT OF THE PRESIDENT TO PRESERVE THE UNION
AND ENFORCE LAWS

Strict duty would require of me nothing more than the exercise of those powers with which I am now or may hereafter be invested for preserving the peace of the Union and for the execution of the laws; but the imposing aspect which opposition has assumed in this case, by clothing itself with State authority, and the deep interest which the people of the United States must all feel in preventing a resort to stronger measures while there is a hope that anything will be yielded to reasoning and remonstrance, perhaps demand, and will certainly justify, a full exposition to South Carolina and the nation of the views I entertain of this important question, as well as a distinct enunciation of the course which my sense of duty will require me to pursue.

NATION IS THE SUPREME POWER UNDER
THE CONSTITUTION

The ordinance is founded, not on the indefeasible right of resisting acts which are plainly unconstitutional and too oppressive to be endured, but on the strange position that any one State may not only declare an act of Congress void, but prohibit its execution; that they may do this consistently with the Constitution; that the true construction of that instrument permits a State to retain its place in the Union and yet be bound by no other of its laws than those it may choose to consider as constitutional. . . . If it should be said that public opinion is a sufficient check against the abuse of this power, it may be asked why it is not deemed a sufficient guard against the passage of an unconstitutional act by Congress? There is, however, a restraint in this last case which makes the assumed power of a State more indefensible, and which does not exist in the other. There are two appeals from an unconstitutional act passed by Congress—one to the judiciary, the other to the people and the States. . . .

SOVEREIGNTY OF THE UNION EXISTED FROM THE OUTSET

In our colonial state, although dependent on another power, we very early considered ourselves as connected by common interest with each other. Leagues were formed for common defense, and before the declaration of independence we were known in our aggregate character as the United Colonies of America. That decisive and important step was taken jointly. We declared ourselves a nation by a joint, not by several acts, and when the terms of our Confederation were reduced to form it was in that of a solemn league of several States, by which they agreed that they would collectively form one nation for the purpose of conducting some certain domestic concerns and all foreign relations. In the instrument forming that Union is found an article which declares that "every State shall abide by the determination of Congress on all questions which by that Confederation should be submitted to them."

SUPREMACY OF THE UNION WAS THE ESSENCE OF THE CONSTITUTION

Under the Confederation, then, no State could legally annul a decision of the Congress or refuse to submit to its execution; but no provision was made to enforce these decisions. Congress made requisitions, but they were not complied with. The Government could not operate on individuals. They had no judiciary, no means of collecting revenue.

But the defects of the Confederation need not be detailed. Under its operation we could scarcely be called a nation. We had neither prosperity at home nor consideration abroad. This state of things could not be endured, and our present happy Constitution was formed, but formed in vain if this fatal doctrine prevails. It was formed for important objects that are announced in the preamble, made in the name and by the authority of the people of the United States, whose delegates framed and whose conventions approved it. The most important among these objects—that which is placed first in rank, on which all the others rest— is "to form a more perfect union." . . .

STATES HAVE MADE BINDING COMPACT

Because the Union was formed by a compact, it is said the parties to that compact may, when they feel themselves aggrieved, depart from it; but it is precisely because it is a compact that they can not. A compact is an agreement or binding obligation. . . .

STATES NOT SOVEREIGN WERE IN CONFLICT WITH FEDERAL GOVERNMENT

No one, fellow-citizens, has a higher reverence for the reserved rights of the States than the Magistrate who now addresses you. . . .

The States severally have not retained their entire sovereignty. It has been shown that in becoming parts of a nation, not members of a league, they surrendered many of their essential parts of sovereignty. The right to make treaties, declare war, levy taxes, exercise exclusive judicial and legislative powers, were all of them functions of sovereign power. The States, then, for all these important purposes were no longer sovereign. The allegiance of their citizens was transferred, in the first instance, to the Government of the United States; they became American citizens and owed obedience to the Constitution of the United States and to laws made in conformity with the powers it vested in Congress. This last position has not been and can not be denied. How, then, can that State be said to be sovereign and independent whose citizens owe obedience to laws not made by it and whose magistrates are sworn to disregard those laws when they come in conflict with those passed by another? . . .

Under the royal Government we had no separate character; our opposition to its oppressions began as united colonies. We were the United States under the Confederation, and the name was perpetuated and the Union rendered more perfect by the Federal Constitution. In none of these stages did we consider ourselves in any other light than as forming one nation. . . .

But it has been shown that in this sense the States are not sovereign, and that even if they were, and the national Constitution had been formed by compact, there would be no right in any one State to exonerate itself from its obligations.

11. The Specie Circular

[The Specie Circular, rarely reprinted but frequently referred to in many pre-Civil War arguments, was a document that returned government finance policy to "hard money." It required that homestead lands payments be made in silver or gold rather than paper. Jackson had favored the measure in 1836 but it remained for Van Buren to assume the deflationary responsibility.]

Issued by the Treasury Department, July 11, 1836

In consequence of complaints which have been made of frauds, speculations, and monopolies, in the purchase of the public lands, and the aid which is said to be given to effect these objects by excessive bank credits, and dangerous if not partial facilities through bank drafts and bank deposits, and the general evil influence likely to result to the public interests, and especially the safety of the great amount of money in the Treasury, and the sound condition of the currency of the country, from the further exchange of the national domain in this manner, the President of the United States has given directions, and you are hereby instructed, after the 15th day of August next, to receive in payment of the public lands nothing except what is directed by the existing laws, viz: gold and silver, and in the proper cases, Virginia land scrip; provided that till the 15th of December next, the same indulgences heretofore extended as to the kind of money received, may be continued for any quantity of land not exceeding 320 acres to each purchaser who is an actual settler or bona fide resident in the State where the sales are made.

In order to ensure the faithful execution of these instructions, all receivers are strictly prohibited from accepting for land sold, any draft, certificate, or other evidence of money, or deposit, though for specie, unless signed by the Treasurer of the United States, in conformity to the act of April 24, 1820. . . .

The principal objects of the President in adopting this measure being to repress alleged frauds, and to withhold any countenance or facilities in the power of the Government from the monopoly of the public lands in the hands of speculators and capitalists, to the injury of the actual settlers in the new States, and of emigrants in search of new homes, as well as to discourage the ruinous extension of bank issues, and bank credits, by which those results are generally supposed to be promoted, your utmost vigilance is required, and relied on, to carry this order into complete execution.

12. Martin Van Buren on Noninterference by Government

From Special Session Message, September 4, 1837

NOT INTENDED TO PROVIDE FINANCIAL AID [9]

Those who look to the action of this Government for specific aid to the citizen to relieve embarrassments arising from losses by revulsions in commerce and credit lose sight of the ends for which it was created and the powers with which it is clothed. It was established to give security to us all in our lawful and honorable pursuits, under the lasting safeguard of republican institutions. It was not intended to confer special favors on individuals or on any classes of them, to create systems of agriculture, manufactures, or trade, or to engage in them either separately or in connection with individual citizens or organized associations. If its operations were to be directed for the benefit of any one class, equivalent favors must in justice be extended to the rest, and the attempt to bestow such favors with an equal hand, or even to select those who should most deserve them, would never be successful.

COMMUNITIES EXPECT TOO MUCH

All communities are apt to look to government for too much. Even in our own country, where its powers and duties are so strictly limited, we are prone to do so, especially at periods of sudden embarrassment and distress. But this ought not to be. The framers of our excellent Constitution and the people who approved it with calm and sagacious deliberation acted at the time on a sounder principle. They wisely judged that the less government interferes with private pursuits the better for the general prosperity. It is not its legitimate object to make men rich or to repair by direct grants of money or legislation in favor of particular pursuits losses not incurred in the public service. This would be substantially to use the property of some for the benefit of others. But its real duty —that duty the performance of which makes a good government the most precious of human blessings—is to enact and enforce a system of general laws commensurate with, but not exceeding, the objects of its establishment, and to leave every citizen and every interest to reap under its benign protection the rewards of virtue, industry, and prudence.

SHOULD AVOID UNNECESSARY INTERFERENCE WITH PRIVATE INTERESTS

I can not doubt that on this as on all similar occasions the Federal Government will find its agency most conducive to the security and happiness of the people when limited to the exercise of its conceded powers. In never assuming, even for a well-meant object, such powers as were not designed to be conferred upon it,

[9] Subheadings added by the author.

we shall in reality do most for the general welfare. To avoid every unnecessary interference with the pursuits of the citizens will result in more benefit than to adopt measures which could only assist limited interests, and are eagerly, but perhaps naturally, sought for under the pressure of temporary circumstances. If, therefore, I refrain from suggesting to Congress any specific plan for regulating the exchanges of the country, relieving mercantile embarrassments, or interfering with the ordinary operations of foreign or domestic commerce, it is from a conviction that such measures are not within the constitutional province of the General Government, and that their adoption would not promote the real and permanent welfare of those they might be designed to aid.

PERMANENT PROSPERITY NOT AFFECTED

The difficulties and distresses of the times, though unquestionably great, are limited in their extent, and can not be regarded as affecting the permanent prosperity of the nation. Arising in a great degree from the transactions of foreign and domestic commerce, it is upon them that they have chiefly fallen. The great agricultural interest has in many parts of the country suffered comparatively little.

13. Lincoln on Proposal to Purchase Slaves

[The steps by which Lincoln hoped to purchase the slaves and end the war are outlined in the main text of this book. Lincoln's arguments on this point were expounded in great detail in his message of December 1, 1862. The portions of the message printed below are available in only a few source books. Seemingly, the failure of the purchase plan, which was succeeded by enforced emancipation, dimmed the record to such an extent that Lincoln's pleas for the compensated freeing of the slaves have been virtually forgotten in some quarters. The other Lincoln papers are not included here because they are generally available elsewhere.]

From Message to Congress, December 1, 1862

On the 22d day of September last a proclamation was issued by the Executive, a copy of which is herewith submitted.

In accordance with the purpose expressed in the second paragraph of that paper, I now respectfully recall your attention to what may be called "compensated emancipation."

In this view I recommend the adoption of the following resolution and articles amendatory to the Constitution of the United States:

Resolved by the Senate and House of Representatives of the United States of America in Congress assembled (two-thirds of both Houses concurring), That the following articles be proposed to the legislatures (or conventions) of the several States as amendments to the Constitution of the United States, all or any of which articles, when ratified by three-fourths of the said legislatures (or conventions), to be valid as part or parts of the said Constitution, viz:

ART. —. Every State wherein slavery now exists which shall abolish the same therein at any time or times before the 1st day of January, A. D. 1900, shall receive compensation from the United States as follows, to wit:

The President of the United States shall deliver to every such State bonds of the United States bearing interest at the rate of —— per cent per annum to an amount equal to the aggregate sum of —— for each slave shown to have been therein by the Eighth Census of the United States, said bonds to be delivered to such State by installments or in one parcel at the completion of the abolishment, accordingly as the same shall have been gradual or at one time within such State; and interest shall begin to run upon any such bond only from the proper time of its delivery as aforesaid. Any State having received bonds as aforesaid and afterwards reintroducing or tolerating slavery therein shall refund to the United States the bonds so received, or the value thereof, and all interest paid thereon.

ART. —. All slaves who shall have enjoyed actual freedom by the chances of the war at any time before the end of the rebellion shall be forever free; but all owners of such who shall not have been disloyal shall be compensated for them at the same rates as is provided for States adopting abolishment of slavery, but in such way that no slave shall be twice accounted for.

ART. —. Congress may appropriate money and otherwise provide for colonizing free colored persons with their own consent at any place or places without the United States.

I beg indulgence to discuss these proposed articles at some length. Without slavery the rebellion could never have existed; without slavery it could not continue.

Among the friends of the Union there is great diversity of sentiment and of policy in regard to slavery and the African race amongst us. Some would perpetuate slavery; some would abolish it suddenly and without compensation; some would abolish it gradually and with compensation; some would remove the freed people from us, and some would retain them with us; and there are yet other minor diversities. Because of these diversities we waste much strength in struggles among ourselves. By mutual concession we should harmonize and act together. This would be compromise, but it would be compromise among the friends and not with the enemies of the Union. These articles are intended to embody a plan of such mutual concessions. If the plan shall be adopted, it is assumed that emancipation will follow, at least in several of the States.

THREE POINTS UNDER ARTICLE I [10]

As to the first article, the main points are, first, the emancipation; secondly, the length of time for consummating it (thirty-seven years); and, thirdly, the compensation.

The emancipation will be unsatisfactory to the advocates of perpetual slavery, but the length of time should greatly mitigate their dissatisfaction. The time spares both races from the evils of sudden derangement—in fact, from the necessity of any derangement—while most of those whose habitual course of thought will be disturbed by the measure will have passed away before its consummation. They will never see it. Another class will hail the prospect of emancipation, but will deprecate the length of time. They will feel that it gives too little to the now living slaves. But it really gives them much. It saves them from the vagrant destitution which must largely attend immediate emancipation in localities where

[10] Subheadings added by the author.

their numbers are very great, and it gives the inspiring assurance that their posterity shall be free forever.

The plan leaves to each State choosing to act under it to abolish slavery now or at the end of the century, or at any intermediate time, or by degrees extending over the whole or any part of the period, and it obliges no two States to proceed alike. It also provides for compensation, and generally the mode of making it. This, it would seem, must further mitigate the dissatisfaction of those who favor perpetual slavery, and especially of those who are to receive the compensation. Doubtless some of those who are to pay and not to receive will object. Yet the measure is both just and economical.

NORTH AND SOUTH BOTH RESPONSIBLE

In a certain sense the liberation of slaves is the destruction of property—property acquired by descent or by purchase, the same as any other property. It is no less true for having been often said that the people of the South are not more responsible for the original introduction of this property than are the people of the North; and when it is remembered how unhesitatingly we all use cotton and sugar and share the profits of dealing in them, it may not be quite safe to say that the South has been more responsible than the North for its continuance. If, then, for a common object this property is to be sacrificed, is it not just that it be done at a common charge?

COMPENSATION COSTS LESS THAN WAR

And if with less money, or money more easily paid, we can preserve the benefits of the Union by this means than we can by the war alone, is it not also economical to do it? Let us consider it, then. Let us ascertain the sum we have expended in the war since compensated emancipation was proposed last March, and consider whether if that measure had been promptly accepted by even some of the slave States the same sum would not have done more to close the war than has been otherwise done. If so, the measure would save money, and in that view would be a prudent and economical measure. Certainly it is not so easy to pay *something* as it is to pay *nothing,* but it is easier to pay a *large* sum than it is to pay a *larger* one. And it is easier to pay any sum *when* we are able than it is to pay it *before* we are able.

The war requires large sums, and requires them at once. The aggregate sum necessary for compensated emancipation of course would be large. But it would require no ready cash, nor the bonds even any faster than the emancipation progresses. This might not, and probably would not, close before the end of the thirty-seven years. At that time we shall probably have a hundred millions of people to share the burden, instead of thirty-one millions as now. And not only so, but the increase of our population may be expected to continue for a long time after that period as rapidly as before, because our territory will not have become full.

PREDICTED POPULATION INCREASE

I do not state this inconsiderately. At the same ratio of increase which we have maintained, on an average, from our first national census, in 1790, until that of

1860, we should in 1900 have a population of 103,208,415. And why may we not continue that ratio far beyond that period? Our abundant room, our broad national homestead, is our ample resource. Were our territory as limited as are the British Isles, very certainly our population could not expand as stated. Instead of receiving the foreign born as now, we should be compelled to send part of the native born away. But such is not our condition.

We have 2,963,000 square miles. Europe has 3,800,000, with a population averaging 73⅓ persons to the square mile. Why may not our country at some time average as many? Is it less fertile? Has it more waste surface by mountains, rivers, lakes, deserts, or other causes? Is it inferior to Europe in any natural advantage? If, then, we are at some time to be as populous as Europe, how soon? As to when this *may* be, we can judge by the past and the present; as to when it *will* be, if ever, depends much on whether we maintain the Union.

Several of our States are already above the average of Europe—73⅓ to the square mile. Massachusetts has 157; Rhode Island, 133; Connecticut, 99; New York and New Jersey, each 80. Also two other great States, Pennsylvania and Ohio, are not far below, the former having 63 and the latter 59. The States already above the European average, except New York, have increased in as rapid a ratio since passing that point as ever before, while no one of them is equal to some other parts of our country in natural capacity for sustaining a dense population.

Taking the nation in the aggregate, and we find its population and ratio of increase for the several decennial periods to be as follows:

YEAR	POPULATION	RATIO OF INCREASE
		Per cent
1790	3,929,827	....
1800	5,305,937	35.02
1810	7,239,814	36.45
1820	9,638,131	33.13
1830	12,866,020	33.49
1840	17,069,453	32.67
1850	23,191,876	35.87
1860	31,443,790	35.58

This shows an average decennial increase of 34.60 per cent in population through the seventy years from our first to our last census yet taken. It is seen that the ratio of increase at no one of these seven periods is either 2 per cent below or 2 per cent above the average, thus showing how inflexible, and consequently how reliable, the law of increase in our case is. Assuming that it will continue, it gives the following results:

YEAR	POPULATION
1870	42,323,341
1880	56,967,216
1890	76,677,872
1900	103,208,415
1910	138,918,526
1920	186,984,335
1930	251,680,914

These figures show that our country *may* be as populous as Europe now is at some point between 1920 and 1930—say about 1925—our territory, at 73⅓ persons to the square mile, being of capacity to contain 217,186,000.

And we *will* reach this, too, if we do not ourselves relinquish the chance by the folly and evils of disunion or by long and exhausting war springing from the only great element of national discord among us. While it can not be foreseen exactly how much one huge example of secession, breeding lesser ones indefinitely, would retard population, civilization, and prosperity, no one can doubt that the extent of it would be very great and injurious.

TIME FACTOR MAKES PAYMENT EASIER

The proposed emancipation would shorten the war, perpetuate peace, insure this increase of population, and proportionately the wealth of the country. With these we should pay all the emancipation would cost, together with our other debt, easier than we should pay our other debt without it. If we had allowed our old national debt to run at 6 per cent per annum, simple interest, from the end of our revolutionary struggle until to-day, without paying anything on either principal or interest, each man of us would owe less upon that debt now than each man owed upon it then; and this because our increase of men through the whole period has been greater than 6 per cent—has run faster than the interest upon the debt. Thus time alone relieves a debtor nation, so long as its population increases faster than unpaid interest accumulates on its debt.

This fact would be no excuse for delaying payment of what is justly due, but it shows the great importance of time in this connection—the great advantage of a policy by which we shall not have to pay until we number 100,000,000 what by a different policy we would have to pay now, when we number but 31,000,000. In a word, it shows that a dollar will be much harder to pay for the war than will be a dollar for emancipation on the proposed plan. And then the latter will cost no blood, no precious life. It will be a saving of both.

As to the second article, I think it would be impracticable to return to bondage the class of persons therein contemplated. Some of them, doubtless, in the property sense belong to loyal owners, and hence provision is made in this article for compensating such.

COLONIZATION CONSIDERED

The third article relates to the future of the freed people. It does not oblige, but merely authorizes Congress to aid in colonizing such as may consent. This ought not to be regarded as objectionable on the one hand or on the other, insomuch as it comes to nothing unless by the mutual consent of the people to be deported and the American voters, through their representatives in Congress.

I can not make it better known than it already is that I strongly favor colonization; and yet I wish to say there is an objection urged against free colored persons remaining in the country which is largely imaginary, if not sometimes malicious.

NO ADDED LABOR COMPETITION

It is insisted that their presence would injure and displace white labor and white laborers. If there ever could be a proper time for mere catch arguments, that time surely is not now. In times like the present men should utter nothing for which they would not willingly be responsible through time and in eternity. Is it true, then, that colored people can displace any more white labor by being free than by remaining slaves? If they stay in their old places, they jostle no white laborers; if they leave their old places, they leave them open to white laborers. Logically, there is neither more nor less of it. Emancipation, even without deportation, would probably enhance the wages of white labor, and very surely would not reduce them. Thus the customary amount of labor would still have to be performed— the freed people would surely not do more than their old proportion of it, and very probably for a time would do less, leaving an increased part to white laborers, bringing their labor into greater demand, and consequently enhancing the wages of it. With deportation, even to a limited extent, enhanced wages to white labor is mathematically certain. Labor is like any other commodity in the market— increase the demand for it and you increase the price of it. Reduce the supply of black labor by colonizing the black laborer out of the country, and by precisely so much you increase the demand for and wages of white labor.

But it is dreaded that the freed people will swarm forth and cover the whole land. Are they not already in the land? Will liberation make them any more numerous? Equally distributed among the whites of the whole country, and there would be but one colored to seven whites. Could the one in any way greatly disturb the seven? There are many communities now having more than one free colored person to seven whites and this without any apparent consciousness of evil from it. *Heretofore* colored people to some extent have fled North from bondage, and *now,* perhaps, from both bondage and destitution. But if gradual emancipation and deportation be adopted, they will have neither to flee from. Their old masters will give them wages at least until new laborers can be procured, and the freedmen in turn will gladly give their labor for the wages till new homes can be found for them in congenial climes and with people of their own blood and race. This proposition can be trusted on the mutual interests involved. And in any event, can not the North decide for itself whether to receive them? . . .

This plan is recommended as a means, not in exclusion of, but additional to, all others for restoring and preserving the national authority throughout the Union. The subject is presented exclusively in its economical aspect. The plan would, I am confident, secure peace more speedily and maintain it more permanently than can be done by force alone, while all it would cost, considering amounts and manner of payment and times of payment, would be easier paid than will be the additional cost of the war if we rely solely upon force. It is much, very much, that it would cost no blood at all.

The plan is proposed as permanent constitutional law. It can not become such without the concurrence of, first, two-thirds of Congress, and afterwards three-fourths of the States. The requisite three-fourths of the States will necessarily include seven of the slave States. Their concurrence, if obtained, will give assurance of their severally adopting emancipation at no very distant day upon the new constitutional terms. This assurance would end the struggle now and save the Union forever.

I do not forget the gravity which should characterize a paper addressed to the Congress of the nation by the Chief Magistrate of the nation, nor do I forget that some of you are my seniors, nor that many of you have more experience than I in the conduct of public affairs. Yet I trust that in view of the great responsibility resting upon me you will perceive no want of respect to yourselves in any undue earnestness I may seem to display.

Is it doubted, then, that the plan I propose, if adopted, would shorten the war, and thus lessen its expenditure of money and of blood? Is it doubted that it would restore the national authority and national prosperity and perpetuate both indefinitely? Is it doubted that we here—Congress and Executive—can secure its adoption? Will not the good people respond to a united and earnest appeal from us? Can we, can they, by any other means so certainly or so speedily assure these vital objects? We can succeed only by concert. It is not "Can *any* of us *imagine* better?" but "Can we *all* do better?" Object whatsoever is possible, still the question recurs, "Can we do better?" The dogmas of the quiet past are inadequate to the stormy present. The occasion is piled high with difficulty, and we must rise with the occasion. As our case is new, so we must think anew and act anew. We must disenthrall ourselves, and then we shall save our country.

Fellow-citizens, *we* can not escape history. We of this Congress and this Administration will be remembered in spite of ourselves. No personal significance or insignificance can spare one or another of us. The fiery trial through which we pass will light us down in honor or dishonor to the latest generation. We *say* we are for the Union. The world will not forget that we say this. We know how to save the Union. The world knows we do know how to save it. We, even *we here,* hold the power and bear the responsibility. In *giving* freedom to the *slave* we *assure* freedom to the *free*—honorable alike in what we give and what we preserve. We shall nobly save or meanly lose the last best hope of earth. Other means may succeed; this could not fail. The way is plain, peaceful, generous, just—a way which if followed the world will forever applaud and God must forever bless.

14. Andrew Johnson on the Restoration of the Union

From First Annual Message to Congress, December 4, 1865

THE PERPETUITY OF THE STATES [11]

The perpetuity of the Constitution brings with it the perpetuity of the States; their mutual relation makes us what we are, and in our political system their connection is indissoluble. The whole can not exist without the parts, nor the parts without the whole. So long as the Constitution of the United States endures, the States will endure. The destruction of the one is the destruction of the other; the preservation of the one is the preservation of the other.

HAZARDS OF MILITARY RULE

I found the States suffering from the effects of a civil war. Resistance to the General Government appeared to have exhausted itself. The United States had recovered possession of their forts and arsenals, and their armies were in the occupation of every State which had attempted to secede. Whether the territory within the limits of those States should be held as conquered territory, under military authority emanating from the President as the head of the Army, was the first question that presented itself for decision.

[11] Subheadings added by the author.

Now military governments, established for an indefinite period, would have offered no security for the early suppression of discontent, would have divided the people into the vanquishers and the vanquished, and would have envenomed hatred rather than have restored affection. . . .

SECESSION NOT AN ADMISSIBLE PRINCIPLE

. . . the true theory is that all pretended acts of secession were from the beginning null and void. The States can not commit treason nor screen the individual citizens who may have committed treason any more than they can make valid treaties or engage in lawful commerce with any foreign power. The States attempting to secede placed themselves in a condition where their vitality was impaired, but not extinguished; their functions suspended, but not destroyed.

But if any State neglects or refuses to perform its offices there is the more need that the General Government should maintain all its authority and as soon as practicable resume the exercise of all its functions. On this principle I have acted, and have gradually and quietly, and by almost imperceptible steps, sought to restore the rightful energy of the General Government and of the States. To that end provisional governors have been appointed for the States, conventions called, governors elected, legislatures assembled, and Senators and Representatives chosen to the Congress of the United States. . . .

PROMISE OF HARMONY

And is it not happy for us all that the restoration of each one of these functions of the General Government brings with it a blessing to the States over which they are extended? Is it not a sure promise of harmony and renewed attachment to the Union that after all that has happened the return of the General Government is known only as a beneficence?

I know very well that this policy is attended with some risk; that for its success it requires at least the acquiescence of the States which it concerns; that it implies an invitation to those States, by renewing their allegiance to the United States, to resume their functions as States of the Union. But it is a risk that must be taken. In the choice of difficulties it is the smallest risk; and to diminish and if possible to remove all danger, I have felt it incumbent on me to assert one other power of the General Government—the power of pardon. As no State can throw a defense over the crime of treason, the power of pardon is exclusively vested in the executive government of the United States. In exercising that power I have taken every precaution to connect it with the clearest recognition of the binding force of the laws of the United States and an unqualified acknowledgment of the great social change of condition in regard to slavery which has grown out of the war. . . .

TREASON TO BE PUNISHED UNDER CIVIL LAW

It is manifest that treason, most flagrant in character, has been committed. Persons who are charged with its commission should have fair and impartial trials in the highest civil tribunals of the country, in order that the Constitution and the laws may be fully vindicated, the truth clearly established and affirmed that treason is a crime, that traitors should be punished and the offense made infamous, and, at the same time, that the question may be judicially settled, finally and forever, that no State of its own will has the right to renounce its place in the Union.

ELECTIVE FRANCHISE A STATE FUNCTION

The relations of the General Government toward the 4,000,000 inhabitants whom the war has called into freedom have engaged my most serious consideration. On the propriety of attempting to make the freedmen electors by the proclamation of the Executive I took for my counsel the Constitution itself, the interpretations of that instrument by its authors and their contemporaries, and recent legislation by Congress. When, at the first movement toward independence, the Congress of the United States instructed the several States to institute governments of their own, they left each State to decide for itself the conditions for the enjoyment of the elective franchise. . . .

But while I have no doubt that now, after the close of the war, it is not competent for the General Government to extend the elective franchise in the several States, it is equally clear that good faith requires the security of the freedmen in their liberty and their property, their right to labor, and their right to claim the just return of their labor. I can not too strongly urge a dispassionate treatment of this subject, which should be carefully kept aloof from all party strife. We must equally avoid hasty assumptions of any natural impossibility for the two races to live side by side in a state of mutual benefit and good will. The experiment involves us in no inconsistency; let us, then, go on and make that experiment in good faith, and not be too easily disheartened. . . .

ECONOMIC JUSTICE FOR THE NEGRO

The freedman can not fairly be accused of unwillingness to work so long as a doubt remains about his freedom of choice in his pursuits and the certainty of his recovering his stipulated wages. In this the interests of the employer and the employed coincide. The employer desires in his workmen spirit and alacrity, and these can be permanently secured in no other way. And if the one ought to be able to enforce the contract, so ought the other. The public interest will be best promoted if the several States will provide adequate protection and remedies for the freedmen. Until this is in some way accomplished there is no chance for the advantageous use of their labor, and the blame of ill success will not rest on them.

I know that sincere philanthropy is earnest for the immediate realization of its remotest aims; but time is always an element in reform. It is one of the greatest acts on record to have brought 4,000,000 people into freedom. The career of free industry must be fairly opened to them, and then their future prosperity and condition must, after all, rest mainly on themselves. If they fail, and so perish away, let us be careful that the failure shall not be attributable to any denial of justice. . . .

15. Andrew Johnson on Reconstruction

From Veto of a Bill to Establish a Freedman's Bureau, February 19, 1866

CREATES ENLARGED POWERS [12]

I share with Congress the strongest desire to secure to the freedmen the full enjoyment of their freedom and property and their entire independence and equality in making contracts for their labor, but the bill before me contains provisions which in my opinion are not warranted by the Constitution and are not well suited to accomplish the end in view.

The bill proposes to establish by authority of Congress military jurisdiction over all parts of the United States containing refugees and freedmen. It would by its very nature apply with most force to those parts of the United States in which the freedmen most abound, and it expressly extends the existing temporary jurisdiction of the Freedmen's Bureau, with greatly enlarged powers, over those States "in which the ordinary course of judicial proceedings has been interrupted by the rebellion." The source from which this military jurisdiction is to emanate is none other than the President of the United States, acting through the War Department and the Commissioner of the Freedmen's Bureau. The agents to carry out this military jurisdiction are to be selected either from the Army or from civil life; the country is to be divided into districts and subdistricts, and the number of salaried agents to be employed may be equal to the number of counties or parishes in all the United States where freedmen and refugees are to be found.

NO LEGAL SUPERVISION OF AGENTS

The subjects over which this military jurisdiction is to extend in every part of the United States include protection to "all employees, agents, and officers of this bureau in the exercise of the duties imposed" upon them by the bill. In eleven States it is further to extend over all cases affecting freedmen and refugees discriminated against "by local law, custom, or prejudice." In those eleven States the bill subjects any white person who may be charged with depriving a freedman of "any civil rights or immunities belonging to white persons" to imprisonment or fine, or both, without, however, defining the "civil rights and immunities" which are thus to be secured to the freedmen by military law. This military jurisdiction also extends to all questions that may arise respecting contracts. The agent who is thus to exercise the office of a military judge may be a stranger, entirely ignorant of the laws of the place, and exposed to the errors of judgment to which all men are liable. The exercise of power over which there is no legal supervision by so vast a number of agents as is contemplated by the bill must, by the very nature of man, be attended by acts of caprice, injustice, and passion.

[12] Subheadings added by the author.

UNWARRANTED MILITARY JURISDICTION

The trials having their origin under this bill are to take place without the intervention of a jury and without any fixed rules of law or evidence. The rules on which offenses are to be "heard and determined" by the numerous agents are such rules and regulations as the President, through the War Department, shall prescribe. No previous presentment is required nor any indictment charging the commission of a crime against the laws; but the trial must proceed on charges and specifications. The punishment will be, not what the law declares, but such as a court-martial may think proper; and from these arbitrary tribunals there lies no appeal, no writ of error to any of the courts in which the Constitution of the United States vests exclusively the judicial power of the country.

While the territory and the classes of actions and offenses that are made subject to this measure are so extensive, the bill itself, should it become a law, will have no limitation in point of time, but will form a part of the permanent legislation of the country. I can not reconcile a system of military jurisdiction of this kind with the words of the Constitution. . . .

NO LONGER AT WAR

If it be asked whether the creation of such a tribunal within a State is warranted as a measure of war, the question immediately presents itself whether we are still engaged in war. Let us not unnecessarily disturb the commerce and credit and industry of the country by declaring to the American people and to the world that the United States are still in a condition of civil war. At present there is no part of our country in which the authority of the United States is disputed. Offenses that may be committed by individuals should not work a forfeiture of the rights of whole communities. The country has returned, or is returning, to a state of peace and industry, and the rebellion is in fact at an end. The measure, therefore, seems to be as inconsistent with the actual condition of the country as it is at variance with the Constitution of the United States. . . .

PROPOSED GRANTS WITHOUT PRECEDENT

The third section of the bill authorizes a general and unlimited grant of support to the destitute and suffering refugees and freedmen, their wives and children. Succeeding sections make provision for the rent or purchase of landed estates for freedmen, and for the erection for their benefit of suitable buildings for asylums and schools, the expenses to be defrayed from the Treasury of the whole people. The Congress of the United States has never heretofore thought itself empowered to establish asylums beyond the limits of the District of Columbia, except for the benefit of our disabled soldiers and sailors. It has never founded schools for any class of our own people, not even for the orphans of those who have fallen in the defense of the Union, but has left the care of education to the much more competent and efficient control of the States, of communities, of private associations, and of individuals. It has never deemed itself authorized to expend the public money for the rent or purchase of homes for the thousands, not to say millions, of the white race who are honestly toiling from day to day for their subsistence. A system for the support of indigent persons in the United

States was never contemplated by the authors of the Constitution; nor can any good reason be advanced why, as a permanent establishment, it should be founded for one class or color of our people more than another. Pending the war many refugees and freedmen received support from the Government, but it was never intended that they should thenceforth be fed, clothed, educated, and sheltered by the United States. The idea on which the slaves were assisted to freedom was that on becoming free they would be a self-sustaining population. Any legislation that shall imply that they are not expected to attain a self-sustaining condition must have a tendency injurious alike to their character and their prospects.

WOULD CREATE A LARGE PATRONAGE

The appointment of an agent for every county and parish will create an immense patronage, and the expense of the numerous officers and their clerks, to be appointed by the President, will be great in the beginning, with a tendency steadily to increase. . . .

SUPPORT NOT NEEDED BY FREEDMEN

Undoubtedly the freedman should be protected, but he should be protected by the civil authorities, especially by the exercise of all the constitutional powers of the courts of the United States and of the States. His condition is not so exposed as may at first be imagined. He is in a portion of the country where his labor can not well be spared. Competition for his services from planters, from those who are constructing or repairing railroads, and from capitalists in his vicinage or from other States will enable him to command almost his own terms. He also possesses a perfect right to change his place of abode, and if, therefore, he does not find in one community or State a mode of life suited to his desires or proper remuneration for his labor, he can move to another where that labor is more esteemed and better rewarded. . . .

AFFECTED STATES NOT REPRESENTED

At the time, however, of the consideration and the passing of this bill there was no Senator or Representative in Congress from the eleven States which are to be mainly affected by its provisions. . . .

DUTY OF PRESIDENT TOWARD COUNTRY AS A WHOLE

The President of the United States stands toward the country in a somewhat different attitude from that of any member of Congress. Each member of Congress is chosen from a single district or State; the President is chosen by the people of all the States. As eleven States are not at this time represented in either branch of Congress, it would seem to be his duty on all proper occasions to present their just claims to Congress. . . .

From Veto of so-called "Civil Rights Bill," March 27, 1866

UNFAIR TO THE WHITE POPULATION

In all our history, in all our experience as a people living under Federal and State law, no such system as that contemplated by the details of this bill has ever before been proposed or adopted. They establish for the security of the colored race safeguards which go infinitely beyond any that the General Government has ever provided for the white race. In fact, the distinction of race and color is by the bill made to operate in favor of the colored and against the white race. They interfere with the municipal legislation of the States, with the relations existing exclusively between a State and its citizens, or between inhabitants of the same State—an absorption and assumption of power by the General Government which, if acquiesced in, must sap and destroy our federative system of limited powers and break down the barriers which preserve the rights of the States. It is another step, or rather stride, toward centralization and the concentration of all legislative powers in the National Government: The tendency of the bill must be to resuscitate the spirit of rebellion and to arrest the progress of those influences which are more closely drawing around the States the bonds of union and peace.

16. Cleveland on the Monroe Doctrine

From Special Message to Congress, December 17, 1895

ESSENTIAL TO AMERICAN INTEGRITY [13]

It may not be amiss to suggest that the doctrine upon which we stand is strong and sound, because its enforcement is important to our peace and safety as a nation and is essential to the integrity of our free institutions and the tranquil maintenance of our distinctive form of government. It was intended to apply to every stage of our national life and can not become obsolete while our Republic endures. If the balance of power is justly a cause for jealous anxiety among the Governments of the Old World and a subject for our absolute noninterference, none the less is an observance of the Monroe doctrine of vital concern to our people and their Government.

Assuming, therefore, that we may properly insist upon this doctrine without regard to "the state of things in which we live" or any changed conditions here or elsewhere, it is not apparent why its application may not be invoked in the present controversy. [Venezuela]

If a European power by an extension of its boundaries takes possession of the territory of one of our neighboring Republics against its will and in derogation of its rights, it is difficult to see why to that extent such European power does not thereby attempt to extend its system of government to that portion of this continent which is thus taken. This is the precise action which President Monroe declared to be "dangerous to our peace and safety," and it can make no difference

---

[13] Subheadings added by the author.

whether the European system is extended by an advance of frontier or otherwise. . . .

IMPLIED IN INTERNATIONAL LAW

Practically the principle for which we contend has peculiar, if not exclusive, relation to the United States. It may not have been admitted in so many words to the code of international law, but since in international councils every nation is entitled to the rights belonging to it, if the enforcement of the Monroe doctrine is something we may justly claim it has its place in the code of international law as certainly and as securely as if it were specifically mentioned; and when the United States is a suitor before the high tribunal that administers international law the question to be determined is whether or not we present claims which the justice of that code of law can find to be right and valid.

The Monroe doctrine finds its recognition in those principles of international law which are based upon the theory that every nation shall have its rights protected and its just claims enforced.

17. T. Roosevelt on Monroe Doctrine

From Fifth Annual Message, December 5, 1905

EFFECTIVE INSTRUMENT FOR PEACE [14]

One of the most effective instruments for peace is the Monroe Doctrine as it has been and is being gradually developed by this Nation and accepted by other nations. No other policy could have been as efficient in promoting peace in the Western Hemisphere and in giving to each nation thereon the chance to develop along its own lines.

That our rights and interests are deeply concerned in the maintenance of the doctrine is so clear as hardly to need argument. This is especially true in view of the construction of the Panama Canal. As a mere matter of self-defense we must exercise a close watch over the approaches to this canal; and this means that we must be thoroughly alive to our interests in the Caribbean Sea.

NO EXCUSE FOR AGGRANDIZEMENT

There are certain essential points which must never be forgotten as regards the Monroe Doctrine. In the first place we must as a Nation make it evident that we do not intend to treat it in any shape or way as an excuse for aggrandizement on our part at the expense of the republics to the south.

We must recognize the fact that in some South American countries there has been much suspicion lest we should interpret the Monroe Doctrine as in some way inimical to their interests, and we must try to convince all the other nations of this continent once and for all that no just and orderly Government has anything to fear from us.

[14] Subheadings added by the author.

There are certain republics to the south of us which have already reached such a point of stability, order, and prosperity that they themselves, though as yet hardly consciously, are among the guarantors of this doctrine. These republics we now meet not only on a basis of entire equality, but in a spirit of frank and respectful friendship, which we hope is mutual.

If all of the republics to the south of us will only grow as those to which I allude have already grown, all need for us to be the especial champions of the doctrine will disappear, for no stable and growing American Republic wishes to see some great non-American military power acquire territory in its neighborhood.

All that this country desires is that the other republics on this continent shall be happy and prosperous; and they cannot be happy and prosperous unless they maintain order within their boundaries and behave with a just regard for their obligations toward outsiders. It must be understood that under no circumstances will the United States use the Monroe Doctrine as a cloak for territorial aggression.

CIRCUMSTANCES AND LIMITATIONS OF OUR INTERVENTION

We desire peace with all the world, but perhaps most of all with the other peoples of the American Continent. There are, of course, limits to the wrongs which any self-respecting nation can endure. It is always possible that wrong actions toward this Nation, or toward citizens of this Nation, in some State unable to keep order among its own people, unable to secure justice from outsiders, and unwilling to do justice to those outsiders who treat it well, may result in our having to take action to protect our rights; but such action will not be taken with a view to territorial aggression, and it will be taken at all only with extreme reluctance and when it has become evident that every other resource has been exhausted.

Moreover, we must make it evident that we do not intend to permit the Monroe Doctrine to be used by any nation on this Continent as a shield to protect it from the consequences of its own misdeeds against foreign nations. If a republic to the south of us commits a tort against a foreign nation, such as an outrage against a citizen of that nation, then the Monroe Doctrine does not force us to interfere to prevent punishment of the tort, save to see that the punishment does not assume the form of territorial occupation in any shape.

The case is more difficult when it refers to a contractual obligation. Our own Government has already refused to enforce such contractual obligations on behalf of its citizens by an appeal to arms. It is much to be wished that all foreign governments would take the same view. But they do not; and in consequence we are liable at any time to be brought face to face with disagreeable alternatives. On the one hand, this country would certainly decline to go to war to prevent a foreign government from collecting a just debt; on the other hand, it is very inadvisable to permit any foreign power to take possession, even temporarily, of the custom houses of an American Republic in order to enforce the payment of its obligations; for such temporary occupation might turn into a permanent occupation.

The only escape from these alternatives may at any time be that we must ourselves undertake to bring about some arrangement by which so much as possible of a just obligation shall be paid. It is far better that this country should put through such an arrangement, rather than allow any foreign country to undertake it.

WILL EXTEND HELP TO SISTER REPUBLICS

This brings me to what should be one of the fundamental objects of the Monroe Doctrine. We must ourselves in good faith try to help upward toward peace and order those of our sister republics which need such help. Just as there has been a gradual growth of the ethical element in the relations of one individual to another, so we are, even though slowly, more and more coming to recognize the duty of bearing one another's burdens, not only as among individuals, but also as among nations.

18. T. Roosevelt on International Peace

From Fifth Annual Message, December 5, 1905

URGES U. S. PART IN HAGUE CONFERENCE [15]

It remains our clear duty to strive in every practicable way to bring nearer the time when the sword shall not be the arbiter among nations. At present the practical thing to do is to try to minimize the number of cases in which it must be the arbiter, and to offer, at least to all civilized powers, some substitute for war which will be available in at least a considerable number of instances. Very much can be done through another Hague conference in this direction, and I most earnestly urge that this Nation do all in its power to try to further the movement and to make the result of the decisions of The Hague conference effective.

SHOULD ARBITRATE MOST CASES

I earnestly hope that the conference may be able to devise some way to make arbitration between nations the customary way of settling international disputes in all save a few classes of cases, which should themselves be as sharply defined and rigidly limited as the present governmental and social development of the world will permit. If possible, there should be a general arbitration treaty negotiated among all the nations represented at the conference. Neutral rights and property should be protected at sea as they are protected on land. There should be an international agreement to this purpose and a similar agreement defining contraband of war.

NUMBER OF WARS HAS DECLINED

During the last century there has been a distinct diminution in the number of wars between the most civilized nations. International relations have become closer and the development of The Hague tribunal is not only a symptom of this growing closeness of relationship, but is a means by which the growth can be furthered. Our aim should be from time to time to take such steps as may be possible toward creating something like an organization of the civilized nations, be-

[15] Subheadings added by the author.

cause as the world becomes more highly organized the need for navies and armies will diminish.

It is not possible to secure anything like an immediate disarmament, because it would first be necessary to settle what peoples are on the whole a menace to the rest of mankind, and to provide against the disarmament of the rest being turned into a movement which would really chiefly benefit these obnoxious peoples; but it may be possible to exercise some check upon the tendency to swell indefinitely the budgets for military expenditure.

REQUIRES "SPIRIT OF SANITY"

Of course such an effort could succeed only if it did not attempt to do too much; and if it were undertaken in a spirit of sanity as far removed as possible from a merely hysterical pseudo-philanthropy. It is worth while pointing out that since the end of the insurrection in the Philippines this Nation has shown its practical faith in the policy of disarmament by reducing its little army one-third. But disarmament can never be of prime importance; there is more need to get rid of the causes of war than of the implements of war.

I have dwelt much on the dangers to be avoided by steering clear of any more foolish sentimentality because my wish for peace is so genuine and earnest; because I have a real and great desire that this second Hague conference may mark a long stride forward in the direction of securing the peace of justice throughout the world. . . . To this aim we should endeavor not only to avert bloodshed, but, above all, effectively to strengthen the forces of right. The Golden Rule should be, and as the world grows in morality it will be, the guiding rule of conduct among nations as among individuals; though the Golden Rule must not be construed, in a fantastic manner, as forbidding the exercise of the police power.

Index

collective bargaining, famous NRA clause on, 155
Colombia and the Panama Canal, 119
Colorado Fuel and Iron Company strike, 128, 129
communications system a handicap to Lincoln, 81
Congress, Lincoln on, 91
consent of the governed, 6, 7
  settlement of, 87
  Washington and the, 24
Constitution:
  and third term, Jefferson on, 41
  on private pursuits, 67, 68
  the new, 14
Constitutional rights in Lincoln's First Inaugural, 77
contradictions typical of American temperament, 41
Coolidge, Calvin:
  a Jacksonian, 52
  a "restful" president, 140
  "do not choose to run" of, 141
  era, abuses of, 141
  era of unprecedented prosperity, 141
  laissez faire policy of, 141
  "little red schoolhouse" president, 140, 141
  personal characteristics of, 140, 141
  plain, unmoneyed man, 140
  political principles of, 140, 141
  prosperity era of, 141
  self-admitted ignorance of tariffs, 141
  successor to Harding, 140
"court packing" bill of F. D. Roosevelt, 157
courts, the, and Thomas Jefferson, 36, 37
credit readjustments under Van Buren, 68
Curtis, G. W., 105
Customs office reforms under Hayes, 106

Dana, Richard H., 105
Davis, Jefferson, Inaugural Address of, 76
dawn of the modern world, 111
debates in Congress, notable, 71
Debs, Eugene V., 126
decade of the '20's, 139
Declaration of Independence, Jefferson and the, 30, 31
decline of national fortunes after Johnson, 99, 100
defense, George Washington on, 174
democracy:
  a war for, 132
  American, a world experiment under Van Buren, 65, 67
"Democratic patriotism" of Wilson, 133
Department of Commerce and Labor, 117
depression, liberal in, 62
depositors' losses:
  during big depression, 143, 144
  under F. D. Roosevelt, all-time high, 144
depression, the big, 143-145
Dewey campaign against F. D. Roosevelt, 164

diary and letters of Wilson, 132
dictatorship, beginnings of, 4
documents bearing on The Liberal Presidents, 173, 174
Draft Act under Wilson, 133
Dumbarton Oaks conference, 163

early England:
  a review of, 18-20
  civil liberty in, 18
Eaton issue and Jackson, 52
economic controls, 9
economic era of Jackson, 44
"economic royalists," F. D. Roosevelt and, 156
educational, literary and social aspects under Wilson, 122
electorial system and popular vote, 5
embargo against France and England, 40
Emergency Farm Mortgage Act, 153
enfranchisement:
  of blacks, 7
  of women, 7
expansion toward the West, 43
extent of sovereignty, 7, 8

Farewell Address of Washington, see Washington, George, Farewell Address
fear psychosis in South, 71
federal:
  finances under Hamilton, 15, 16
  income tax under Wilson, 128
federal authority:
  Jackson advocate of, 46
  "nullification" and the, 56, 57
Federal Farm Board, 142
Federal Reserve Act, 128
Federal Trade Commission, 128
  establishment of, 128
  successor to Bureau of Corporations, 117
Federalist, The, on business regulation by government, 114, 115
fiat money, Hayes and, 107
financial:
  and industrial power, 113, 114
  crash of 1929, 143-145
  crisis under Van Buren, 66, 67
  fraternity and Jackson, 54-56
  policy of Hayes, 107, 108
first patterns for the presidency, 12
Florida:
  Jackson governor of, 50
  Jackson's conquest of, 49, 50
foreign:
  policy of Jefferson, 40-41
  relationships as challenge to government, 23-24
forestry, park and preserves, T. Roosevelt on, 121
Fort Sumter:
  evacuation of, 78
  key to Lincoln's strategy, 78

DATE DUE

OCT 2 2 '65			
MAY 1 3 1971			
GAYLORD			PRINTED IN U.S.A.